The Nazi Revolution

PROBLEMS IN EUROPEAN CIVILIZATION SERIES

The Nazi Revolution

Hitler's Dictatorship and the German Nation

Fourth Edition

Revised and Edited by
Allan Mitchell
University of California, San Diego

HOUGHTON MIFFLIN COMPANY   Boston   New York

Senior Sponsoring Editor: Jean Woy
Assistant Editor: Keith Mahoney
Project Editor: Nicole Ng
Associate Production Coordinator: Deborah Frydman
Senior Manufacturing Coordinator: Michael O'Dea

Cover Design by Alwyn Velasquez, Lapis Design
Cover Image by Hubert Lanzinger, 1934, *Der Bannertraeger*
(Adolf Hitler as standard-bearer, US-Army Center of Military
History, photograph by Erich Lessing/Art Resource)

Printed in the U.S.A.

Library of Congress Catalog Card Number: 96-76936

ISBN: 0-669-41694-0

456789-MP-08 07 06 05 04

Contents

Preface

Conservatively estimated, somewhere in the world at least five hundred books are published every decade on the subject of Nazi Germany. This is not to reckon the literally countless number of scholarly articles, popular essays, and editorials that pour from the presses. Accordingly, even the most diligent specialists are daunted by the task of keeping abreast of all the available evidence and interpretation. At the end of the twentieth century, Nazism thus continues to provoke both intellectual debate and commercial activity on a large scale.

It is no wonder, then, that this edition follows closely on the heels of its predecessor. About fifteen years separated the second edition of this volume from the first, and again the third from the second. Yet barely half of that time, well less than a decade, elapsed before the need arose for a fourth. Truer today than ever is the sentence I wrote scarcely seven years ago: "The tempo of research and writing about Nazism remains astonishingly rapid."

Changes in the text have been made throughout. The most obvious one is splitting the opening section into two. This alteration allows a fuller treatment of the theoretical background — specifically, the so-called *Sonderweg* debate — and it permits a greater concentration on the practical means by which the Nazi regime managed to replace the tottering Weimar Republic in 1933. It seemed advisable to separate these topics by inserting an additional section. Otherwise, an effort has been made to update many of the readings in order to take account of recent advances in scholarship. Naturally every selection required an agonizing reappraisal, as the question inescapably arose whether students would be better served by one essay or another. Finally, the editor has to reach a decision to part with some authors in order to include alternatives. The sole responsibility for those difficult choices is, of course, mine.

Not simply for the sake of formal symmetry, I have retained the format of five excerpts in each section. My own experience as a college and university teacher has dictated that arrangement, which allows for coherence as well as variety in discussion of the topics at hand. The only exception to that rule in this edition is the final unit on the social impact of Nazism, where I have chosen to introduce seven essays in all. Yet even in this instance there are actually only five themes to be considered, because two of them — on the role of women and on the fate of Jews — are presented in pairs. As always, however, my intention has been to avoid juxtaposition of extreme views with stark (but often artificial) alternatives. Rather, I hope to encourage a nuanced analysis of several diverging perspectives on any given topic.

For his assistance in bringing so many possibilities and so much controversy into a manageable form, I want to thank my student and friend Barnet Hartston.

A.M.

Chronology of Events

1871	German Empire (Second Reich) founded.
1889	Adolf Hitler born in Austria.
1907–14	Hitler's Vienna and Munich years.
1914	World War I begins.
1918	World War I ends.
	German (Weimar) Republic established.
1919	Treaty of Versailles signed.
	Hitler joins German Workers' Party (later NSDAP, or Nazi Party).
1922	Mussolini seizes power in Italy.
1923	France occupies Germany's Ruhr District after German default on reparations payments.
	Hyperinflation in Germany wipes out savings of most middle-class families.
	Failed Beer Hall Putsch in Munich (November) leads to Hitler's arrest and imprisonment.
1924	Hitler writes *Mein Kampf* and is released from prison.
1924–30	Relatively prosperous period in Germany.
1927	Ban on Hitler's speeches is lifted.
1928	NSDAP receives 2.6 percent of votes in elections for Reichstag.
1929	Stock-market crash on Wall Street marks onset of Great Depression.
1930	NSDAP receives 18.3 percent of votes in elections for Reichstag.
1931	Collapse of Creditanstalt Bank in Vienna plunges Germany into financial crisis and depression.
1932	Hitler runs second to Hindenburg in presidential election; NSDAP becomes largest German party with 37.4 percent of votes in Reichstag elections.

1933   Hitler becomes chancellor (January).
        Reichstag fire and Enabling Act pave way for establishment of the Nazi dictatorship (February–March).
        NSDAP declared only legal political party in Germany (July).
        Secret German rearmament begins.

1934   "Blood purge" of Röhm and SA, as well as of other opponents (June).
        Nazi coup in Austria fails (July).
        Hindenburg dies; Hitler becomes Führer (August).

1935   Saar district returns to Germany after plebiscite (January).
        Germany begins open rearmament in violation of Versailles Treaty.
        Anglo-German agreement permits Germany to rebuild navy.
        Nuremberg Laws define Jews' degraded status in Germany.

1936   Rhineland remilitarized (March).
        Four Year Plan marks onset of economic planning for war.
        Olympic Games in Berlin.
        Civil war erupts in Spain, in which Germany aids Franco's Nationalists (July).
        Hitler and Mussolini announce "Rome-Berlin Axis" followed by the Anticominterm Pact (Germany, Italy, and Japan).

1937   Hitler reveals plans for systematic conquests at secret meeting with military leaders.

1938   Germany annexes Austria (March).
        Czechoslovak crisis and Munich conference lead to German annexation of Sudetenland (September).
        Kristallnacht marks the beginning of violent persecution of German Jews (November).

1939   Germany occupies Bohemia-Moravia; Slovakia becomes a German puppet state (March).
        Franco triumphs in Spanish Civil War (March).
        Hitler-Stalin pact (August).
        Germany invades Poland, precipitating World War II (September).

1940 Germany conquers Denmark, Norway, Low Countries, and France (March–June).
    Battle of Britain (June–September).

1941 Germany conquers Yugoslavia and Greece (April).
    Germany attacks Soviet Union (June).
    Japanese attack Pearl Harbor and Germany declares war on the United States (December).

1942 Mass extermination of European Jews begins.
    Germany fails to take Suez Canal (March–November).
    Battle of Stalingrad marks turn of tide against German army in Soviet Union (September–November).
    Allies invade North Africa (November).

1943 Allies begin massive air raids on German cities.
    Allies invade Italy; Germans rescue Mussolini (July).

1944 Allies invade France (June).
    Attempt on Hitler's life fails; anti-Nazi conspirators are purged (July).
    German counterattack on western front fails (December).

1945 Allied armies cross the Rhine and Soviet army besieges Berlin (March–April).
    Hitler commits suicide (April).
    Third Reich collapses (May).
    Surviving major Nazi leaders are tried at Nuremberg, and most of them are executed (November).

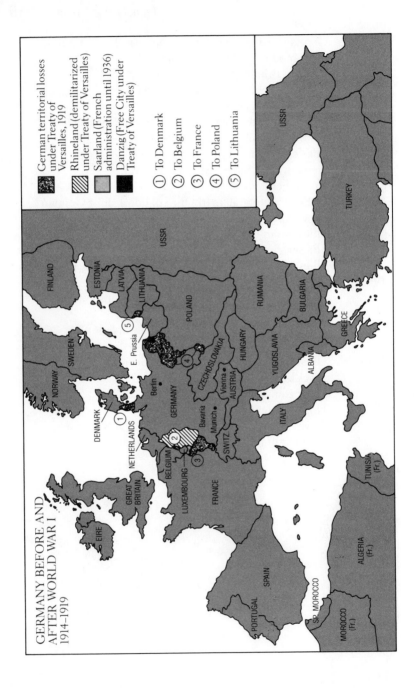

GERMANY BEFORE AND
AFTER WORLD WAR I
1914–1919

German territorial losses
under Treaty of
Versailles, 1919

Rhineland (demilitarized
under Treaty of Versailles)

Saarland (French
administration until 1936)

Danzig (Free City under
Treaty of Versailles)

① To Denmark
② To Belgium
③ To France
④ To Poland
⑤ To Lithuania

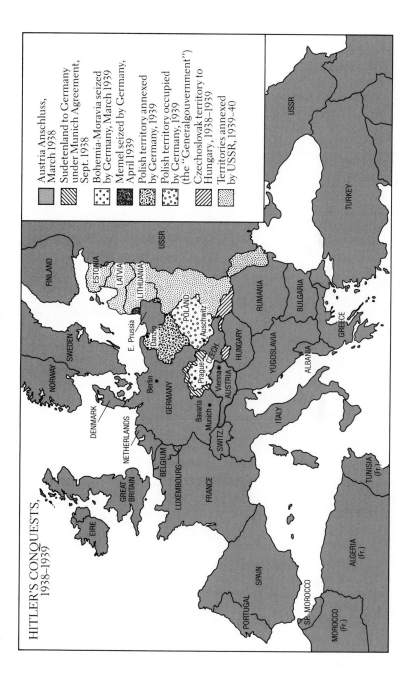

HITLER'S CONQUESTS,
1938–1939

Austria Anschluss,
March 1938

Sudetenland to Germany
under Munich Agreement,
Sept. 1938

Bohemia-Moravia seized
by Germany, March 1939

Memel seized by Germany,
April 1939

Polish territory annexed
by Germany, 1939

Polish territory occupied
by Germany, 1939
(the "Generalgouvernement")

Czechoslovak territory to
Hungary, 1938–1939

Territories annexed
by USSR, 1939–40

USSR

TURKEY

FINLAND

ESTONIA

LATVIA

LITHUANIA

USSR

SWEDEN

NORWAY

E. Prussia

Danzig

POLAND

Auschwitz

RUMANIA

BULGARIA

GREECE

DENMARK

Berlin

Prague

CZECH.

HUNGARY

YUGOSLAVIA

ALBANIA

NETHERLANDS

GERMANY

Bavaria

Munich

Vienna

AUSTRIA

GREAT
BRITAIN

EIRE

BELGIUM

LUXEMBOURG

SWITZ.

ITALY

FRANCE

PORTUGAL

SPAIN

SP. MOROCCO

MOROCCO
(Fr.)

ALGERIA
(Fr.)

TUNISIA
(Fr.)

Introduction

No brief period in human history has been so intensively scrutinized as that of Nazi Germany. And for good reason. No twelve years have made so much difference in the lives of millions of people. The epicenter of this extraordinary phenomenon was obviously Germany, where the National Socialist regime after 1933 organized and launched a European war that soon spread worldwide. Others shared some responsibility for the resulting conflict and incredible destruction, but the identity of the main aggressors cannot be in doubt. Hence the reader will find no war-guilt debate in the pages that follow.

Rather, critical assessment of the Nazi era has principally involved two other controversies. The first concerns the continuities and discontinuities of German history. Nazism was so far beyond the pale of European normality, so exceptional in its character and so monstrous in outcome, that a natural reflex after 1945 was to consider it an aberration from the past. But most historians soon began to question that view and to point out that Nazi ideology in fact had profound roots in German tradition. Moreover, the nation's authoritarian institutions and reactionary social forms were all too well suited as seedbeds for dictatorship. Gradually these arguments, emphasizing the unbroken sweep of German history, began to prevail. Citizens of the twenty-first century should be still more able than past generations to perceive the before, during, and after of Nazism, which are closely linked. To choose one striking example among many, the development of a social security system has been a continuous thread from Bismarckian times through the Nazi years to the present. Indeed, one may find among the scholars represented in this volume a virtual consensus that the experience of Nazism needs to be integrated into the continuum of German history. That trend seems clear and definitive; hence it could not fail to be reflected here.

Meanwhile, another debate has appeared that is related but as yet unresolved. If it is true that German history is continuous, in what ways was it comparable to that of other Western nations? Was its course separate and essentially unique, or did it bear a resemblance to the rest? Once more, the outlandish nature of Nazism lends immediate credence to the notion that the German historical path was special, a *Sonderweg*. But some scholars have effectively challenged that thesis, at least in its most uncompromising form, and even its hardiest proponents have been persuaded to concede some ground in defense. It is manifest, after all, that the German transition from a rural to an industrial society was part of a general European current, and, despite the lack of a full-scale social revolution, Germany did manage to develop a thriving bourgeoisie, a strong working-class movement, and forms of representative government, all of which served to mitigate absolutism. Still, the issue of separateness remains on the agenda, and basic differences of viewpoint are detectable in some of the recent writings contained in this anthology.

Specialists will note and perhaps lament the absence of any direct reference among the present essays to the so-called "historians' debate" (*Historikerstreit*). Yet there is little reason to dwell here on this unfortunate professional altercation that visibly thrived on mutual insults and misstatements. Better it is for students and teachers to leave polemics aside and to concentrate on the primary tasks of historical interpretation, namely, the evaluation of evidence and the formulation of informed opinions. This volume has been designed with those objectives in view, as an aid in the classroom and as a guide to understanding one of the most troubling passages in all the annals of mankind.

Before beginning, the reader may well wonder about the title of this volume. What was really so revolutionary about a political movement that contained many conservative elements and claimed to want nothing more than a restoration of German greatness?

In its simplest terms, the answer comes in three parts. First, Nazism was an abrupt turnabout from the tendencies of representative democracy at least since the French Revolution. For all of its erring byways, the course of European development in the nineteenth century was usually away from political absolutism. But the Nazis deliberately aimed to turn democracy on its head. In their view, the German *Volk* would freely choose to identify itself with a single leader, who would personally embody the General Will and thus abolish existing democratic institutions. The blunt reality of Nazism was that the wishes of one man were supposed to be beyond contradiction. He would decide what was best for the German nation, and his intuitive judgment would be accepted by all citizens as infallible.

Second, under this new regime any meaningful distinction between the public and private spheres was all but abolished. In times past the social norm was to maintain such a distinction and jealously to guard privacy and individual rights. Such was the prevailing ethic of European liberalism throughout the nineteenth century, and if that conception had somewhat eroded by 1933, nothing previous was remotely comparable to the radical intentions of complete state control under Nazism. Again, a volte-face occurred in this regard that can only be described altogether as revolutionary.

Finally, Nazism espoused a startling change of values and attitudes, specifically in respect to race. While the fundamental tenets of Social Darwinism were enunciated long before, there had never been such a radical departure in ethical theory or actual means of its application. Biological struggle became political practice, and only the fittest were to survive. They, in the Nazis' primitive binary perspective, were the so-called Aryans, whereas the perceived enemies of mankind, justifiably doomed to perish, were the Jews. Anti-Semitism thus remained at the core of Nazi thought, even when it was at times conveniently dissimulated. In this way, too, Nazism was truly and appallingly revolutionary.

Although these brief observations are largely self-evident, it is well that they be plainly and firmly stated at the outset. To study Nazism as a historical subject requires a certain scholarly detachment and a tolerance for ambiguity. But these laudable qualities should not be equated with moral indifference. Indeed, if ever a case could be made for maintaining an elementary sense of morality, it is here.

The Nazi Revolution

Proclamation of the German Reich, 1871. This painting depicts William I being proclaimed Emperor of Germany in the Hall of Mirrors at Versailles. In the foreground is Otto Von Bismark, the architect of German unification. (Corbis-Bettman)

PART

I

The Nazi Movement and German History

Variety of Opinion

Many threads of development can be traced to the fact that Germany had never experienced a successful bourgeois revolution.

Hans-Ulrich Wehler

The real strands of continuity across the divide of the First World War can best be followed if we look at what did happen in Imperial Germany rather than at what did not.

David Blackbourn

On the whole the latest comparative research on the bourgeoisie has substantiated the essence of the Sonderweg *thesis.*

Jürgen Kocka

It seems clear that the Sonderweg *concept as originally formulated can no longer serve.*

Charles S. Maier

What separated Germany was that so much of the potential for fascism became actual.

Allan Mitchell

We begin with a cluster of writers who attempt to locate the Nazi years within the long course of German history. Obviously Nazism was related to Germany's past as well as to its future, but precisely what was the nature of that relationship? For such a complex problem, as these historians testify, simple answers will not suffice.

Hans-Ulrich Wehler *draws a straight line from the autocratic regime of the German Kaiserreich, established in 1871, to the onset of Nazi dictatorship. He sees Germany as a land without a democratic revolution, and he emphasizes an unbroken tradition of elitism that allowed modernization but maintained the iron discipline of the imperial state until the military defeat of 1918. Thereupon the old political leadership was temporarily displaced, but the economic and social power of the elites remained unshaken. They merely resorted to more clever manipulations during the interim of the Weimar Republic (1918–1933). Meanwhile, Wehler argues, genuine democratic reform was blocked and outdated reactionary institutions stayed in place. When the crisis of the Great Depression struck Germany with full force about 1930, therefore, the Republic was unable to cope and the Nazis stepped forward. In all of this, Wehler stresses, there was a distinct continuity.*

David Blackbourn *takes exception to Wehler's categorical portrayal of political manipulation by the old elites, and he challenges the neat theory of continuity. He charges Wehler with overstating the peculiarity of German history by assuming that it deviated from a "normal" path of democratic development on the British model. In reality, Blackbourn contends, Germany resembled other Western countries in its general tendency toward a modern bourgeois industrial capitalism. In this respect the only real difference was that Germany went farther — ultimately much farther — in the direction of fascism.*

Jürgen Kocka *directly addresses the* Sonderweg *theory. Some speculation about the separate path of Germany's development actually began well before the First World War. Since then it has undergone a number of permutations. Kocka recognizes various weaknesses of this thesis, and indeed he defines four telling criticisms of it. But he nonetheless remains convinced that an emphasis on the peculiarities of Germany's history represents the soundest approach to the study of Nazism.*

Charles S. Maier *is less persuaded that the* Sonderweg *thesis can survive the withering fire to which it has been submitted. To be sure, he acknowledges that certain forms of the German political and social structure were distinctive. Yet he returns to the underlying similarities* among European nations, of which Germany was not alone to display authoritarian traits.

Allan Mitchell *adds a brief comment in hopes of clarifying the central issues of this debate. Three paradoxes are proposed that may not be as self-contradictory as they seem at first glance. Maybe there is a middle way between advocates and adversaries of the Sonderweg thesis. In any event, we may conclude that the power and resilience of the German nation have been major components of European history throughout the twentieth century, and the Nazi period must consequently be viewed within that larger context.*

These five statements supply ample proof that our conceptions of the past are bound to change. As Nazism recedes into time, inevitably it comes to be examined in different perspectives. Even when moral judgment remains firm, historical interpretations must evolve.

Hans-Ulrich Wehler

The Case for Continuity

Many threads of development can be traced to the fact that Germany had never experienced a successful bourgeois revolution. This resulted in a lack of questioning and opening up, or at least loosening up, of traditional structures. The unbroken tradition of government by pre-industrial power-élites, the prolongation of absolutism among the military, the weakness of liberalism and the very early appearance of deliberalising measures suggest on the surface a depoliticising of society, but one which deep down favoured a continuation of the *status quo*. The same can be said of the barriers to social mobility, the holding over of differences and various norms between separate estates, which is such a revealing aspect of Imperial Germany, and the essentially élitist character of education. Much of this resulted from the political weakness and defeats suffered by the bourgeoisie in the

From Hans-Ulrich Wehler, *The German Empire, 1871–1918*, trans. by Kim Traynor, 1985. Copyright © Berg Publishers, Ltd., 1985, New York/Oxford. Reprinted by permission of the publisher and the author.

nineteenth century, and all these factors, which are given here only as examples, had assumed their importance during a phase of historical development which was uninterrupted by a successful revolution. They were further strengthened by the success of Bismarck's policies for legitimising the *status quo*. This achievement did not preclude a partial modernisation of the economy, since after 1848 the strategy of "revolution from above" at first had the effect of strengthening the nascent industrial system. Nor did it rule out other achievements. Technical education was so well organised against the various efforts to resist its progress that the flow of scientific and technological innovations began relatively early on and was subsequently maintained. Many of the big cities profited from the retreat of liberalism's leading lights into local government, as well as from the bureaucratic tradition. It was not by chance that, after the 1890s, German local government, together with its communally-run public services, was regarded as a model by the American "progressives." While it is true that in 1895 more than 170,000 workers, punished as a result of their involvement in strikes, knew what it was to be on the receiving end of a system of class justice, the law nevertheless ensured a high degree of physical safety in the towns and rural districts. This was as true for workers and for members of national minorities, as for other social groups. Anyone who thinks highly of American party democracy should also look at the darker side of life in the United States — at, for example, the jungles of New York's immigrant quarters or the lynch justice of the South, to which for decades after the Civil War at least one Black per day fell victim. Party politics, lynch justice and life in the big cities may not appear commensurable with the above; but any comparing of systems inevitably draws upon positive or negative aspects of each, for which direct comparisons are difficult to find. In the German Empire it was not only discipline and repression which ensured social cohesion — whatever their undeniable effects, both subtle and obvious — but the conditions of everyday life. All protests to the contrary, the majority of Germany's citizens did not find these so oppressive that the crises of the Empire developed into a revolutionary situation before the war.

As regards the ruling élites' ability to adapt to changing circumstances, we must again enquire into the reasons for the system's relative stability, the traditional bases for which have been pointed out several times. We can only say, in the language of modern theory, that "pathological learning" was in evidence in several areas. The retention or introduction of class-based electoral laws, the reaction to fundamental social conflicts and the creation of income taxes, the Zabern affair of 1913 or the belated repeal of the clauses on language in the Imperial Law of Associations in April 1917 — all reveal, even if measured solely in terms of a pure self-interest in upholding the system, such an extreme narrow-mindedness that Bethmann Hollweg's judgement would seem to be borne out. History, his associate, Riezler, recorded, would reveal "the lack of education, the stupidity of militarism and the rottenness of the entire chauvinistically minded upper class." This is what directly paved the way for the revolutionary crisis of 1918. In other areas where the élites endeavoured to hold on to their inherited positions of power, their successes outweighed the risks involved. There is no denying that the system of connections between the nobility, the ministerial bureaucracy, the provincial authorities and the district administrators — who were a veritable pillar of stability east of the river Elbe — created political tensions. But the myth of the bureaucracy's neutrality and the patina of inherited traditions, together with the preference shown to powerful interests, kept these below the danger-mark for a considerable time. Without doubt, the combination of compulsory military service with a social militarism in everyday life, in school subjects and in various organisations, created areas of friction. But the gains made in terms of the stability which these elements helped to achieve more than made up for this friction throughout the period up to and including the first years of the war. In both cases, it was not until November 1918 that the true extent of the population's strong dislike of the bureaucracy and the military could be seen.

Most effective of all, perhaps, were those strategies which, also depending on the ruling élites' capacity to learn, combined an ability to adapt to modern forms of politics and propaganda with, at the same time, a stubborn defence of their inherited positions of power. The unholy trinity of social imperialism, social protectionism and social militarism provides more than sufficient examples of this. In this case of social imperialism, the ruling élites' reaction to industrialisation was closely linked to its usefulness in stabilising the social and political hierarchy of privilege. In the case of social protectionist measures, institutional arrangements of future import, such as state legislation on social insurance, were combined with welfare measures and rights which were not essentially liberal, but reactionary, so long as they led to an increase in the numbers of "friends of the Empire." In the case of social militarism, which was intensively encouraged, privileges of social status handed down from the past were defended by means of modern techniques of political campaigning pursuing carefully thought-out aims. The same is true of the early forms of state interventionism. Even a modern-style pressure group like the Agrarian League reveals quite clearly how this ability to adapt to modern methods of organisation and propaganda was entirely compatible with the continued promotion of traditional interests. All in all the entire process, which Hans Rosenberg has described as "the pseudo-democratisation" of the old agrarian elite, showed an often astonishingly flexible readiness on the part of the ruling élites to move with the times while all the more ruthlessly defending their traditional positions behind the façade.

All these strategies, measures and processes of pathological and ingenuous learning were interwoven. Together with a combination of traditionalism and partial modernisation, they were able, on the one hand, to preserve the stability of an historically outdated power structure over a surprisingly long period. Time and time again they achieved the necessary social cohesion. On the other hand, they added, especially in the long run, to an unmistakably increasing burden. The various interests and traditions thus protected became all the more difficult to reconcile with the growing demands for equality, a share of power and liberation from an increasingly intolerable legacy. Just as the economic successes of German industrialisation threw up enormous social and political problems, so the successful defence of traditional political, social and economic power relationships exacted its price. The costs were all the greater and more numerous as a result. The accumulation of unsolved problems which eventually had to be faced, the petrification of institutions which had outlived their usefulness and were in need of reform and the obstinate insistence on prerogatives which should no longer have been the sole property of the privileged few, pronounce their own judgement on the extent to which the ruling élites were prepared to adapt. So do the continual recourse to evasive strategies and attempts to divert attention from the need for internal reforms, as well as the decision to accept the risk of war rather than be forced into making concessions. In practice, the ruling élites showed themselves to be neither willing nor able to initiate the transition towards modern social and political conditions when this had become necessary. This is not a judgement based on theoretical speculation but on processes which culminated in the breakdown of the German Empire in revolution and the end of the old regime. This hiatus now belongs among the undisputed facts of history and cannot be explained away. It represented the bill that had to be paid for the inability of the German Empire to adapt positively to change.

The fact that this break with the past did not go deep enough and that the consequences of the successful preservation of outworn traditions remained everywhere visible after 1918, accounts for the acute nature of the problem of continuity in twentieth-century German history. Instead of bewailing "the distortion of judgement caused by the category of continuity," in arguments which patently seek to defend the German Empire's record, we should, in keeping with the essential requirements of an historical social science, face up to the problems of continuity and seek to analyse them further, rather than encourage an escapist attitude. This does not, of course, mean we should offer superficial explanations based on the "great men" approach to history (from Bismarck to Hitler via Wilhelm II and Hindenburg); rather we should investigate the social, economic, political and psychic structures which, acting as matrices, were able to produce the same, or similar, configurations over a long period of time. Conversely, we should also analyse those factors which gave rise to anomalies and discontinuity. The question as to whether, in fact, certain conditions favoured the emergence of charismatic political leaders in Germany should be re-examined against the background of these structures.

In the years before 1945, and indeed in some respects beyond this, the fatal successes of Imperial Germany's ruling élites, assisted by older historical traditions and new experiences, continued to exert an influence. In the widespread susceptibility towards authoritarian policies, in the hostility towards democracy in education and political life, in the continuing influence of the pre-industrial ruling élites, there begins a long inventory of serious historical problems. To this list we must add the tenacity of the German ideology of the state, its myth of the bureaucracy, the superimposition of class differences on those between the traditional late-feudal estates and the manipulation of political anti-Semitism. It is because of all these factors that a knowledge of the history of the German Empire between 1871 and 1918 remains absolutely indispensable for an understanding of German history over the past decades.

David Blackbourn

German Peculiarity in Question

All national histories are peculiar, but some appear to be more peculiar than others. Few historians of modern Germany, whether native or non-native, can escape awareness of that. Historians of other countries are also engaged in some manner with examining national myths: 1688 and the English genius for gradualism, 1789 and the French revolutionary tradition, Easter 1916 and the Irish nationalist mystique. The work of revisionism, in each of these cases, has frequently been a matter of debunking, questioning the pieties of the myth, and pointing up its paralyzing as well as emancipating features. But post-war historians of Germany have seen themselves presented with a still more daunting task. They have been concerned not just with residual elements of myth, but with explaining why the course of German history led to 1933. . . .

What can be said about these ways of looking at the German past? First, of course, their questions and answers have produced much of the most illuminating work on modern German history during the last decades. In no way has the present essay sought to belittle these achievements. Secondly, these perspectives on the past are clearly not identical with each other. They emerged from different milieus and betray different casts of mind and temperament. In many points of detail and interpretation they would make odd, even incompatible, bedfellows. But there are certain basic questions and answers which they share. They view 1933 as the final outcome of a particular historical continuity; they see that continuity as the product of German peculiarity; and they see a crucial element of that peculiarity in the aberrant behaviour of the German bourgeoisie. While these approaches are therefore neither identical with each other, nor of course the only ones in which modern German history has been discussed, they nevertheless have sufficient common threads and sufficient stature to be worthy of critical attention. If there is a figure in the carpet it is German peculiarity, of which in turn the failure of the bourgeoisie to conduct itself like a "proper" bourgeoisie is a central motif. It is dissatisfaction with this way of looking at things that has prompted the present essay. . . .

I have also questioned the idea of "manipulation" with which historians have commonly described the cynical preservation of class interests (particularly those of a "pre-industrial élite"). This, once again, does not entail denying the elements of political dishonesty which characterized Imperial Germany; but it is easy to misidentify the range of would-be manipulators, and to approach the question of political manipulation itself one-sidedly. I am skeptical of accounts that depict the political process, in Gramsci's words, as "a continuous *marche de dupes*, a competition in conjuring and sleight-of-hand." It does greater justice to a complex historical process to recognize that if we are to talk of manipulation at all — and I prefer the term demagogy — we should at least recognize that it was a two-way process which was politically unpredictable and potentially dangerous. This approach need be neither ingenuous nor "populist." The purpose of questioning the idea of manipulation by a particular élite is not to substitute a view that everything happened "from below" (which might be called the populist heresy), or that it happened because of the entry of "the masses" into politics (the older conservative orthodoxy). The intention here has been to try to add the missing dimension to accounts that habitually present the sound of only one hand clapping. Similarly, I have not sought to deny the elements of continuity that link the history of Imperial Germany with the Weimar Republic and the Third Reich. It would hardly be necessary to make such a disclaimer, perhaps, had apologist historians not insisted on portraying the Third Reich as an "accident." The real question about continuity is not "whether" but "in which ways?" I have offered an implicit answer to the second of these questions by suggesting that we examine nineteenth-century

Pillars of the Reich. Hitler is shown at a Nazi party rally in 1934, flanked by members of his staff: (to his left) Julius Streicher, managing editor of *Der Stürmer* (The Fighter), the Nazi party newspaper; (to his right) Rudolf Hess, head of the political section of the party and third deputy of the Führer; Viktor Lutze, head of the SA following Röhm's death; and Heinrich Himmler, head of the SS. (UPI/Corbis-Bettman)

Germany itself from a rather different perspective. This arises partly, of course, from a desire that Imperial Germany especially be treated less as a mere prelude to what followed. In terms of continuity, however, this could be put in more positive terms. To return to the opening remarks of the essay, the real strands of continuity across the divide of the First World War can best be followed if we look at what did happen in Imperial Germany rather than at what did not.

Perhaps a final observation is called for on the dangers of complacency, moral as well as historical, if we insist too much on a certain kind of German peculiarity. While he was preparing *Doctor Faustus,* Thomas Mann warned of creating "a new German myth, flattering the Germans with their own 'demonism'." Nearly forty years on, we see this problem at its most acute in the ephemera which has helped to establish the Third Reich as a macabre, but chic, chamber of horrors. That is what Hans-Jürgen Syberberg meant by referring to the Third Reich as "our Disneyland." Historians cannot dismiss this problem with an impatient gesture, for it raises moral implications for their own work. The charge of "trivializing" the Third Reich has been raised in recent acrimonious exchanges between historians of the 1930s, and the general issue is clearly present beneath the surface of the *Sonderweg* debate. My own view is that serious historians are perhaps most likely to "trivialize" modern German history in an involuntary manner: by exaggerated emphasis on the absoluteness of German peculiarity, which indirectly bolsters the morbid mystique of German history. There is a pedagogic, as well as a historical, argument for denting that mystique, just as there is a parallel case for not placing swastikas routinely on the covers of books dealing with twentieth-century Germany. That does not mean that we should write the history of Germany as if it were like the history of everywhere else; only that we should not write it as if it were quite unlike the history of anywhere else. The distinctiveness of German history is probably best recognized if we do not see it (before 1945) as a permanent falling-away from the "normal." In many respects, as I have tried to show, the German experience constituted a heightened version of what occurred elsewhere. This is true of Germany's dynamic capitalism, and of the social and political consequences it generated. It is true of the complex mesh of private and public virtues and vices which were characteristic of German bourgeois society. It is true of a widespread sentiment like cultural despair, and of the crass materialism which unwittingly reinforced it. It is true, I believe — although not all will want to accept this — of the way in which these and other phenomena discussed above combined to produce Germany's exceptionally radical form of fascism. What stamps the German case as distinctive is, of course, the particular, uneven combination of these elements. This is not an attempt to smuggle peculiarity in again through the back door. As we have also seen, this unevenness of economic, social, and political developments was not in itself peculiarly German: Germany was much more the intensified version of the norm than the exception. That it so often appears exceptional probably owes a good deal to the distorting focus of a more acceptable myth — that of a benign and painless "western modernization." There is much to be said for shifting our emphasis away from the *Sonderweg* and viewing the course of German history as distinctive but not *sui generis*: the particular might then help to illuminate the general, rather than remaining stubbornly (and sometimes morbidly) peculiar. That would be less likely to encourage apologetics than to disarm them. It might also enlarge rather than diminish our sense of modern Germany as a metaphor of our times. We recognize the richness of allusion when Walter Benjamin called Paris the "capital of the nineteenth century." We should be similarly open to the full meaning of Germany as the "tragic land" of the twentieth century. Our historical and moral sense of that tragedy is sharpened, not blunted, if we decline to view it solely as the final culmination of German peculiarity.

Jürgen Kocka

The Theory of a *Sonderweg*

In the late nineteenth and early twentieth centuries, many people were convinced of the existence of a special "German path" of development which set the Reich apart — in accordance with its particular

From Jürgen Kocka, "The German Identity and Historical Comparison: After the *Historikerstreit*," in Peter Baldwin (ed.), *Reworking the Past*. Copyright © 1987 by Fischer Taschenbuch Verlag GmbH, Frankfurt am Main. Reprinted by permission of Beacon Press, Boston.

geographic position and historical tradition — in a positive way from France and England. They regarded the nonparliamentary character of the German "constitutional monarchy" as an advantage. Many were proud of the strong government that stood above the parties, the respected and efficient German bureaucracy, and the long tradition of reforms from above which distinguished Germany from the Western principles of revolution, laissez-faire, and party government. German "culture" seemed superior to Western "civilization" — an ideology that culminated in the "ideas of 1914." After the First World War, some scholars, like Otto Hintze and Ernst Troeltsch, began to relativize this positive variant of the *Sonderweg* thesis. After the Second World War it had ceased to be convincing at all. Since then, the idea of a positive German *Sonderweg* has played little role in comparative interpretations of German history.

After 1945, a liberal-democratic, critical version of the *Sonderweg* thesis emerged. Its progenitors included Friedrich Engels and Max Weber. Emigrés and other critics of National Socialism also played an important part in its formulation. The essence of this critical variant of the *Sonderweg* thesis was its attempt to explain why Germany, in contrast to other highly developed and comparable countries of Northern and Western Europe, turned to fascism or totalitarianism during the crisis of the interwar period. Identifying the causes of National Socialism became the central issue of historical interpretation. The new *Sonderweg* thesis embodied Germans' attempt to explain "the German catastrophe" from a comparative perspective and to acknowledge it as an oppressive, yet undeniable, part of their historical heritage, while at the same time distancing themselves from it.

The great importance of short-term factors in the collapse of the Weimar Republic and the rise of National Socialism were, of course, not overlooked from this perspective. Who could possibly have disregarded the consequences of Germany's humiliating defeat in World War I? It was also generally recognized that the difficulties of international economic relations between the wars and the Depression intensified the problems of the first German republic and ultimately contributed to Hitler's rise.

Yet, at the same time, researchers looked back to the eighteenth and nineteenth centuries to uncover the deeper roots of the Third Reich. Through comparisons with England, France, the United States, or simply "the West," they attempted to identify the peculiarities of German history, those structures and processes, experiences and turning points, which, while they may not have led directly to National Socialism, nevertheless hindered the long-term development of liberal democracy in Germany and eventually facilitated the triumph of fascism. Many authors made various contributions to the elaboration of this argument, usually without actually using the word *Sonderweg*. . . .

Adherents of this interpretative approach naturally understood that the defeat in World War I and the 1918/19 revolution represented a deep break with the past and changed the inherited constellation of power in Germany. The traditional authoritarian state, the civil service, and the army lost much of their former legitimacy, the old elites were partially replaced, and a parliamentary democracy was erected. The labor movement was one of the winners in this process. The Social Democrats may have split, but they also gained power. The development of the welfare state made rapid progress. Yet in spite of all this, according to the *Sonderweg* thesis, many of the old problems remained and contributed to the special weaknesses of Weimar democracy. As a result, the Republic collapsed in the face of the Depression, whereas the more stable democracies of Western and Northern Europe survived.

As is well known, there is much to be said for this argument. Because parliamentarization had been hindered for so long, the new system — born of defeat — was not powerful enough to defuse the deep social tensions that emerged in the wake of war and economic turbulence. The core elements of the Wilhelmian party system were still in place after the revolution; the parties had not learned in time how to act in a parliamentary manner, how to accept the compromises necessary in a democracy. Traditional attitudes and elitist expectations remained characteristic among large segments of the upper class — among the Junkers, the upper bureaucracy, the officer corps, the judiciary, and portions of the bourgeoisie — and these traditional, pre-democratic, and in part premodern attitudes and claims increasingly conflicted with the realities of Weimar.

All of this explains why a substantial portion of the upper class was hostile to the new democratic republic and helped bring it down. Segments of the petty bourgeoisie also continued to direct their usual demands at the state. These demands turned into protests against the new political system once the republic showed itself incapable of protecting the lower middle classes against the challenges of modernization. Despite Berlin and the flourishing of modernism in Weimar, the illiberal elements of German political culture survived and gained in strength. In complicated and circuitous ways, it was the Nazis who benefited from this trend.

From this perspective, then, it was not only economic crisis, explosive class antagonisms, and the destabilizing consequences of modernization that brought on the crisis of Weimar. These "modern" factors were certainly important, but they were, after all, present also in other countries. In Germany, however, such factors were intensified by premodern structures and traditions which, though under attack, continued to make their presence felt. This was the legacy of the *Sonderweg.*

The multifaceted interpretation sketched out above (dubbed the "*Sonderweg* thesis" more often by its critics than by its supporters) has never enjoyed universal support. In recent years it has come under increasing fire. The chief objections can be briefly summarized as follows:

1. To view German history only in relation to 1933 (or 1933–45) is a one-sided approach. As National Socialism recedes ever further into the past, it becomes less and less reasonable to interpret German history of the nineteenth and twentieth centuries principally in terms of Weimar's collapse and the triumph of Nazism. German history before 1933 is more than just a prelude to 1933. It is also part of the prehistory of 1988, for example; and moreover it is an epoch in its own right.

2. According to another objection, the notion of a German *Sonderweg* presupposes that a "normal" path of development existed, from which Germany deviated. If "normal" is taken to mean "average," "probable," or "most frequent," then it would be difficult to show that the French, English, or American patterns of development represented "normality" — completely leaving aside the fact that they are ill-suited to be lumped together in a single "Western" model.

If "normal" is meant in the sense of "norm," then the difficulties multiply. For if "the West" is taken as a normative standard from which Germany deviated to its own detriment, then this implies a subjective value judgment — and with it the danger of an idealization of "the West." This objection has gained in resonance as doubts increasingly arise concerning the Western model of modernization.

3. Recent empirical studies seem to show that the causal significance of premodern attitudes, structures, and elites for the crisis of the Weimar Republic has perhaps been exaggerated. Instead, greater emphasis is placed on the consequences of defeat and inflation, the world economic crisis, and the supposedly precipitous construction of a welfare state. Other authors have taken up an older line of argument and stressed that rapid modernization itself led to social and cultural *anomie* and tensions, which in turn intensified the Weimar crisis and destabilized the system. The failure of Weimar was thus the result of the "contradictions of classic modernism."

4. Recent interpretations of the Wilhelmian Empire have strongly emphasized its modernity: its achievements in the areas of education, science, and architecture, its allegedly well-developed bourgeois character — in civil law, the press, the theater, and other areas of culture. In addition, a comparative approach appears to show that those characteristics long interpreted as the peculiar weaknesses of the German bourgeoisie — the influence of the aristocracy on the upper bourgeoisie, for example — were in fact phenomena shared across all European nations.

In light of these and other criticisms, the Sonderweg thesis must be rethought, made more precise, and partially modified. . . .

What is one to make, then, of the empirical objections to the *Sonderweg* thesis? First of all, no serious historian would argue that the peculiarities of German history led directly and of necessity to 1933. Without question, there were many additional causal factors — from the consequences of defeat to the personality of Adolf Hitler — and it might still have been possible to prevent the Nazi victory as late as the end of 1932. Nevertheless, the structures and processes identified in the *Sonderweg* literature intensified the difficulties of the Weimar Republic and facilitated the rise of the Nazis. Recent research has added new elements to the overall picture and shifted emphases, yet the broad outlines of interpretation have not been revised. The rejection of the Weimar Republic by broad sectors of the upper class, antidemocratic nationalism, the difficulties of the parliamentary system, the power of large landowners and the officer corps, illiberal elements of the political culture, the weakness of the democratic and republic camp: such factors help explain the collapse of the Republic and are themselves the product of preceding processes and structures identified by the *Sonderweg* thesis. References to the "contradictions of classic modernism" fit well into the contemporary atmosphere skeptical of modernization, but other countries were also modern — and yet they escaped Germany's fate.

In addition, much has changed over the past few years in the interpretation of the Wilhelmine Empire and, with it, a central element of the inherited *Sonderweg* thesis. The "feudalization of the upper bourgeoisie" turns out to have been much less advanced than had long been thought, and at any rate the close connections between upper bourgeoisie and aristocracy was a phenomenon common throughout Europe. The German middle class was indeed relatively weak in an economic and political sense when compared to its counterparts in the West, but in Germany as a kind of compensation, a precocious and strong bourgeoisie of culture and learning [*Bildungsbürgertum*] emerged. The continuing power of liberalism on the local level also made up to some degree for its weakness on the national level.

Other examples could also be mentioned, but on the whole the latest comparative research on the bourgeoisie has substantiated the essence of the *Sonderweg* thesis: there were peculiarities in the relationship between aristocracy and bourgeoisie which confirm the weaknesses of the German middle classes. The fairly marked differentiation of the bourgeoisie in Germany was a function of its relatively weak powers of attraction and integration. The many "unbourgeois" characteristics of middle-class society during the Wilhelmine Empire can be accounted for in this way. The bureaucratic tinge to German bourgeois culture also highlights one of its most painful limits.

Comparative research over the past several years has repeatedly confirmed this peculiarity — among others — of German development: the importance and continuity of a bureaucratic tradition. German development distinguished itself from that in both East and West by the presence of a precocious, efficient, respected, and influential professional civil service and a long tradition of successful reforms from above. A strong, authoritarian state emerged which achieved much and became the object of widespread, and not unjustified, admiration. But the price paid for this, in a certain sense, was the specific weakness of bourgeois-liberal virtues.

The bureaucratic tradition influenced many different spheres of life: the formation of classes and status groups, the educational system, the structure and mentality of the bourgeoisie, the labor movement and the party system, the organization of large-scale industry, even the social theories of Max Weber. It facilitated the early development of a welfare state, but also helped to block the parliamentarization of the Empire and its member states up to 1918. The various social groups looked to the state for initiatives, and when these state-oriented expectations were disappointed they were easily transformed into protests directed at the existing system. The bureaucratic and authoritarian character of deeply rooted ideas, modes of behavior, and attitudes certainly helps to explain why there was so little resistance during the 1930s and 1940s to atrocities committed by the state.

Charles S. Maier

Differences or Deviance?

Is there any persuasive power left to the *Sonderweg*? If every nation has its own *Sonderweg*, deviant behavior is a meaningless concept. Still, as Jürgen Kocka has pointed out, among those countries with which Germans chose to compare themselves, Germany alone chose an authoritarian path. The Germans picked their own relevant universe of comparable countries — and diverged significantly. But even if the historian seeks to jettison the case-history approach, is there no valid model of German national development that explains the vulnerability to authoritarianism? Was Nazism, then, merely the contingent product of immediate political factors? Is German national identity to be pronounced unproblematic? Alternatively, was National Socialism an ailment of capitalism in crisis that happened to strike the country that had lost World War I and had been subjected to a humiliating peace treaty?

It seems clear that the *Sonderweg* concept as originally formulated can no longer serve. To adduce a stunted bourgeoisie or a middle class overawed by Junkers and military prestige will no longer adequately

From Charles S. Maier, *The Unmasterable Past: History, Holocaust, and German National Identity.* Harvard University Press: Cambridge, Mass. Copyright © 1988 by the President and Fellows of Harvard College. Reprinted by permission of the publisher.

account for the annexationist fervor of 1914 or the vulnerability of Weimar democracy. Many historians will still object: Surely the Germany of 1914 relied more than other countries on military solutions, whether Bismarck's wars of unification or heavy-handed diplomatic pressure in the years before the outbreak of war. It took greater pride in military splendor, had its elites more attuned to drums and trumpets than inveterately civilian Britain. But even in this respect the comparison is less clear-cut than often remembered. If militarism seemed endemic within Germany — "Kennst Du das Land, wo die Kannonen blühen?" so Erich Kästner parodied Goethe in the 1920s — Englishmen outside their island exercised a military and racialist domination throughout an empire extending from Ireland in the west to the Raj and Capetown and Hong Kong. Germany, it might be countered, was "authoritarian" and stratified. And yet Britain's class society was as profoundly elitist as Germany's. There was more velvet glove and less iron hand, but no bared arm. It is hard to find indices of German stratification and even of class arrogance for which Britain lacked equivalents. . . .

As Marc Bloch insisted fifty years ago, comparison involves establishing differences as well as similarities. Moving beyond the case-history approach should not preclude trying to understand real distinctiveness. The fact that German bourgeois achievements were long underrated does not mean that political life in Berlin was equivalent to that in London or Paris. Bureaucrats, the court, parliaments, and parties played different roles. Inherited titles conferred prestige everywhere, but the power they brought varied from country to country. Despite the battering that the *Sonderweg* thesis has undergone, despite the correct insistence that Germans enjoyed a vigorous civic life, political organization, and public debate, the countries were run differently. Paul Kennedy has updated the argument forcefully: "Whatever the area selected — controls by the representative over the executive, prerogatives of the monarch, role of the army, management of the economy, freedom of the press, supervision of the educational system — the German position was more authoritarian and state-directed."

Kennedy's summary, however, slights the fact that the British elites neither desired nor required so assertive a state apparatus. The political conflicts of the seventeenth and eighteenth centuries ended by confirming that the British upper classes would govern their national society for their own benefit. Analogous crisis in Germany, especially

in Prussia, had a different outcome. Urban patriciates and rural nota-
bles were overawed. They remained influential at the local level but
were constrained to enroll as civil servants or army officers if they
wished to play a national political role. The bargain was made attractive by affixing noble titles to state service and letting landlords have
increased power over their local peasants and peasant lands. Subsequent chances to redress power relationships were not really exploited:
hence the "failures" of liberalism in 1815, 1848, and 1862. As of the
early twentieth century, the German parliament played less crucial a
role, could not limit discretionary royal authority, and certainly em-
anated no executive power of its own. Political analysts believed the
difference lay in the constitutional prohibition on Prussian/German
cabinet officials' sitting in the Reichstag (hence belonging to a party
coalition), but this was only one of several distinctions.

Perhaps the salient difference between the German regime and
the others lay in the role of parties. . . .

German parties were certainly strong in terms of organization.
They were ideologically coherent, they had important links with interest groups and newspapers, and their basic array survived the upheaval
of 1918, if not of 1933 and 1945. But the historian must distinguish dimensions of strength: if cohesiveness was high, the passion to govern
was low. When the parties inherited sovereign power in the debacle of
November 1918, they were unprepared to exercise it. German party
leaders had not wanted to rule per se. They wanted to be consulted,
certainly sought policies favorable to their economic interests, and (especially in the case of the Catholics) insisted on recognition from government ministers that their support was indispensable. Success was
measured by standing within the party organization, not domination
of a national agenda. Parties served as transmission belts. Parliament
confronted an executive that in theory was independent of the parties,
even if they could make life difficult. The result, as Max Weber noted
ruefully during World War I, was merely negative. England could be
rightly termed a democratic state (*ein Volksstaat*); "whereas a parliament of the ruled that can exert only a negative politics with respect to
a ruling bureaucracy represents the plaything of an authoritarian
state." In England, access to government remained crucial. Parties as-
pired to decision-making power; their representatives constituted the
executive. So, too, in France. If not permanent parties, major parliamentary coalitions demanded decisive power. The great clashes of the
pre-1914 Third Republic involved issues laden with implications as to

who ruled — the church or the republic — and whose values would be hegemonic.

Another distinction potentially handicapped German parliamentarism. Its capacity to live with a majority of the left without a civil war or an authoritarian coup remained untested before the revolution of 1918. In Britain and France governing coalitions replaced each other according to electoral outcomes. Had the Labour Party or French Socialists emerged with decisive blocs of delegates before World War I, they probably would have been admitted to a share of cabinet power. In Germany electoral results did not mandate different coalitions. And the prospect of a majority dependent upon Social Democratic delegates appeared more frightening and might have triggered some sort of authoritarian coup. Nonsocialists accepted SPD power as a lesser evil in the revolution of 1918, but many of them preferred an authoritarian political solution rather than permit the party to play a leading role after 1930. The capacity of the German political system to allow for peaceful alternation of coalitions was precarious.

Stressing these impediments to democratization does not require endorsing a German *Sonderweg*. History sometimes repeats its opportunities. Setbacks are not always permanent. Parties and parliament would probably have acquired more power (if only by default) had World War I not suspended "normal" political conditions. Granted, every move toward "opening" — the effort to quash the Kaiser after the *Daily Telegraph* interview, the reformist electoral victories in the elections of 1912 — provoked a conservative backlash. Nonetheless, over the long term, a new political equilibrium that conceded more influence to a parliamentary majority and did not rely upon quarantining the SPD was certainly one plausible scenario. The *Sonderweg* approach, however, allows little scope for the transformative impact of what might be termed "normal crises." Every apparent reform becomes at best a pseudo-reform that only stabilizes the old elites.

The *Sonderweg* thesis, moreover, purports to explain political outcomes according to societal factors, and societal factors of a special sort. It implies that the flaws in German politics resulted from some deficiency in the society or underlying culture. Granted that German institutions differed from those in other Western countries, granted that they placed liberal-democratic outcomes under a greater handicap — did they differ because of proximate factors or did they differ because of "deeper" reasons? It is the search for allegedly more profound (or "structural") causes that distinguishes the analyses of Marx and Engels, Weber and Veblen, and their recent heirs. The structural difficulties, moreover, are of a particular kind. The societal factors that allegedly have weighed so fatefully on German politics are the residues of an earlier, prebourgeois era.

The concept of the *Sonderweg* implies a theory of belated development. Other societies, which are viewed as normative, shed their feudal past through one form of bourgeois revolution or another. Not so the Germans. According to the scenario, the remnants of a premodern society of estates or *Stände* remained embedded in semimodernized form. Archaic guilds remained until the 1850s, then crystallized in public-law corporations, thus inhibiting the rise of a modern citizenry and producing petit-bourgeois chauvinists obsessed with status, as fictionally exemplified by Heinrich Mann's *Untertan*. The bourgeoisie won reserve officer status in the army by virtue of their education and internalized the rigid outlook of that antidemocratic caste. The East Elbian Junkers preserved outmoded rights of justice over the peasantry until 1872 and informal jurisdiction thereafter. In 1849 they extracted a skewed suffrage that enhanced their political preponderance in Prussia; and in 1878 they extracted a protectionist tariff that allowed them to remain on the land as feudal agrarian capitalists. The bureaucracy, with its dependence on the monarch and its life tenure of secure office, discouraged more meritocratic hierarchies. "No economic reasons are responsible for the political immaturity of the German bourgeoisie," declared Weber in his celebrated inaugural lecture of 1892. "The reason lies in its unpolitical past . . . And the serious question for the political future is whether it isn't now too late to catch up." In effect, the caterpillar of the old regime went into the cocoon of nineteenth-century social transformation and emerged . . . a fatter and more rapacious caterpiller.

What critics of the *Sonderweg* idea have objected to is the notion that a "backward" societal substructure inevitably led German politics to turn out so miserably. On the one hand, they argue, when German politics turned out badly it did so because of deficiencies at the level of politics alone: miscalculation, arrogance, hostility to compromise, narrow economic goals. A major piece of evidence in this regard is the new interpretation of the Weimar electoral returns: the voting results suggest that Nazism was a broad political protest, not the work of a frightened lower middle class. Second, the critics question the indices of backwardness. Too many of Germany's urban dwellers formed political associations, organized, sought votes, read newspapers. Too many Junkers were deeply involved with banks and industries. Too few shopkeepers and small independent businessmen persisted to be a decisive influence on the grass-roots upheaval against the Weimar Republic. And to argue from the negative case, too many British shopkeepers had the same petit-bourgeois, often chauvinist mentality that identified with imperial success and kowtowed to social superiors. Why should the behavior in England known as "deference politics," which supposedly helped entrench parliamentary liberalism, be condemned as a prop of the *Obrigkeitsstaat* (authoritarian state) in Germany? The liberal societies were hardly free of premodern legacies (and at all levels of society). Each polity rested upon a cumulative sedimentation of social structures. Insofar as political patterns corresponded to social organization, they did not reflect any one level of social or economic development. Thus each nation's politics involved organizational forms, conflicts, rivalries, and outcomes that transcended any one-to-one determination by those elements.

Allan Mitchell

The Three Paradoxes of Nazism

No history of a modern nation arouses greater passion, or so much confusion, as that of Germany. To state the obvious: German history matters to all of us because it is a crucial aspect of *human* history; it is a part of everyone's past.

Yet the historical record, like our personal experience, is often muddled. While the scholarly debates rage on, students may be forgiven for wondering just where to begin in exploring issues of such infinite complexity. By some historians we are assured that the most appropriate starting point is a notion of Germany's "separate path" (*Sonderweg*). No comparable European nation produced an Adolf

Hitler, provoked a Second World War, and pursued a course of maniacal genocide. Surely, they argue in effect, the proof is in the pudding.

The validity of this thesis thus hinges directly on the stunning events that occurred during the twelve years of German history after 1933. True, no person can legitimately question the enormity of those events. But a nagging question remains whether they were the inevitable outcome of that history. A serious problem with the *Sonderweg* theory, in other words, is that it tends to remove contingency from history. Suppose Hitler had been killed, as well he might have been, during his 1923 Putsch in Munich. Would the dreadful developments that began to unfold a decade later necessarily have come to pass? And would we still be forced to acknowledge Germany's special status among European nations had the Weimar Republic survived?

Because no certain response to such imponderables is possible, we would do well to use caution as we roam in the valley between the imposing proponents of a *Sonderweg* and their no less formidable detractors. For our journey into German history we need some reliable signposts. Arguably there are three ahead, each of which may be read as a paradox:

1. *Germany's history was unique but not isolated.* To state that every European nation took a separate path to modernity may be a banality, but it is one that we should seriously take to heart. Doubtless German tradition was distinctive from any of its neighbors and competitors, but so was *their* individual history distinctive from others. Hence it is an absurd proposition that Germany was different from "the West" — as if the collective experience of the French was coterminus with that of the British, the Italians, the Scandinavians, or the Americans (not to mention regional differences within those vast populations). It only makes sense to view each of these historical and geographical units as a unique entity, and Germany as one among them. All passed along the same broad path to modernity, each in its own fashion, some more successfully than others.

This pluralistic conception need not beg the question of what was "modern" in the nineteenth and twentieth centuries. With a greater or lesser degree of precision we can indicate what we mean by that term: democratic political forms of representative government, advancing technology and public transportation, industrialization and urbanization, a measure of social welfare with an organized medical profession, corporate banking and business institutions, patronage of the arts and sciences, an elaborate system of schools and universities, a consequent rise in literacy, trade unionism, and so on. All the nations of Europe and North America shared in these developments, and Germany was no exception. Exceptional was solely the German variant, unique in degree but not in kind. If so, what we need to analyze is the peculiar chemistry of the German people, those ingredients that made them distinctive from others who were undergoing essentially the same evolutionary process.

2. *Nazism was not an exception but an exaggeration.* This second axiom logically follows from the first, and it contains two paradoxical corollaries. In the first place, Germany was not alone in succumbing to fascism, or at least in absorbing into its body politic certain fascist traits. Whether or not the early twentieth century can aptly be described as "the fascist epoch" (as does Ernst Nolte) is moot. But it is certain that traces of fascism and its ugly twin racism were everywhere to be found, not just in the obvious cases of Mussolini's Italy and Franco's Spain, but also in France, England, and the United States.

The second corollary, however, is that none of the other nations went so far in the implementation of a dictatorship. What separated Germany was that so much of the potential for fascism became actual. To grasp the phenomenon of Nazism, therefore, we need to examine those elements of the German pattern that allowed the general fascist surge to progress beyond the bounds of decency. Impediments to fascism did exist in Germany, as elsewhere, but they were decisively breached in 1933 and they crumbled in the Nazi torrent thereafter. Hence, willingly or not, the Germans faced the grim reality of a fascist state control that far exceeded any other in its ruthlessness and, ultimately, its destruction of innocent lives. Although deeply embedded in the general historical trends of the modernizing Occident, therefore, Germany's intense and devastating experience under Nazi rule will forever set its past apart from the rest of humanity.

3. *Nazism was an extraordinary episode but an integral part of European history.* As a new millennium opens, we are now able to look back at the entirety of the twentieth century. And in this retrospect, it is remarkable to observe how similar the balance of European power appears at the end of the century when compared to its outset. If, some years ago in the midst of the Cold War, one had assessed Europe's

condition, matters would have seemed otherwise. At that time Europe and, with it, Germany were divided, half dominated by the Soviet Union. But after 1989 a dramatic change occurred that revealed the enduring character of the European constellation. As it turns out, the primary fact of European history in the twentieth century (uncomfortable as it is for some to admit) has been the supremacy of Germany. Such a configuration was already evident by 1900 as a result of Germany's political unification and intensely rapid industrialization after 1870. While the Kaiserreich of that era bestraddled Central Europe, Russia (then as now) played the secondary role of a somewhat distant flanking power, usually considered by others to be backward and vaguely menacing. The other flank was occupied by Great Britain, as ever aloof but always an estimable factor in the European equilibrium — a part it continues to perform, despite a loss of empire, thanks to its atomic power and its special relationship to North America. Meanwhile, on the Continent itself there exists once more, as a century ago, a scene of muffled competition between France and Germany, in which the former is badly outmatched by its colossal Teutonic neighbor, again unified and thriving with unprecedented industrial might.

If this scenario is nearly accurate, then the essential (or, one may virtually say, normal) alignment of European nations in the twentieth century has revolved about the preeminence of Germany. The irrepressible vitality and sheer magnitude of the German nation, superior in strength to its rivals, are fundamental factors too often awkwardly avoided in discussions of the *Sonderweg* thesis. Withal, what we have witnessed in the century just past is an astonishingly powerful performance by a people that has suffered so much (often self-inflicted) adversity: the humiliating defeat of 1918 and the futile restrictions of the Treaty of Versailles, the economic debacle of the Great Depression, the awesome physical destruction and complete moral bankruptcy of 1945, and the lengthy political division into two mutually hostile states dominated by foreign superpowers. Yet through it all Germany has somehow survived and indeed prevailed. Truth to tell, for better and worse, it has been the German century.

In this historical perspective the advent, course, and collapse of Nazism gain their full meaning. Nazism was no accident, no breakdown, no detour. It was in fact the most emphatic assertion of Germany's continental supremacy. The truly perplexing issue of twentieth-century

Europe, then, has not been the reality of German dominance but the means. By employing fascist methods imposed by military force, the regime of Nazi Germany became an outrage and an obscenity. No sane person can lament its demise. But that condemnation has an inverse: a recognition of what is fair and legitimate in the desire of the German people to excel as a nation and to inspire the future of a prosperous Europe. So long as those objectives are pursued by just and peaceful means, we have every reason to wish them well.

The Old and New Germany. President Paul Von Hindenburg, followed by his Chancellor, Adolf Hitler, is greeted by enthusiastic crowds in Potsdam following a carefully orchestrated ceremony designed to link National Socialism with Prussian Conservatism. (Library of Congress)

II The Seizure of Power

Variety of Opinion

Support for the NSDAP was not uniform and was influenced by the same factors which determined support for the other parties.

Geoffrey Pridham

Support for National Socialism . . . was, however, by no means confined to the lower middle class or to socially marginal declassés.

Thomas Childers

Hitler became Reich Chancellor. His appointment was quite unnecessary.

A. J. Nicholls

Hitler always found obedient instruments to carry out his eccentric radicalism.

Joachim C. Fest

Nazi violence took on a new significance as the storm troopers were able, virtually unhindered, to mount a campaign of terror during the first half of 1933.

Richard Bessel

*Next we turn to consider the practical means by which the Nazi move-
ment conducted the long march to political prominence. The ascent was
steep, and not without obstacles and pitfalls. Yet the party pressed on with
an astonishing display of maneuver, ruse, and tenacity — all of which
are evident in the accounts that follow.*

Geoffrey Pridham *writes about the early days of the Nazi party,
when it was an obscure rightist splinter group in the southern German
state of Bavaria. There, in 1923, Adolf Hitler and his cohort burst onto
the scene during a bizarre attempt to bring down the Weimar Republic
by executing a military putsch in Munich. The inglorious failure of that
episode brought Hitler a certain notoriety and a chance to rethink his
tactics. From this base, Pridham explains, Nazism gradually moved
northward as it developed a dynamic leadership and mass appeal.*

Thomas Childers *analyzes the electoral strategy of the Nazi party,
which solicited votes from all segments of German society in an attempt
to transcend the narrow bounds of region, confession, and class. While
he recognizes Nazism's obvious attraction for adult lower-middle-class
males, Childers shows that it also made conspicuous inroads with the
affluent bourgeoisie, youth, women, and even some blue-collar workers.
Hitler's party had the least success among those social groups that already had stable political affiliations: Catholics who voted for the Center party (Zentrum) and industrial workers who supported either the
Social Democratic party (SPD) or the Communist party (KPD). Childers
sees the Nazi organization (NSDAP) as an agent of protest whose platform was anticapitalist, antimodernist, and to its core anti-Semitic.*

A. J. Nicholls *narrates the final months of political crisis in late
1932, when the Weimar Republic collapsed and Hitler emerged as chancellor. Franz von Papen and Kurt von Schleicher, two representatives of
the old elites, unsuccessfully attempted to bail Germany out of difficulty
with one last manipulation. At the same time, within the Nazi camp,
Gregor Strasser posed a possible alternative to Hitler, whose party was
showing signs of electoral fatigue and financial exhaustion. Already in
his late eighties, President Paul von Hindenburg sought a solution and
foolishly agreed to a desperate gamble: Hitler was allowed to enter the
cabinet as a minority member, where he might be controlled by his more
respectable colleagues. But, as we know, this calculated risk was a fatal
mistake. Within a few weeks Hitler would sweep the others aside.*

Joachim C. Fest *describes the Nazi political takeover amid an initial popular euphoria, and he identifies what was unique about this*

German form of fascism. The key, Fest contends, lay in a fanatical sense of morality, as though the Nazis succeeded because they were able to convert Germany into one huge Boy Scout camp. In all of this there was a loss of reality. Traditional standards of behavior were suspended and replaced by a special mission to fulfill a higher law. Thus, the first excitement of Nazism soon led to a widespread moral confusion.

Richard Bessel supplies the details of how Nazi squads of bullies, the SA, were able to throttle open or latent opposition through terrorist tactics. These included smashing property, ransacking offices, beating, torturing, and in scattered instances even killing individuals. A determined campaign of brutal physical intimidation was especially directed against the old trade-union movement. Those disinclined to cooperate were suddenly put at great risk. By these means, after the Nazis had risen to power, they quickly tightened their grasp.

Hence, within ten years, a small and floundering gang of Bavarian rowdies managed to reach the pinnacle of the German state. Once ensconced there, the Nazis set about to consolidate their conquest and to subdue all sectors of society. Better than their opponents, they realized that — in politics as on the playing field — a good offense is the best defense.

Geoffrey Pridham

The Roots of Nazism

The Nazi "seizure of power" in 1933 brought a political revolution in Germany, but the relative ease and rapidity with which the Nazis secured control over the state can only be explained in the context of the enduring political crisis of the preceding years. The Weimar Republic had failed to establish its legitimacy making it vulnerable during a time of economic and political upheaval. The Depression of the early

1930s crystallized the weaknesses of its political structure and accelerated the disintegration of its authority. The NSDAP assumed at the same time the role of the main opposition force in the state and infiltrated many different levels of German political life. Although it acted generally within constitutional bounds, the NSDAP nevertheless managed to present itself not only as an alternative government but also as an alternative political system. This distinction became clouded towards the end of the Weimar period, when the Republic became less of a democracy in reality and moved towards an authoritarian régime.

The rise in popular support for the NSDAP within the space of a few years was still phenomenal in spite of all these conditions, for in 1928 it had counted as merely one of a number of small parties in terms of electoral support. The party's reputation at this time was based not on its success in attracting voters but on the dramatic event of the Munich Putsch and the notoriety of its leader as a mob orator. A study of the NSDAP in Bavaria offers many lessons on how the party achieved its success. These may be summarized under the general headings: the character of the NSDAP as a totalitarian movement; the nature and extent of its mass appeal; and the relationship between the NSDAP and the state.

Firstly, the party's rise in prominence in the early 1930s was made possible by the fact that it had already established an elaborate leadership structure and laid the organizational basis for its expansion as a mass movement. The NSDAP emerged from the period of its prohibition after the Putsch in a state of weakness owing to the divisions among its leaders and activists and its limited appeal to the public. Its principal strength then was the figure of Hitler, who had succeeded in surrounding himself with the myths associated with the Putsch by the right-wing opposition to the Weimar Republic. It was already apparent at this stage that Hitler's charismatic leadership was entirely separate from internal party disputes and conflicts over policies and tactics, a factor which remained constant throughout the years of the party's rise to power and proved crucial during the critical months which preceded Hitler's appointment as Chancellor.

The pull of Hitler's *Führer* appeal among his followers was especially strong in Bavaria, where his release from prison late in 1924 soon led to rival party groups dissolving their differences and submitting themselves without question to his control. Hitler encountered less difficulty in reasserting his authority in Bavaria than anywhere else in the country because his party had its strongest roots here, as it had certain "Bavarian" associations which in fact made it less attractive among party circles in Northern Germany and because of the proximity of party headquarters which allowed Hitler to make greater use of direct contact with local party leaders there. But the memory of the Munich Putsch proved to be a double-edged sword. While it enhanced Hitler's image in the eyes of the extreme Right, it also dominated the view of Hitler held by the Bavarian authorities. Their decision to ban Hitler from making public speeches for two years shortly after the party was refounded neutralized the main asset enjoyed by the NSDAP.

The situation appeared stable when the ban on Hitler's speeches was lifted in 1927, but it was nevertheless evident that the NSDAP constituted a different kind of party from the others on the extreme Right of German politics, not to mention the moderate parties in the Weimar Republic. If the NSDAP was most akin ideologically to the Nationalist Party (DNVP), it had more in common in terms of party structure with the Communists (KPD) from whom it borrowed ideas on methods of organization and techniques of mass agitation. The NSDAP and the KPD were similar in their attention to new methods of propaganda, although the former used these more successfully in mobilizing wider sections of the electorate. Both parties would be classified as totalitarian, but the main difference between them was the prominence given to ideology by the Communists and the emphasis on the *Führer* figure in the case of the Nazis.

The "*Führer* principle," which had held the party together during the years of its eclipse in the mid 1920s, now became more elaborately systematized. The changes in organization during 1928–29 involved a rearrangement of departments at headquarters, alterations in the regional structure of the party to coordinate it with the electoral system, as well as a more methodical and centralized approach to party activities. . . .

The continuous emphasis on propaganda activities and electoral success which followed created a momentum of its own among party activists. The image of activism which the party cultivated and its promise of a new kind of involvement in politics accounted for the increasing attraction felt by young people towards the NSDAP. A generational gap emerged between the totalitarian parties — for the KPD was also successful in winning the active support of young people — and the older traditional parties. This momentum furthermore reduced the possibilities of conflict within the party by providing a common focus of activity, although tension and differences were still apparent over adaptation to new techniques in rural propaganda, attempts to initiate a party press and in some cases over the development of specialist organizations. When the momentum lapsed, as during the second half of 1932, the consequences were seen in the rise in internal party tension. Such conflict arose also from Hitler's deliberate policy of "divide and rule" as well as the existence in spite of the party's growing bureaucracy of a state of semi-anarchy with the overlapping of authority created by the proliferation of party offices. All these problems had no adverse effect on the central feature of the NSDAP, namely loyalty to the *Führer*, and in fact the accusation of insufficient loyalty to him was often used in internal party disputes. It was this characteristic together with the party's professional methods of organization and superior techniques of propaganda which distinguished it from conventional protest parties on the extreme Right.

Secondly, the NSDAP was distinguished by the unprecedented degree with which it attracted mass support. Its achievement could be attributed partly to its successful organization, but the answer must also lie in the nature of its popular appeal. There were two main sources of its electoral support: firstly, the liberal and conservative parties in the towns and the peasant parties in the countryside; and, secondly, the new voters. The NSDAP succeeded largely in attracting the support of the middle classes, although it endeavoured to present itself as an integrative force which claimed to represent different interests in society, a claim strengthened by the flexibility of its propaganda and its development of specialist organizations. The NSDAP came the closest there was in the Weimar period to a "people's party" (*Volkspartei*) appealing across classes and interests. . . .

Support for the NSDAP was not uniform and was influenced by the same factors which determined support for the other parties. The most important of these factors was confession. It is clear from the voting patterns of the NSDAP in Bavaria that support for the party was much higher among Protestants than among Catholics. The confessional factor was evident too at the local level of politics where Protestant and Catholic communities were neighbours in the same area and even cut across economic interests, for the NSDAP faced more problems in winning over the peasantry in Catholic areas than it did in the Protestant areas of rural Franconia. The reason for the importance of the confessional factor was firstly the existence of a strong Catholic party, and secondly the fact that in the case of Bavaria Catholic interests were allied with regional patriotism. There were certain similarities between the Bavarian People's Party and the NSDAP, for both managed to appeal across classes and both were essentially "ideological" rather than interest parties, but the substructure of politics in the traditional region of "Old Bavaria" was weighted in favour of the BVP. This party owed the stability of its vote until 1933 to the active and moral support of the Catholic associations and the Catholic Church as well as to its ability to project its own "fundamental view of life" which offered a form of emotional security in a time of crisis. . . .

Thirdly, the NSDAP's rise to power has finally to be examined with reference to its relationship with the state. The case of Bavaria again throws interesting light on how such a totalitarian party operated in a parliamentary system like that of the Weimar Republic. Hitler had chosen the path of "legality" out of necessity, but this did not exclude the violent element in the Nazi movement for it rather contained it. Hitler managed to siphon off the energies of the most revolutionary wing in the party, the SA, by using them as fuel for his electoral locomotive. Yet political violence was endemic in German politics then and helped to make a sham of Weimar democracy. It was evident not so much in the form of political assassinations, which had marked the early years of the Republic, as the way in which it intruded into everyday politics — through the existence of party military organizations, and the change in the political atmosphere with the growth of civil warfare during the last critical years of the Republic. Such a state of affairs seriously affected the authority of the Republic and brought about a polarization of politics, which could only benefit a party promising a new form of law and order.

The NSDAP's attitude to Bavarian particularism was to some extent a barometer of its general attitude towards the state. Whereas previously the party had camouflaged its centralist tendencies and sought to take refuge in Bavarian hostility to the Reich, it showed less sympathy for Bavarian susceptibilities once it gained a wide popular following and was no longer dependent on the goodwill of the Bavarian Government. The Reichstag Election of 1930 was an important stage in this development, for electoral success blessed the Nazis with political respectability and made adherence to their cause not merely one of ideological conviction or hostility to the Republic but also one of political opportunism. The party's change of attitude to Bavarian particularism became clear during the summer of 1932, when the government in Munich found itself in conflict with the new Reich Chancellor over his decision to lift the ban on the SA. By this time, Bavaria had assumed a different role in the Weimar Republic. It was no longer the patron of right-wing extremism, as it had been in the early 1920s, and had become now a source of resistance to the growth of authoritarian tendencies in national politics.

Bavaria's importance as an individual state during the political crisis which enveloped Germany in the early 1930s was reduced, however, by the general disintegration of authority in the Weimar state and the dramatic rise in popular support for the NSDAP. The Bavarian Government proved incapable in the face of these developments to resist the Nazi "seizure of power" and was further weakened by its adherence to the conventional rules of politics at a time when they were becoming less relevant. The NSDAP had succeeded in pervading German political life by working within the system, but at the same time it had not lost its essential revolutionary characteristics in the form of its radical energies, its aim to create a new political order and its promise to bring new social élites and a younger generation to the summit of politics.

Thomas Childers

The Party's Electoral Appeal

From its first campaign in the spring of 1924 to the pinnacle of its electoral fortunes eight years later, the NSDAP remained an enigma

From *The Nazi Voter: The Social Foundations of Fascism in Germany, 1919–1933*, by Thomas Childers. Copyright © 1983 by The University of North Carolina Press. Reprinted by permission.

in German political life. Unlike their more established rivals, the National Socialists were never content to anchor their movement securely along the traditional lines of social, religious, and regional cleavage that had structured the German party system since its formation in the last half of the nineteenth century. Instead, they were determined to transcend those widely accepted restrictions on their potential constituency to become the first genuine party of mass integration in German political history. National Socialist electoral strategy, with its consistent efforts to mobilize support in every sector of the economy, in every occupational group, in every region, and in the major Christian confessions, vividly reflected that ambition. Although the party shifted the emphasis of its campaign strategy after 1928, revising the urban plan and concentrating more pointedly on the middle-class electorate, it never abandoned its efforts to cultivate a broader constituency. . . .

Although the NSDAP succeeded in exploiting the widespread disaffection with the traditional liberal and conservative options, support for the party was unevenly distributed among the different groups of the middle-class electorate. Indeed, support for National Socialism varied in duration and degree and sprang from a wide variety of motives. It was, however, by no means confined to the lower middle class or to socially marginal declassés. The nucleus of the NSDAP's following was formed by the small farmers, shopkeepers, and independent artisans of the old middle class, who constituted the most stable and consistent components of the National Socialist constituency between 1924 and 1932. It was among these groups that the fear of social and economic displacement associated with the emergence of modern industrial society was most pronounced, and it was among these groups that the NSDAP's corporatist, anti-Marxist, and anticapitalist slogans struck their most responsive chord. Nazi sympathies within the old middle class certainly intensified and broadened after the onset of the depression, but the persistence of those sympathies even in the period of relative prosperity between 1924 and 1928 strongly suggests that this support did not represent a spasmodic reaction to immediate economic difficulties but expressed a congenital dissatisfaction with long-term trends in German economic and social life. . . .

Although National Socialist sympathies among lower-middle-class white-collar employees were less developed than expected, the NSDAP found a surprisingly large following in more established social circles. By 1932 the party had won considerable support among the upper middle-class student bodies of the universities, among civil servants, even in the middle and upper grades, and in affluent electoral districts of Berlin, Hamburg, and other cities. Motivations were myriad, including fear of the Marxist left, frustrated career ambitions, and resentment at the erosion of social prestige and professional security. Yet, while sizable elements of these groups undoubtedly felt their positions or prospects challenged during the Weimar era, they cannot be described as uneducated, economically devastated, or socially marginal. They belonged, in fact, to the established elites of German society.

Just as the Nazis were winning support from elements of both the upper- and lower-middle classes, they also secured a significant constituency within the blue-collar working class. Usually ignored or dismissed as unimportant, the NSDAP's prominent solicitation of a working-class following and its success in the endeavor, were exceptional in the context of German electoral politics. Aside from the confessionally oriented Zentrum, the NSDAP was alone among the non-Marxist parties in its efforts to establish an electorate within the blue-collar population. Even after 1928, the party refused to concede the blue-collar electorate to the left and continued to invest a surprising amount of energy to win working-class voters. Nor were those efforts — which led the traditional bourgeois parties to denounce the Nazis as Bolsheviks — without effect. Despite hostility and indifference from the organized industrial *Arbeiterschaft*, the party's appeal found considerable resonance among that sizable body of workers in handicrafts and small-scale manufacturing. These workers were usually employed in small shops or in government enterprises and were rarely integrated into either the organized working class or the entrepreneurial *Mittelstand*. Their support was loudly trumpeted in the Nazi press and was extremely important in establishing the public image the Nazis sought to project, allowing them to maintain, with some degree of credibility, that they had succeeded in bridging the great social divide of German electoral politics.

The generational and sexual composition of the Nazi constituency was also broader than traditionally assumed. Usually treated as the party of youth, the NSDAP, in fact, found its greatest electoral support among groups composed of older voters. The party effectively pursued the vote of the *Rentnermittelstand*, 53 percent of whom were over sixty years of age. Similarly, less than 10 percent of the shopkeepers, self-employed artisans, and other entrepreneurs in the old middle class were under thirty. In addition, the male-dominated NSDAP attracted a steadily increasing percentage of women voters after 1928. In the final elections of the Weimar era, women appear to have surpassed men in the Nazi electorate.

By 1932 the NSDAP could, therefore, approach the German electorate claiming the coveted mantle of a *Volkspartei*. Its constituency was certainly broader than that of the traditional bourgeois parties or of the Marxist left. Yet, even after the NSDAP's dramatic surge between 1929 and 1932, the limits of its expansion were clearly defined by the two most prominent predictors of German electoral behavior, class and religion. Although the Nazis had won adherents within the blue-collar electorate, they proved unable to establish a significant foothold within the industrial working class. Among workers in the major industrial sectors, electoral sympathies continued to be divided chiefly between the SPD and KPD. Even as unemployment soared after 1928, working-class radicalism found political expression in a Communist vote, not in support for National Socialism. The fragmentation of political loyalties that had increasingly splintered the middle-class electorate after 1924 did not infect the constituencies of the Marxist left. While the liberal, conservative, and special interest parties virtually collapsed between 1930 and 1932, the Marxist parties maintained a remarkably strong and stable electoral base. Despite their efforts to cultivate a working-class constituency, the Nazis were confronted by a solid bloc of blue-collar support for the Marxist left that showed no signs of disintegration even at the apex of Nazi electoral fortunes.

The NSDAP also encountered a major obstacle to its ambitions in the Catholic population. Although the party won an increasing percentage of the Catholic vote after 1928, its electoral base remained far smaller in Catholic Germany than in Protestant areas. Catholic support for National Socialism was by and large concentrated in the same occupational and social groups that formed the mainstays of the party's constituency in Protestant areas, but the NSDAP was never able to undermine the solid foundation of Catholic support for the Zentrum. Backed by the Church, the Zentrum, like the Marxist parties, offered its followers a well-defined belief system vigorously reinforced by an extensive network of political, social, and cultural organizations. Although a vote for the Zentrum after 1930 was hardly an enthusiastic endorsement of the Weimar system, the strong Catholic support for the party continued to impose a solid barrier to the potential expansion of the National Socialist constituency.

Given these limitations to the appeal of National Socialism, what does the composition of the Nazi constituency reveal about the social foundations of fascism in Germany? First, the most consistent electoral support for the party was concentrated in those social and occupational groups that harbored the greatest reservations about the development of modern industrial society and that expressed, through their organizations, socially exclusive, corporatist views of their socioeconomic position. By the same token, its appeal was weakest in that segment of the population most prominently identified with modern industrial society, the industrial working class. Even within the new middle class, where electoral sympathies were scattered across the political spectrum, support for National Socialism was concentrated to a surprising extent in the traditionally conservative civil service. . . .

Nazi antimodernism was, therefore, not a simple assault on modern technology or a promise to dismantle one of the world's most advanced industrial economies and return to a romanticized agrarian past. It was instead a fundamental rejection of the social and political implications of modernization, a rejection that found its most vivid expression in the NSDAP's visceral attacks on both Marxist socialism and liberal capitalism. It was in the party's relentless offensive against these manifestations of modern political and economic life that the NSDAP's anti-Semitism was most prominently displayed before 1933. While Rosenberg and other party theorists continued to develop — and publish — the radical racial doctrine that formed the true core of National Socialist ideology, the party's day-to-day political literature tended to emphasize a more familiar form of social and economic anti-Semitism. This strategy of linking Jews with both "supercapitalism" and bolshevism proved doubly effective for the Nazis. On the one hand, it allowed the NSDAP to exploit an already deeply engrained form of anti-Semitic sentiment in German political culture during a period of protracted economic distress; on the other, it lulled even those parties that took public stands against the NSDAP's obsession with "the Jewish question" into the mistaken assumption that it was merely another ephemeral manifestation of that traditional anti-Semitism which had surfaced periodically in the German party system since 1890. . . .

Yet, even at the height of its popularity at the polls, the NSDAP's position as a people's party was tenuous at best. If the party's support

The Voice of Authority. Propaganda chief Joseph Goebbels preached the Nazi gospel and many believed. His clear diction and ironic wit made Goebbels an effective advocate of his cause. (UPI/Corbis-Bettmann)

was a mile wide, it was at critical points an inch deep. The NSDAP had managed to build a remarkably diverse constituency, overcoming regional divisions, linking town and country, spanning the social divides, and shrinking the gap between confessions. Yet, the basis of that extraordinary electoral alliance was dissatisfaction, resentment, and fear. As a result, the Nazi constituency, even at the pinnacle of the party's electoral popularity, remained highly unstable. Indeed, the fragmentation of the NSDAP's volatile electorate was already under way in November 1932. Whether the Nazis would have been able to maintain their appeal under improving economic conditions remains, of course, a moot question, but for a party of protest such continued success is doubtful. Even in the flush of their victories in 1932, Nazi leaders were aware of the party's vulnerability. "Something has to happen now," Goebbels noted in his diary following the NSDAP's victory in Prussia during April. "We have to come to power in the near future or we will win ourselves to death in these elections." It therefore remains one of history's most tragic ironies that at precisely the moment when the party's electoral support had begun to falter, Hitler was installed as chancellor by representatives of those traditional elites who had done so much to undermine the parliamentary system in Germany and who still believed that the National Socialist movement could be safely harnessed for their reactionary objectives.

A. J. Nicholls

The Final Step to Power

Hitler was determined to receive the Chancellorship and wreak his vengeance on the "Marxists." President Hindenburg, on the other hand, set his face against both Hitler and a cabinet based on parliament. If the Nazis entered the Government it would be as subordinates in a presidential régime. During these months Hitler showed great political courage in refusing anything but the highest post. There were important men in his party, the most prominent being

Gregor Strasser, who felt that the Nazi wave had reached its crest and that the time had come to taste the fruits of office. There was reason in this. Hitler's intransigence was beginning to alarm some of his wealthy business patrons. They found von Papen, who was sympathetic to industrial interests, more attractive than earlier Chancellors, and they detected ominous signs of social radicalism in the SA. Some of them cut their links with the Nazis and others became less generous. In the party as a whole the frenzied activism of the previous months could not be maintained without tangible achievements.

The danger to the Nazis was demonstrated in the autumn of 1932 when von Papen, faced with a completely uncooperative Reichstag, dissolved it yet again. On 6 November Germans trooped to the polls once more. Electoral participation was still high, although not the astonishing 83 per cent registered in July. For the first time since 1928 the Nazis lost votes in a Reichstag election, their share of the poll falling from 37.4 per cent to 33.1 per cent. The German Nationalists, who had begun to stress their difference with the Nazis, gained nearly 800,000 votes, and the People's Party improved its position slightly, though it only returned eleven deputies. Von Papen could claim that he was making ground, despite the fact that his supporters were still a tiny minority. He and President Hindenburg were quite prepared to go on governing without parliament — a breach of the constitution — until they were ready to implement a complete programme of constitutional reform. Von Papen had drawn up a number of public-works schemes which he hoped would ease the unemployment situation. If the army and the President kept their trust in him he might survive.

It was here that von Papen's political inexperience revealed itself. His unpopularity was so widespread that even his colleagues feared a civil war if the government openly violated the constitution on his behalf. Such fears had been increased at the beginning of November, when Nazis and Communists had collaborated to organise a transport strike in Berlin. Acts of sabotage and violence accompanied this extremist alliance. Upbraided by his wealthier sympathisers, Hitler replied that, unless he allowed his rank and file to take such action, they would desert to the Communists. Reichswehr commanders were alarmed lest their soldiers should have to fight the SA and the Communists. They thought the Poles might take the opportunity to attack Germany. Their anxiety was almost certainly exaggerated. A partnership between Nazis and Communists would have been difficult to maintain and would have aroused fierce opposition from such disparate political elements as the Reichsbanner and the Stahlhelm. Nevertheless, von Schleicher, now convinced that von Papen was a liability, stressed the dark side of the military picture, and his cabinet colleagues agreed with him. Von Papen resigned.

On 2 December von Schleicher himself became Chancellor. It was an exposed position which he had not coveted. Power without responsibility had been his goal. In one important respect he was even weaker than von Papen. His relations with the President had grown cooler since the previous spring. Von Papen had quite replaced him in Hindenburg's favour.

Von Schleicher was an ingenious man who did not lack courage. Having failed once more to negotiate with Hitler, he attempted to create popular support for his government by cutting across normal party lines. Gregor Strasser, still regarded as Hitler's main rival within the Nazi Party, had previously indicated that he might be willing to break with his chief and take office under another Chancellor. Von Schleicher also tried to appeal to the trade unions with schemes of work creation. He envisaged projects for compulsory youth training and cheap labour for farmers. Had he remained in office, he was even prepared to consider nationalising the coal and steel industry.

Imaginative though these ideas were, they quickly collapsed in practice. Strasser was forced to resign his offices in the Nazi Party on 8 December. The Christian and Social Democratic Trade Unions rebuffed von Schleicher. In desperation he turned to the Social Democrats but, fortified with the belief that the Nazi tide had turned, they refused to join his government. Schleicher was forced to ask Hindenburg for the power to govern unconstitutionally — something which had been refused to von Papen.

The President had no desire to accept this. Besides, it was not necessary. Von Papen had been negotiating with Hitler, and had convinced Hindenburg that the Nazi leader should be given the post of Chancellor. Von Papen was confident he could control Hitler. Schleicher had to resign. He greatly feared that Papen would be his successor. The Reichswehr leaders thought that this really would lead to a civil war in which 90 per cent of the nation would be against them. Their apprehension soon disappeared. On 30 January Hitler became Reich Chancellor.

His appointment was quite unnecessary. His coalition government, in which Hugenberg's Nationalists were the only other party represented, had no majority in the Reichstag. The Nazis could not have threatened the State if they had been denied power. Their movement was waning. A further period of frustration might have finished them off. It was perhaps for this reason that Hitler became attractive to men of property in Germany. If his mass support ebbed away the beneficiaries would either be the democratic Weimar parties or the Communists. The dream of national resurgence based on an authoritarian régime would then have been destroyed.

In any case, von Papen and his friends thought they could manage the Nazis. Hitler's men had only two major posts in the Reich government, those of the Chancellor and Minister of the Interior. Von Papen was Vice-Chancellor and Prime Minister of Prussia, and had the ear of the President. A general, Blomberg, headed the Defence Ministry. Hugenberg was Minister of Economics and Food, and Seldte, the Stahlhelm leader, Minister of Labour. There seemed little danger that the Nazis would overwhelm their colleagues.

Within a month Hitler had demonstrated how complacent von Papen had been. Having made a show of negotiating for a coalition with the Centre, Hitler persuaded his colleagues to dissolve the Reichstag for a third general election. He promised them that he would not change the complexion of his cabinet even if he won. The election campaign was conducted under quite unfair conditions, because the authority of the state was at Hitler's disposal. Göring had been appointed Prussian Minister of the Interior, and thus controlled police power in almost two-thirds of Germany. He recruited 50,000 "auxiliary police," most of whom were Nazi storm-troopers. The regular police were purged and ordered to protect Nazis and Nationalists against "Marxist" attack.

On 27 February the Reichstag in Berlin was set on fire by a young Dutchman of extreme left-wing opinions. Using this as a pretext to claim that Germany was threatened by a Bolshevik *coup*, Hitler issued a presidential decree "for the Protection of the People and the State." For many years this was to be one of the main foundations of Nazi tyranny. It swept away constitutional safeguards against arbitrary arrest and the suppression of free speech. A wave of arrests followed. Hitler's opponents believed that the Reichstag fire had been a Nazi plot. This now seems unlikely, but the issue is not an important one. The Nazis had made preparations to take emergency action before the fire, and, had it not occurred, other excuses would have been found.

The Reichstag elections on 5 April did not give Hitler an absolute majority, despite the enormous pressure exerted on the electorate. But with almost 44 per cent of the vote, and in coalition with Hugenberg's Nationalists, Hitler could command a simple majority in the Reichstag.

The Burning of the Reichstag, February 27, 1937. Berliners watch the flames rise from the Reichstag building. The fire, allegedly set by a young Dutch Communist, gave Hitler the necessary pretext to gain emergency powers from Hindenburg. (Ullstein Bilderdienst)

The opposition to him was completely incapable of offering effective resistance. The Centre Party had already shown itself willing to collaborate with Hitler, and its leader, prelate Kaas, now desired only to safeguard the religious freedom of German Catholics. The parties of the moderate right had already been destroyed as an electoral force in the summer of 1932. The Communists were arrested or forced into hiding. Only the Social Democrats tried to put a brave face on defeat. When, on 23 March 1933, Hitler presented the Reichstag with an enabling law empowering him to rule by decree, the Social Democrats were the one group to vote against it. With that last gesture of defiance, their Weimar Republic was finally interred. Hitler was the master of Germany.

Joachim C. Fest

Enthusiasm and Confusion

The dramatic ceremonial with which Hitler took over the chancellorship, the accompaniment of torchlight parades and mass demonstrations, bore no relationship to the constitutional importance of the event. For, strictly speaking, January 30, 1933, brought nothing more than a change of administrations. Nevertheless, the public sensed that the appointment of Hitler as Chancellor could not be compared with the cabinet reshufflings of former years. Despite all the vaunted intentions of the German Nationalist coalition partners "to keep the frustrated Austrian painter on the leash," the Nazis from the start made ready to seize full power and to apply it in revolutionary ways. All the efforts of Papen and his fellows to play a part in the oratory, the celebrating, or the directing of affairs only gave the impression of breathless running to keep up. Numerical superiority in the cabinet, influence with the President, or in the economy, the army, and the bureaucracy could not conceal the fact that this was their rival's hour.

After January 30 a mass desertion to the Nazi camp began. Once again the axiom was proved that in revolutionary times principles are cheap, and perfidy, calculation, and fear reign supreme. This was true, but not the whole truth. For the massive political turncoatism bespoke not only lack of character and servility. Quite often it represented the spontaneous desire to give up old prejudices, ideologies, and social restrictions and to join with others in making a fresh start. "We were not all opportunists," wrote the poet Gottfried Benn in retrospect, speaking as one of the vast host of people who were carried along by the force of the spreading revolutionary mood. Powerful traditional parties and associations cracked under the propagandistic onslaught; and even before they were forcibly dissolved and banned they left a leaderless following to its own devices. The past — republic, divisiveness, impotence — was over and done with. A rapidly shrinking minority did not succumb to the frenzy. But such holdouts were driven into isolation; they saw themselves excluded from those celebrations of the new sense of community, from those who could reveal in mass oaths in cathedrals of lights, in addresses by the Führer, in mountaintop bonfires and choral singing by hundreds of thousands of voices. Even the first signs of the reign of terror could not mute the rejoicing. The public mind interpreted the terror as an expression of a ruthlessly operating energy for which it had looked all too long in vain.

These concomitants of enthusiasm are what have given Hitler's seizure of power its distressing note. For they undermine all the arguments for its having been a historical accident, the product of intrigues or dark conspiracies. Any attempt to explain the events of those years has always had to face the question of how Nazism could so rapidly and effortlessly have conquered the majority, not just attained power, in an ancient and experienced civilized nation. And how could it have thrown that majority into a peculiarly hysterical state compounded of enthusiasm, credulity, and devotion? How could the political, social, and moral checks and balances, which a country belonging to the "nobility of nations" after all possesses, have so glaringly failed? Before Hitler came to power, an observer described what he considered the inevitable course of events: "Dictatorship, abolition of the parliament, crushing of all intellectual liberties, inflation, terror, civil war; for the opposition could not simply be made to disappear. A general strike would be called. The unions would provide a core for the bitterest kind of resistance; they would be joined by the Reichs-banner and by all those concerned about the future. And if Hitler won over even the Army and met the opposition with cannon — he would find millions of resolute antagonists." But there were no millions of resolute antagonists and consequently no need for a bloody coup. On the other hand, Hitler did not come like a thief in the night. With his histrionic verbosity he revealed, more perhaps than any other politician, what he had been aiming for through all the byways and tactical maneuvers: dictatorship, anti-Semitism, conquest of living space.

Understandably enough, the euphoria of those weeks gave many observers the impression that Germany had rediscovered her true self. Although the Constitution and the rules of the political game as played in the republic remained valid for the time being, they nevertheless seemed curiously obsolete, cast off like an alien shell. And for decades this image — of a nation that seemed to have found itself in exuberantly turning away from the European tradition of rationality and humane progress — determined the interpretation of events. . . .

Without doubt there were unmistakably German features in National Socialism; but they are of a different and more complex kind than those set forth by Vermeil or Shirer. No genealogy of evil, no single explanation, can do justice to the nature of the phenomenon. Nor should we see its seeds only in the obviously dark and ominous elements in the German past. Many naïve attitudes, or at any rate attitudes that for generations caused no trouble, and even some virtues and commendable values, made the success of Nazism possible. One of the lessons the era has to teach us is that a totalitarian power system need not be built up upon a nation's deviant or even criminal tendencies. A nation cannot decide, like a Richard III, to become a villain. Historical, psychological, and even social conditions comparable to those in Germany existed in many countries, and frequently only a fine line separated other nations from Fascist rule. The Germans were not the only people to arrive late at the sense of nationhood, or to be behindhand at developing democratic institutions. As for the unbridgeable gulfs between liberal and socialist forces, between the bourgeoisie and the working class, these, too, were not peculiarly German. We may also question whether revanchist yearnings, bellicose ideologies, or dreams of great power status were more pronounced in Germany than in some of her European neighbors. And even anti-Semitism, decisively though it governed Hitler's thinking, was surely not a specifically German phenomenon. In fact, it was rather weaker among the

Germans than in most other peoples. Racial emotions did not, at any rate, win the masses over to National Socialism or kindle their enthusiasm. Hitler himself was cognizant of this, as his efforts to play down his anti-Semitism during the final phase of his struggle for power plainly showed.

During the same era many Fascist or Fascist-oriented movements came in power — in Italy, Turkey, Poland, Austria, and Spain, for example. What was peculiarly German about National Socialism emerges most clearly by comparison with the systems in these other countries: it was the most radical, the most absolute manifestation of Fascism.

This fundamental rigor, which came out on the intellectual as well as the administrative plane, was Hitler's personal contribution to the nature of National Socialism. In his way of sharply opposing an idea to reality, of elevating what ought to be above what is, he was truly German. The failed local politician, subletting a room on Thierschstrasse, sketched triumphal arches and domed halls that were to assure his posthumous fame. Ignoring mockery, the Chancellor did not reckon in generations, but in millennia; he wanted to undo not merely the Treaty of Versailles and Germany's impotence but nothing less than the consequences of the great migrations. Whereas Mussolini's ambition aimed at restoring a lost historical grandeur, whereas Maurras called for a return to the *ancien régime* and the *"gloire de la Déesse France,"* whereas all the other Fascisms could do no better than invoke a past golden age, Hitler set himself a goal more grandiose than anything the world had ever seen: an empire stretching from the Atlantic to the Urals and from Narvik to Suez. His pure master race seeking its rightful place would fight for and win this empire. Would other countries oppose him? He would crush them. Were peoples located contrary to his plans? He would resettle them. Did the races fail to correspond to his image? He would select, breed, eliminate until the reality fitted his conception. He was always thinking the unthinkable; in his statements an element of bitter refusal to submit to reality invariably emerged. His personality was not without manic characteristics. "I confront everything with a tremendous, ice-cold lack of bias," he declared. He seemed authentically himself only when he spoke and acted with the utmost radicality. To that extent, National Socialism cannot be conceived apart from Hitler.

Among the things that set Nazism apart from the Fascist movements of other countries is the fact that Hitler always found obedient instruments to carry out his eccentric radicalism. No stirrings of pity mitigated the concentrated and punctilious harshness of the regime. Its barbarous features have often been ascribed to the deliberate application of cruelty by murderers and sadists, and such criminal elements continue to loom large in the popular mind. To this day types of this sort appear in literary works, whip in hand, as the personifications of Nazism. But the regime had quite another picture of itself. No question about its making use of such people, especially in the initial phase; but it quickly realized that lasting rule cannot be founded upon the unleashing of criminal instincts. The radicality that constituted the true nature of National Socialism does not really spring from the license it offered to instinctual gratification. The problem was not one of criminal impulses but of a perverted moral energy.

Those to whom Nazism chiefly appealed were people with a strong but directionless craving for morality. In the SS, National Socialism trained this type and organized it into an elite corps. The "inner values" that were perpetually being preached within this secular monastic order — the theme of many an evening meeting complete with romantic torchlight — included, according to the prescript of Heinrich Himmler, the following virtues: loyalty, honesty, obedience, hardness, decency, poverty, and bravery. But all these virtues were detached from any comprehensive frame of reference and directed entirely toward the purposes of the regime. Under the command of such imperatives a type of person was trained who demanded "cold, in fact, stony attitudes" of himself, as one of them wrote, and had "ceased to have human feelings." Out of his harshness toward himself he derived the justification for harshness toward others. The ability to walk over dead bodies was literally demanded of him; and before that could be developed, his own self had to be deadened. It is this impassive, mechanical quality that strikes the observer as far more extreme than sheer brutality. For the killer who acts out of an overpowering social, intellectual, or human resentment exerts a claim, however small, upon our sympathy.

The moral imperative was supplemented and crowned by the idea of a special mission: the sense of taking part in an apocalyptic confrontation, of obeying a "higher law," of being the agent of an ideal. Images and slogans alike were made to seem like metaphysical commandments, and a special consecration was conferred upon relentlessness. That is how Hitler meant it when he denounced those who cast doubt on his mission as "enemies of the people." This fanaticism, this fixation upon his own deeper insight and his own loftier missionary aims, reflected the traditional German false relationship to politics, and beyond that the nation's peculiarly distorted relationship to reality in general. The real world in which ideas take form and are experienced by people, in which thoughts can be translated into despairs, anxieties, hatreds, and terrors, simply did not exist. All that existed was the program, and the process of putting it across, as Hitler occasionally remarked, involved either positive or negative activity. The lack of humanitarian imagination (which comes to the fore whenever Nazi criminals are brought to trial, from the Nuremberg Trials on) was nothing but the expression of this loss of a sense of reality. That was the characteristically German element in National Socialism, and there is reason to believe that various connecting lines run far back into German history.

Richard Bessel

Tightening the Grip

The formation of the Hitler government on 30 January 1933 changed the position of the SA fundamentally. Limitations upon the activities of the storm troopers hitherto — the need of the Nazi Party to avoid alienating public opinion, the threat of effective counter-measures by the police, and the possibility of intervention by the Reichswehr — were swept away. Nazi violence took on a new significance as the storm troopers were able, virtually unhindered, to mount a campaign of terror during the first half of 1933. While Hitler and his cabinet colleagues owed their new posts to neither a 'seizure of power' by the Nazi movement nor an upsurge in popular support but to a 'backstairs intrigue', the terror campaign of the SA helped the Nazi leader to consolidate his position and to transform a right-wing coalition government into the Nazi dictatorship. The activities of the SA in 1933 in effect constituted an 'uprising of the small-time Nazis', which to a

From Richard Bessel, *Political Violence and the Rise of Nazism: The Storm Troopers in Eastern Germany 1925–1934.* Copyright © 1984 by Yale University Press. Reprinted by Yale University Press.

considerable extent determined the pace and shape of the Nazi takeover. . . .

Immediately after assuming office Hitler submitted to Reich President von Hindenburg a formal request to dissolve the *Reichstag* and hold fresh elections, which were scheduled for 5 March. Thus for the next few weeks the main focus of SA activity was the elections which Göring, speaking to Ruhr industrialists on 20 February, claimed 'certainly would be the last for ten years, probably for one hundred years'. In some places bands of SA men attacked trade-union offices, meeting places of the left-wing parties and the homes of prominent Communists and Socialists. However, with the storm troopers mainly preoccupied with election campaigning, such violence was still on a relatively small scale.

A major escalation in the campaign against the Left was signalled in mid February when Göring, acting as Prussian Interior Minister, issued a series of decrees which opened new possibilities for Nazi violence. On 15 February Göring formally ordered the Prussian police to cease any surveillance of Nazi organisations; on 17 February he ordered that the police were not to interfere with the SA, SS or the *Stahlhelm* and were to avoid doing anything which might create the impression that they were persecuting the storm troopers, whom they were to support 'with all their powers'; and on 22 February, allegedly in response to the 'increasing disturbances from left-radical, and especially Communist, quarters', he ordered the formation of the 'auxiliary police' (*Hilfspolizei*) to be composed of members of the SA, SS and the *Stahlhelm*.

These measures were followed by an increase in SA violence (much of which preceded the *Reichstag* fire), and once again the Social Democrats proved particularly vulnerable. On the evening of 21 February, for example, a band of storm troopers attacked the 'Otto-Braun-Haus' in Königsberg, smashing windows but failing to get inside. On 26 February the SPD headquarters in Beuthen were occupied by the SA; the swastika flag was raised, rooms were searched and documents of the local miners' union branch were destroyed, and thereafter the building was placed under SA guard with the agreement of the police. . . .

Nevertheless it was after the elections that the really decisive assault was mounted. By early March the storm troopers, together with the police, had been able to paralyse the SPD and drive the KPD underground. Yet the organisational supports of Social Democracy — most importantly the trade unions — remained largely intact. But once the elections were past, the SA, freed of the need to assist with the campaigning of the NSDAP, could turn its attention to the root-and-branch destruction of the SPD and the trade-union movement.

The first major blow in eastern Germany was struck in Königsberg, immediately after the elections. On the night of 5 March the SA attacked and occupied the 'Otto-Braun-Haus', demolishing the local SPD and *Reichsbanner* offices in the process. The one-time nerve centre of East Prussian Social Democracy was transformed into an SA headquarters in which Socialists and Communists were beaten, tortured and — in the case of the KPD *Reichstag* deputy Walter Schütz — killed. Three days later the ADGB headquarters in Breslau fell to the storm troopers. Early in the morning of 8 March a group of about 250 SA men passed in front of the Breslau trade-union offices. According to the Nazis, shots were fired at the storm troopers from within the building; according to the defenders, the Nazis stormed the building unprovoked in order to hoist a swastika flag. In any event, the storm troopers had tried to occupy the union headquarters, there was gunfire, and as a result four people were injured seriously and one killed. Afterwards the SA searched the building, accompanied by members of the police force including the Breslau Police President and his deputy. Eleven occupants were arrested, and as soon as the police left and the search was entrusted solely to the SA, the storm troopers, some of whom were *Hilfspolizei*, proceeded to wreck the interior. . . .

The SA offensive against the trade unions gathered momentum as March progressed. On 13 March the ADGB headquarters in Görlitz were occupied by police and SA men, trade-union officials arrested and a portion of the building taken over by the SA. On 15 March storm troopers broke into trade-union offices in Reichenbach; and on the night of 18 March the SA assaulted the headquarters of the Pomeranian SPD in Stettin, wrecked the interior of the building, destroyed the SPD archive and printing presses and converted the cellar into a torture chamber for political opponents. On 20 March SA and SS men attacked the trade-union headquarters in Schneidemühl, which they had occupied for a short period the week before, threatened that any resistance would be met with armed force, destroyed furniture, stole whatever cash and useable articles could be found, and together with the police, arrested a number of union officials. On 21 and 22 March groups of SA men searched trade-union offices in Stargard, seizing the property which could be carried away. On 29 March in Greifswald, where police had shut the ADGB offices more than two weeks previously, SA men occupied the building during a police search and raised the swastika flag. By the end of March there remained hardly a single major town in eastern Germany where the Social Democratic trade unions could still function normally. By assaulting trade-union offices one-by-one, the SA managed to destroy what only weeks before had seemed the strongest bulwark against a Nazi takeover.

In one sense the violence against the Left during March and April 1933 may be seen as uncoordinated and even anarchic: there is no evidence that the attacks on Social Democratic targets were carried out on orders from Berlin or Munich; the assaults often appear simply to have been the spontaneous actions of bands of young men eager to prove themselves and settle old scores. However, the attacks on SPD and trade-union offices displayed a remarkably uniform pattern; if the activities of the SA in early 1933 spelt chaos, this was a structured chaos. The storm troopers were asserting in a perhaps incoherent but nonetheless unmistakable manner that they now were on top, that the former strongholds of their enemies now were *their* turf, that the old authority of the Socialist movement was at an end. Here it is important to remember that the principal target of this campaign was not the Communists (who already had borne the brunt of police repression and many of whom already had gone underground), but the generally older and more respectable Social Democrats who had been identified with the Weimar system. Thus in the components of the violence we can see an attack upon symbols of authority: in the removal of the old black-red-gold republican flag and the raising of the Nazi colours, in the destruction of the records of the trade unions, in the wrecking of property, in the public humiliation of Social Democratic functionaries, and in the conversion of many a 'Volkshaus' into an SA den where the building's former occupants could be tortured. Yet by March 1933 this attack on 'authority' carried very little risk, for the SPD and its allies already had been robbed of their press and positions of political power and were clearly on the defensive. . . .

The effects of this campaign of repression were devastating. Within roughly two months of Hitler's appointment as Reich Chancellor open opposition to the Nazis virtually had disappeared. For example, in the East Prussian *Kreis* Darknehmen Nazi Party leaders proudly boasted in mid-March that neither the SPD nor the KPD could hold meetings anywhere in the district, since these would either be prohibited or broken up; SPD supporters were prevented from canvassing from house to house; local Communist functionaries had been arrested; and KPD candidates were forced to withdraw their names from the Party lists for the *Kreistag* elections on 12 March. In Allenstein the local Nazi propaganda chief reported cheerfully in early April that neither the SPD nor the KPD were still active in the region; by the end of April only 23 members of the SPD were left in Allenstein and the membership of the ADGB trade unions had dropped to 167 from approximately 400 two months before. And in nearby *Kreis* Ortelsburg the district Nazi propaganda leader noted in April that the Communists and Social Democrats no longer showed any signs of activity, 'since virtually all the functionaries of the SPD and KPD are in custody'. Not only did such repression largely destroy the once impressive organisational networks of the working-class parties; it also isolated the working-class movement from the working class. By terrorising left-wing activists, raiding the offices of left-wing organisations, closing down left-wing newspapers, preventing Socialists and Communists from distributing printed material, driving members away from trade unions and making it clear that left-wing political activity now involved considerable physical danger, the Nazis made great strides in early 1933 toward cutting off the Left from its working-class constituency.

During the weeks after the formation of the Hitler government, support by the Nazi leadership for the terror campaign of the SA was conspicuously muted. Had the offensive failed, the Nazi leadership probably would have been no less prepared to distance itself from it than had been the case in late 1932. With the important exception of Göring, government and party leaders stressed the need for discipline and expressed concern that the political process set in motion not get beyond their control. If the storm troopers took the initiative on Göring's encouragement, which certainly helped to legitimise the violence of the SA, then they listened only to those messages from the Nazi leadership which they liked and ignored those which they did not. The crucial assault on the trade unions during March and April appears to have been neither planned nor organised by the top party or government leadership, and in a sense this proved an advantage: the piecemeal nature of the offensive made effective resistance virtually impossible. Divided and on the defensive, not knowing where or when the next blow might be struck, unsure which of the hundreds of incidents might constitute the proper occasion for all-out resistance to the Nazi regime, faced with the combined forces of the SA, SS, *Stahlhelm*, police and, potentially, the army, the Left was in a hopeless position.

On 10 April the Hitler government proclaimed that henceforth 1 May would be a holiday, a 'Day of National Labour'. A goal for which the trade unions had striven for decades was achieved by a government whose supporters had smashed the trade-union movement to pieces. The festivities planned for 1 May were to be followed by a systematic offensive against the trade unions the next morning: the SA and SS were entrusted with the tasks of occupying all offices of the Social Democratic unions and arresting leading figures of the trade-union movement. After weeks of watching and waiting while their supporters attacked the citadels of 'Marxism', the Nazi leaders had decided to celebrate the removal of the Left from German political life.

On the evening of 1 May Goebbels noted in his diary: 'Tomorrow we are going to occupy the trade-union offices. Resistance is not expected anywhere.' Goebbels' expectations were well-founded: most trade-union headquarters were occupied already and most leading figures on the Left were either in jail or exile. The real battle had already been fought, and the campaign against the trade unions on 2 May was essentially a piece of political theatre. At the same time, however, it offered a convenient opportunity for a mopping-up operation: in Stettin, for example, the *Gau* headquarters of the *Reichsbanner* were shut, the ADGB offices again occupied, and all the property of the unions seized; in Königsberg the trade-union offices were converted into headquarters of the newly created 'German Labour Front', which seized the property of the unions as well as of the 'Konsum' organisation; and in Schneidemühl the union offices, already occupied for some time by the SA, were turned over to the NSBO, while the SA, together with the local police, arrested a number of former trade-union functionaries. The terror campaign which SA groups had been carrying out for weeks received an official government stamp of approval.

The character of the Nazi assault on the Left underlines the extent to which the 'seizure of power' was driven from below. The initiative of the SA committed the Hitler government to the complete destruction of the trade unions; while the government in Berlin and the party leadership in Munich looked on, the storm troopers dismantled organised labour. Once this had been accomplished and it became apparent that the destruction of the SPD and the trade unions involved little risk, the Nazi leaders readily took advantage of the situation created by their most violent and active supporters. The result was a defeat for the German labour movement of incalculable proportions.

The Master Demagogue. By combining the strengths (and flaws) of his natural personality with artfully contrived gestures, Hitler fashioned a charismatic presence that enabled him to achieve absolute power over an entire nation. (Wide World Photos)

PART

III The Personality of the Leader

Variety of Opinion

> *It is pointless to speculate about possible breakdowns suffered during his adolescence, Oedipal complexes, unrequited love, etc.*
>
> Karl Dietrich Bracher

> *Though he often experienced difficulty in establishing human relationships with individuals, his rapport with a mass audience was exceptional.*
>
> Alan Bullock

> *There was little in this Jewish conspiracy theory that was new, or which could not be found in the ravings of anti-Semites in other countries.*
>
> Michael Burleigh and Wolfgang Wippermann

> *Hitler's huge platform of popularity made his own power position ever more unassailable, providing the foundation for the selective radicalization process in the Third Reich by which his personal ideological obsessions became translated into attainable reality.*
>
> Ian Kershaw

> *Aided by the insights of psychoanalysis, let us set forth here our best guesses as to the causes of Hitler's feelings of guilt. One possibility can quickly be eliminated. Hitler felt no remorse whatever over the calculated murder of millions.*
>
> Robert G. L. Waite

The fate of the Nazi movement and the life of Adolf Hitler were inseparable. Born on the Austrian bank of the Inn River, literally a stone's throw from Bavaria, Hitler grew up believing in a greater Germany. His party, created in the chaos of post-1918 Munich, eventually provided the path to that end. Personal and political ambitions thereby became fused. To comprehend Nazism, then, it is essential to examine the life of its virtually undisputed Führer.

Karl Dietrich Bracher *begins by stripping away the layers of myth that surround Hitler's youth and exposing the banal reality. He takes careful account of the research of other scholars, but he refuses to elaborate far beyond the available documentation. This is a comparison of fantasy and known fact, not a psychological probing. Yet Bracher does recognize the psychopathic nature of Hitler's world-view (*Weltanschauung*), and he attempts to delineate the sources of Hitler's racism and passionate German nationalism.*

Alan Bullock *introduces us to Hitler the orator, a man whose fanatical beliefs did not deter him from developing clever techniques of swaying a crowd. Behind this public facade lay a twisted personal philosophy, revealed by his autobiography* Mein Kampf, *in which the young Hitler explained with chilling frankness his hatred for what he considered to be a Jewish conspiracy against Germany. With a closed mind and a polished style, he prepared for the moment when his chance would come.*

Michael Burleigh and Wolfgang Wippermann *further explore Hitler's racist theories, specifically his unyielding anti-Semitism. They illustrate how all of his allegedly modern social ideas were thoroughly corrupted by absurd notions of German racial purity and superiority. "The Jew" was behind every cut and hurt of German history, Hitler was convinced, and therefore the struggle to rid society of this scourge could be elevated to the status of a holy mission. In this rhetoric, the authors say, there was a terrible logic that was bound to lead to a single conclusion.*

Ian Kershaw *draws our attention from the actual personality of Adolf Hitler to his public image. The Führer's appeal far exceeded that* of the Nazi party. It provided the mortar of his regime and made possible the realization of his most obsessive imaginings, even when they were not fully shared by the German population. The distinction between reality and propaganda thereby became blurred, all the better to delude the masses and to secure their loyalty. The greater the degree of Hitler's successes, and hence of his popularity, the less need there was for strong-arm methods to squelch opposition. But once Hitler's fortunes began to wane, Kershaw adds, the use of terror was necessarily increased to replace his crumbling image.

Robert G. L. Waite has boldly ventured onto the bogs of psychobiography in hopes of fathoming Hitler's emotional life. He concludes that the Führer was a man driven by feelings of guilt and inferiority, by fears about the impurity of his own blood, and by his warped sexuality. Thus Hitler developed a morbid concern with the possibility of defeat, a constant preoccupation with suicide and death, a predilection for religious imagery, and a rabid antipathy for all things Jewish. Any such application of Freudian psychoanalysis to history necessarily remains highly speculative when compared to more conventional approaches. Yet Waite believes the serious student must confront these matters squarely rather than leave them to salacious gossip.

These essays leave no doubt about the importance of Adolf Hitler to the Nazi movement. But was he indispensable to its triumph? Would the preexisting deeper currents of the German nation, not created by Hitler, have found a similar outlet without him? Obviously, no definitive answer can be offered to such questions. We can only conjecture here on the basis of the baleful events to which Hitler lent his stern face.

Karl Dietrich Bracher

Fantasy and Fact

The triumph of National Socialism over the Weimar Republic and its realization in the Third Reich are so closely connected with the life of

From *The German Dictatorship*, Third Edition, by Karl Dietrich Bracher. Copyright © 1970 by Praeger Publishers, Inc., New York. Reprinted by permission of Praeger Publishers, Inc. and George Weidenfeld and Nicholson, Ltd.

Adolf Hitler that one tends to equate the two. National Socialism has also been called "Hitlerism" and "nothing other than the projection of the will of the man Adolf Hitler into the realm of ideas and words," coming into existence with Hitler and also disappearing with him. And the rise, triumph, and defeat of National Socialism undoubtedly cannot be divorced from Hitler. But National Socialism is more than the gigantic mistake of misguided followers, the product solely of the demonic powers of one individual. Some of the intellectual and political currents which fed National Socialism and made possible the emergence of a man like Hitler have already been mentioned. His life must be seen against the background of fin de siècle Austria, and his political rise falls within the framework of postwar Germany and Europe, burdened by grave intellectual and social problems.

Neither Hitler himself nor his closest collaborators, such as National Socialism's chief ideologist, Alfred Rosenberg, or the guiding spirit of Jewish extermination, Reinhard Heydrich, measured up to the prerequisites of the biological postulates of National Socialism: race and ancestry. Official data about Hitler were confined to scant information about his date of birth, scarcely detailed enough for that "small Aryan pass" which he later demanded of all his subjects. Whatever facts about his background have been unearthed give the lie to his story of the harsh early life of an ambitious genius frustrated by circumstances. Still more interesting are the many questions that remain unanswered, beginning with the name and ancestry of the Austrian customs official Alois Hitler; Adolf Hitler, the fourth child of Alois's third marriage, was born on April 20, 1889, in the border town of Braunau am Inn. The name "Hitler" is possibly of Czech origin; the family originally came from the Waldviertel, an Austrian border region near Bohemia. But even this much is not certain, for Alois Hitler, the illegitimate son of a servant girl by the name of Maria Anna Schicklgruber, did not change his name to Hitler until 1876, when he was forty. The identity of Alois's father is not known; Maria Schicklgruber presumably had brought the child with her from the city where she had worked, and, five years after her return, at the age of forty-seven, had married a miller's helper by the name of Georg Hiedler. Almost thirty years after her and Hiedler's deaths, Alois Schicklgruber, with the help of a stepuncle and a gullible village priest, had his birth "legitimized," a step he believed essential to his career and one his stepuncle thought he owed his ambitious ward.

Thus, neither Adolf nor Alois could rightfully claim the name of Hitler. Later rumors and speculations, reaching the top echelons of National Socialism, thought it highly probable that Hitler had a Jewish grandfather and ascribed the radicalization of anti-Semitism to Hitler's pathological eagerness to repress this fact. However, no conclusive evidence has thus far been turned up. Recent findings indicate that the name of Grandmother Schicklgruber's last employer in Graz was Frankenberger — by no means invariably a Jewish name — and his son might possibly have fathered her child.

Such digressions are as sensational as they are questionable and pointless, for, though well meaning, they are rooted in racist superstitions. Hitler's early years and development, particularly his Vienna period, offer ample explanation for his intellectual and psychological development. He grew up in the secure household of a minor civil servant, by no means as impoverished a home as later legend had it. The nice house of his birth, the family property, and his father's pension would indicate that Hitler's years of poverty were the result of his own failure. The father, contrary to his son's later claims, was not a chronic alcoholic, but, rather, a comparatively progressive man with a good job; the mother devoted herself to the care of their home and children. The only thing that seemed to be lacking was a sensible education. The note of self-pity struck by Hitler in making the sad fate of his early years responsible for his failures, culminating in the moving story of the young orphan who finally had to leave home to earn his living, is as contrived as it is untrue.

In 1892, the family moved from Braunau to Passau (Bavaria) and in 1894, to Linz (Austria). Alois Hitler retired a year later, and for a while ran a farm in the Traun valley; in 1898, he purchased a house in Leonding near Linz. Thus, the symbolic significance which Hitler in *Mein Kampf* ascribed to his being born in Braunau, where in 1812 a patriotic bookdealer by the name of Palm was executed for anti-Napoleonic activities, also has little foundation, for Hitler spent part of his formative years in the Bavarian border town of Passau and the rest in Linz, the capital city of Upper Austria. His school career in Linz (he had to repeat his fifth year and was transferred to another school in his ninth) was a fiasco; Hitler was not only labeled indolent, but his performance in mathematics and shorthand as well as in German was considered unsatisfactory — a judgment borne out by his later style. Contrary to his claims in *Mein Kampf*, his grades in geography and history were only passing; his only above-average marks were in drawing and gymnastics. One of his teachers called him lopsidedly talented, uncontrolled, high-handed, dogmatic, ill-tempered, lacking in perseverance, and despotic.

After the death of his father (1903), his mother afforded the high-school dropout two-and-a-half years of idleness (1905–1907), which he spent daydreaming, occasionally drawing, and going to the theater. At this time, the sixteen-year-old began to manifest some of the traits that marked the later political fanatic and demagogue: utter self-involvement to the point of hysterical self-pity, a mania for untrammeled speechifying and equally grandoise and uncontrolled plan making, combined with listlessness and an inability to concentrate, let alone work productively. The serious lung disease which Hitler invoked to explain the way he lived is pure invention. A sentence in *Mein Kampf* about the end of his school career is most revealing: "Suddenly I was helped by an illness." The life he led after failing at school was exactly the sort of life that appealed to him. The irresponsible lack of restraint of his Vienna years may be seen as a direct consequence of his two years of idleness. It is simply not true that financial need was responsible for his life in Vienna. Even after the death of his overindulgent mother in late 1907, Adolf and his sister, Paula, were financially secure.

The Hitler myth has it that the seventeen-year-old, forced to earn his living, had to go to that decadent metropolis, Vienna. The fact is that in 1906, his mother treated him to a trip to Vienna, where he passed the time sightseeing and going to the theater, particularly to his beloved Wagner operas. The next year was spent in the protected setting of his mother's house. Neither school nor work was allowed to interrupt his routine. The only "work" he did was occasional drawings, and his grandiose plans for the rebuilding of Linz foreshadowed the extravagant ideas of the master builder of the Third Reich. These youthful fantasies reemerged in the "monumental" designs he prepared after his entry into Linz in 1938. The pre-Vienna period of this "work-shy dreamer" already contained the seeds of the type of life and thoughts which have come to light in studies of Hitler's early years. An episode of 1906 is typical: he had an idea for a large-scale research project, complete with housekeeper and cook, which was to afford him and his musician friend August Kubizek the necessary leisure and comfort for the study of "German art" and the formation of a circle of "art lovers," said project to be realized through the purchase of a winning lottery ticket. According to his friend, "Adolf Hitler could plan and look into the future so beautifully that I could have listened to him forever." Equally typical is the violence with which he reacted to the news that he had won neither the first nor any of the other lottery prizes: it was the fault of the "entire social order." This episode offers an almost uncanny preview of the later Hitler.

It is pointless to speculate about possible breakdowns suffered during his adolescence, Oedipal complexes, unrequited love, etc. Understandably enough, the relatives of the young man of leisure who refused to entertain any idea about simply "working for a living" began to pressure him to learn a trade. Having failed in his efforts to gain admission to the Vienna Academy of Art (September 1907), he gave no thought to the possibility of any other profession. He stayed on in Vienna, living the comfortable life of the "art student," without telling his ailing mother the truth. After his mother's death, he still was not under any immediate financial pressure; there was a substantial inheritance in addition to his orphan's allowance, which he continued to collect until his twenty-third year under the pretext of being enrolled at the Vienna Academy. Later, he also inherited a fairly substantial sum from an aunt. All these facts underscore the dishonesty of the piteous note struck in his autobiography.

The nineteen-year-old Hitler floundering in Vienna did not, contrary to the self-image of *Mein Kampf,* have any definite political orientation. His "nationalism" was in line with the national German tendencies prevalent in Linz, and his knowledge of history, in which he allegedly excelled at school, was limited. As late as the 1930s, his history instructor, Leopold Pötsch, of whom he speaks highly in *Mein Kampf,* did not want to be part of this myth. As to the "Jewish problem," Hitler also had little knowledge and no firm opinions. His family doctor was Jewish, and Hitler used to send him hand-painted postcards from Vienna. He also accepted money gifts from him, yet in 1938, after the Anschluss, the doctor was driven into exile. Against these facts we have Hitler's contention that while in Linz he had already learned "to understand and comprehend the meaning of history" and that the Austrian nationality conflict had taught him that the meaning of history was to be found in the battle for the "nation" (*Volkstum*) and in the victory of "völkisch nationalism" (*Mein Kampf,* pp. 8 ff.). Yet, some of the basic traits and thoughts which took shape during his five-and-a-half years in Vienna were, according to Kubizek, his patient audience, already to be found in the endless speeches and grandiose plans of his Linzer days. The experiences of Vienna, Munich, and World War I lent them substance and embellished them with the up-to-date content and impulses which so profoundly were to shape Hitler the political man.

He was driven to Vienna not by "need and harsh reality" but by the desire to escape work, the need to learn a trade, and the wish to continue the life-style of the "future artist," a pose which he was unable to maintain any longer under the watchful eyes of his relatives in Linz. He kept on urging his friend Kubizek to join him in Vienna. In the ensuing months, he was an almost daily visitor to the opera, went sightseeing, developed grandiose plans for a musical drama and for all sorts of building projects, while Kubizek, who had been as unaware of his friend's academic failure as the family, enrolled in the Vienna Conservatory. Hitler, as he proudly stated, was supreme master of his time. The harsh life of the "common laborer" who had to earn his "crust of bread" is one of the heart-rending myths of his autobiography. Between 1909 and 1913, the unsuccessful art student and self-designated "artist" and "writer" was introduced to the political ideas and currents that were to furnish the decisive concepts and stimuli for his later career. The political and social conflicts and emotions in the Vienna of that era offered material and food for a radical critique of society, and the unbridgeable gap between Hitler's wants, ambitions, and fantasies and naked reality made him accept and enlarge on this critique. It was the same impulse that later, in crisis-ridden postwar Germany, drove so large a segment of the lower middle class, its feelings of superiority threatened, into the arms of the radical-Right doctrine of salvation — a sociopolitical flight into an irrational political creed thriving on hatred and fear and demanding to be saved from conflict through the institution of a total "new order."

The rejection of Hitler's second application for admission to the Art Academy in the fall of 1908 seems to have been a turning point in his life. He broke off his friendship with Kubizek and became submerged in the shadowy world of public shelters (1908–1909) and homes for men (1910–1913), though the allowance and the gifts from relatives continued. Moreover, the "hard labor" referred to in *Mein Kampf* should have brought him additional funds. During this period, Hitler discovered the political and social slogans then in vogue, an encounter reminiscent of his earlier introduction to art. Contrary to his testimony,

Hitler had read few books and had not really concerned himself with the political and social problems of his environment. A chance reading of books, occasional pamphlets, and generalizations based on subjective impressions combined to form the distorted political picture which, in almost pristine form, became the "weltanschauung" that dominated Hitler's future life and work.

The only work he did was an occasional copying of picture postcards which his fellow inmates of the men's home sold for him. He spent most of his time piecing together his weltanschauung from obscure sources. Its essence was extreme nationalism and a radical racial anti-Semitism. The literature which stimulated Hitler's interest in politics forms the subject of a comprehensive study. Among his reading matter was a periodical with the resounding name of *Ostara*, the German goddess of spring, a publication which, from 1905 on, was widely sold in the tobacco kiosks of Vienna. It gave voice to the eccentric and bloodthirsty race mythology of Adolf Lanz (1874–1954), an ex-monk who called himself Lanz von Liebenfels. His program called for the founding of a male order of blue-eyed, blond "Aryans." His headquarters were in a castle in Lower Austria which he had bought with the help of industrialist patrons. There Lanz hoisted the swastika banner in 1906 as the symbol of the Aryan movement. This pathological founding father of an "Aryan" hero cult was the author of *Theozoology* (1901), a work offering a particularly abstruse mixture of an extreme, pseudoreligious racism. Apparently, Hitler got in touch with Lanz personally in 1909, asking for copies of *Ostara* that were missing from his own collection. Lanz's views, and similarly fantastic notions from the "European underground," which later were to make their way into the Ludendorff movement, helped to shape Hitler's political ideology. Lanz's works disseminated the crass exaggerations of the Social Darwinist theory of survival, the superman and superrace theory, the dogma of race conflict, and the breeding and extermination theories of the future SS state. The scheme was simple: a blond, heroic race of "Arioheroes" was engaged in battle with inferior mixed races whose annihilation was deemed a historico-political necessity; "race defilement" was not to be tolerated, and the master race was to multiply with the help of "race hygiene," polygamy, and breeding stations; sterilization, debilitating forced labor, and systematic liquidation were to offer a final solution.

Such pamphlets were fatal reading for an unstable youth with few ideas of his own, even though, as Hitler himself confessed, his

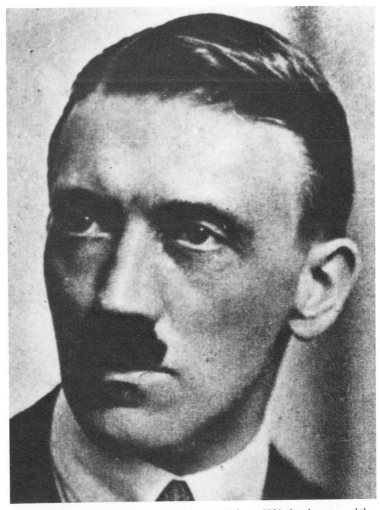

The Young Hitler. Even as an aspiring politician, Hitler in 1921 already possessed the riveting gaze that projected his steely determination to achieve national prominence and power. (© Topham/The Image Works)

middle-class, liberal background initially led him to rebel against these teachings. This literature took on great significance against the background of impressions received by a footloose youth on the lowest rung of the social ladder in the capital city of a multinational monarchy. Hitler's acquaintance with Marxist socialism also was not the product of close study, as he claimed, but of obscure subjective impressions marked by the sort of class and cultural snobbery which was still part of him and which he now directed toward social and political issues. A passage in *Mein Kampf* (p. 25), precisely because of its exaggeration, throws interesting light on its author and the substance of his weltanschauung: "At that time I read ceaselessly and very thoroughly." (He never is specific about his reading matter; his "books," according to his own account of the genesis of his anti-Semitism [p. 59], are polemical pamphlets bought "for a few pennies.") The passage continues: "What free time I had left from my work was spent on my studies. In a few years I thus created for myself the basis of the knowledge on which I still feed. During that time I formed a picture of the world and an ideology which has become the granite foundation of my deeds. I only had to add a little more knowledge to that which I had acquired at that time; I did not have to revise anything."

Who else can say this of his impressions at the age of twenty? This passage is more revealing of the level of his Viennese "studies" (mostly, endless debates between the idle smart aleck and his fellow inmates at the shelter) and of the substance of the later National Socialist ideology than the most probing analysis. What Hitler "learned" in Vienna, and subsequently elevated to the status of a "constructive ideology," was that monomaniacal, obsessive, unseeing yet effective method of political argumentation which led from the evenings in the men's shelter of Vienna to the endless monologues of the demagogue.

In addition to inventing the story of the day laborer who while on the job had his eyes opened to Marxism and its Jewish "backers," Hitler also makes mention of the anti-Semitic movement of the Austro-Pan-German nationalist von Schönerer. The actual impact of this anti-monarchist, anti-Marxist social movement, the Austrian version of a decidedly national "German socialism," is hard to assess, but its nationalist, völkisch battle cries undoubtedly are among the roots of National Socialism. They furnished the young Hitler with a political framework for his personal and social resentments against a society in which his adolescent daydreams and wants found neither response nor expression.

The substance of the ideas which Hitler made into the "granite foundation" of his future policies has been paraphrased repeatedly. It is nothing more than a sweeping rejection of and opposition to tolerance and cosmopolitanism, democracy and parliamentarianism, Marxism and Jewry, which, in primitive equation, were called the primary evils of the world. Even then, however, the core, probably the only "genuine" fanatically held and realized conviction of his entire life, was anti-Semitism and race mania. An enormously oversimplified scheme of good and evil, transplanted to the biological and racial sphere, was made to serve as the master key to the history of political thought. Hitler's fanatical hatred of the Jews defies all rational explanation; it cannot be measured by political and pragmatic gauges. The fact that an entire nation followed him and furnished a legion of executioners does demonstrate, however, that we are confronted not merely with the inexplicable dynamics of one man, but with a terrible disease of modern nationalism, whose desire for exclusivity and war against everything "alien" constitutes one of the root causes of anti-Semitism.

The psychopathic features of Hitler's weltanschauung were discernible even then: the social envy of the failure and the discrepancy between his exalted vision of personal prestige and the poverty of the unemployed man who held ordinary work in disdain both played a role. The much-abused Nietzsche once called anti-Semitism the ideology of the "those who feel cheated." Unconfirmed rumor has it that Hitler arrived at the "awareness" that the creative person — and he, being a painter, belonged to this category — gets cheated by the sly, worldly, aggressive Jewish trader after he himself had had an unpleasant experience with a Jewish art dealer. Such personal resentments may have contributed to the rationalization of his perverse anti-Semitism.

At about that time, Hitler had also become a "fanatical nationalist." At its highest pitch, nationalist ideology appeals to mass insanity, assuming the force of a collective psychosis in which the annihilation of the enemy spells one's own success and salvation. The anti-Semitic atmosphere of the Vienna of that time provided Hitler's new eclectic philosophy with the firm base on which militant nationalism could develop to its most extreme form and be carried to the point of absurdity. The Jews are the cause of all misfortune; ruthless battle against them holds the key to national if not universal salvation; this precept formed the base of Hitler's later nationalism and imperialism, which ultimately combined forcible expansion beyond the national boundaries with the missionary zeal of a German war on "world Jewry." After Hitler became chancellor, he confided to intimates that he had been compelled to resort to nationalism because of "the conditions of the times," but that he had always been convinced that "we have to get rid of this false conception" of democracy and liberalism and in its place "set up . . . the conception of race, which has not yet been politically used up."

The "studies" and "harsh lessons" of his Vienna years, which Hitler said were the foundation of his entire career, thus provided the immature youth with the kind of banal, limited semieducation which is among the most dangerous impulses for the destructive forces of our time. Just as he failed to persevere in school and work, this rambling autodidact failed to gain real insight into the problems of the time. His tirelessly fundamental, global "debates" with Marxism and democracy, despite their manic repetition, also never went beyond generalities and platitudes. In *Mein Kampf*, he describes the method of reading and studying through which he acquired his pseudoeducation: he always knew how to separate the wheat from the chaff and to extract the true content of everything. In this way, he gathered a store of semi-information which he put to good use; his was a "pigeonhole mind" (*Heiber*), lacking the ability to see things in their context. But, at the same time, he satisfied his adolescent "striving for self-worth" (*Daim*) and also developed a set of ideas of whose simplicity he was to furnish proof. When, in 1924, Hitler proudly told a Munich court that by the time he left Vienna he had become "an absolute anti-Semite, a mortal enemy of the entire Marxist philosophy, Pan-German in my political convictions," he was probably telling the truth (*Mein Kampf,* pp. 130 ff.).

In May 1913, a year later than stated in *Mein Kampf*, Hitler suddenly turned up in Munich, after more than five years of obscurity. The reasons for his abrupt departure from Vienna are not clear. One might think he was telling the truth when he said that he was prompted by a dislike for the Habsburg Empire and a yearning for the Bavarian art capital, were it not for the recent revelation of an embarrassing episode. It seems that this future ideologist of combat, the "military genius," had evaded military service in 1909–1910, just as he had evaded all other duties, quite unlike those reviled "homeless" Marxists and Jews. Like all of Hitler's major "decisions" — leaving school, moving to Vienna, going to war, entering politics, again going to war, and, finally, his egocentric fall — the road to Munich was also an escape route, this time from military service. This is attested to also by the fact that the then twenty-four-year-old Hitler, who, in fact, remained a citizen of Austria until 1925, called himself "stateless." When arrested and extradited to Salzburg at the request of Austria, he fawningly told the court about his sad life, and, in fact, his poor physical condition saved him from punishment and conscription. Hitler's long letter of explanation (January 1914) to the Linz authorities hints at the legend of later years. When he writes, "I have never known the lovely word 'youth,' " it almost reads like a "draft for *Mein Kampf*" (Jetzinger). This shameful affair, the documents of which became the object of a feverish search after Hitler's invasion of Austria, testifies to his dishonesty and cowardice and to the mendacity of a weltanschauung whose rigorous precepts were valid only for others.

He fared no better in Munich than he had in Vienna. The sale of his bad paintings brought in little. The future looked no rosier in Germany. The outbreak of World War I almost seemed like salvation. A rare photograph of that time shows Hitler, wearing a dashing artist's hat, among the masses at the Odeonsplatz cheering the news that war had been declared. Carried away by the popular enthusiasm, he felt liberated from his unproductive, unsuccessful life. As a volunteer not expected to act or decide independently, freed from the purposeless existence of the occasional painter and coffeehouse habitué incapable of establishing personal relationships, he now found himself subject to a discipline which, unlike the disreputable camaraderie of the Vienna shelter, also satisfied his dreams of national and social grandeur. Hitler later justified and glorified the fact that he served in the German army rather than that of his homeland by denouncing the Habsburg Empire, however inconsistent this may have seemed with his critical attitude toward Wilhelmian Germany. The fact that once more he found himself in a male community indelibly affected his future life and ideas. "Destiny," which he liked to invoke, had pointed the way: "To me, those times were like a deliverance from the vexing emotions of my youth . . . so that, overcome by passionate enthusiasm, I fell to my knees and thanked heaven out of an overflowing heart" (*Mein Kampf*, p. 177). The war seemed to put an end to all problems of daily life in a society in which he had not been able to find his way and which, in typically egocentric fashion, he held responsible for his failure. This, not the dramatically stilted phrase of 1918 ("I, however, decided to become a politician"), was the decisive turning point; war as the transmutation of all values, battle as the father of all things, was the dominant force of Hitler's future life. Hence the eagerly sought-for prolongation of the war beyond the peace agreement into the crises and civil-war atmosphere of the Weimar Republic became the basis of Hitler's activities.

Little worth mentioning happened to Hitler during the war years. Though as a courier he remained a mere corporal, he did have occasion to distinguish himself. He remained a loner, nonsmoker, teetotaler, and lover of sweets, a model patriot and tireless polemicist against Jews, Marxists, and defeatists; he had little in common with the ordinary soldier. The pronounced ascetic-heroic "idealism," the bent toward the undeviatingly radical, the rejection of "ordinary" and erotic pleasures, the feeling of superiority and the sacrificing of personal interests for a "higher ideal" — all these were already hinted at in his monologues and schemes in Linz. Later, Hitler permitted these tendencies to be magnified into an effective myth of a demigod free from ordinary human needs and failings. This, too, was, in effect, an escape, an "escape into legend" (Heiden).

It was the discipline of war and the "front-line acquaintance" with the clear and simple military hierarchy of order and values which were to shape Hitler's sense of values and turn this unstable dreamer unable to come to terms with the bourgeois world of work and order into the rigid fanatic with incredibly oversimplified ideas of war and order. This military male order was the model for the future armed party organizations, for the ideal of a "national community" ready for battle, and for the leader idea; it was elevated to the guiding principle of the political, social, and intellectual life of the country. Therefore Germany's defeat, news of which reached Hitler in the field hospital of Pasewalk, where he was being treated for gas poisoning, not only touched his patriotic feelings but affected his very existence: he was faced with the prospect of returning to his miserable prewar existence. The war simply could not be over, and if, as Hitler was convinced, it had been lost because of defeatism on the home front and the Jewish-Marxist "stab in the back," then this conviction had to be validated by continuing the fight at home. This "national" necessity took on existential significance for Hitler. Ever since those liberating days of 1914, the private and now "professional" life of Hitler, a man with little education and no personal ties, had been based on perpetuating the state of war. It was this which lay at the root of the fanatical energy with which Hitler turned the war into his motivating principle. That is how he looked at politics as a career — as a means for gaining power which would make possible a new war, this one, however, fought according to his ideas until final victory was won.

Hitler's turn to politics also was not the logical outcome of his own decision and resolution, as the legend of *Mein Kampf* would have it. It, too, was an escape from regular work; once again, having returned to Munich, he let events force a decision on him, one, however, to which he held fast. But, initially, Hitler did little to translate into fact his alleged decision of November 9, 1918, "to get into politics." Fearing civilian life, he clung to the security of military service and witnessed, from his barracks, the brief turmoil of the Munich *Räterepublik* (April 1919). Only later was he given the opportunity, for the first time in his life, to exercise a political function. His "nationalistic" zeal in the service of a commission engaged in ferreting out revolutionary elements among the troops persuaded his superiors to make him an "information officer" responsible for the nationalist education and control of his comrades. Since this assignment involved contact with rightist groups, he found himself, in September 1919, as an observer at a meeting of one of the numerous new small right-wing parties, the German Workers' Party, in a Munich beer hall.

This chance happening was to make history and decide Hitler's career. Drexler's group of sectarians and beer-hall politicians gathered at this meeting to listen to a speech by the engineer Feder about the abolition of capitalism and the rule of finance capital; the speech was not very impressive. But Hitler felt at home in this uncritical assemblage, and so when informed some time later of his admission into the party, though he himself had never applied, he accepted. He became Party Comrade No. 55, and, simultaneously, the seventh member of the executive committee. Hitler may have been incapable of taking the initiative, let alone of founding a political party, but, once a decision had been made without his active help, he zealously threw himself into the new role of politician. In view of the disarmament provisions of the Versailles treaty, his days in the rump army were probably numbered anyway; now he found the framework which might possibly combine the ideas of his Vienna days with a wartime order, offering him a chance to use his modicum of "learning" to secure his existence and to compensate for his fear of the demands of a civilian life in which he had failed.

Alan Bullock

Fanaticism and Calculation

It is important to remember that we are talking of a period of history before television, video cassettes and tape-recorders had been invented, and when both radio and the cinema were in their infancy. If television had been available to him — or radio, either, before he came to power — there is no doubt Hitler would have made the greatest possible use of them. No politician has ever been more enthusiastic or better informed about technology. This is illustrated not only by his record in the Second World War, but by his passion for motor cars and his use of aeroplanes to build up the image of himself and his party. But the focus of his activity in these early years was the mass public meeting: one a week to begin with, most of the time in Munich, sometimes in nearby towns, with Hitler himself acting as the organizer as well as the principal speaker. This was the best way in which to attract attention and to win over recruits.

Many descriptions have been given of Hitler as an orator and of the hypnotic effect he produced on an audience. His early efforts were crude by comparison with his speeches of the 1930s, with their elaborate stage-management and the confidence which came from years of experience. But the elements on which he built were there from the beginning.

His aim, repeatedly stated in *Mein Kampf,* was not to persuade an audience by argument, but to appeal to their feelings:

> *The psyche of the broad masses is accessible only to what is strong and uncompromising. Like a woman whose inner sensibilities are not so much under the sway of abstract reasoning, but are subject to a vague emotional longing for the strength that completes her being, and who would rather bow to a strong man than dominate a weakling — so the masses prefer a ruler to a suppliant and are filled with a stronger sense of mental security by a doctrine that brooks no rival than by liberal teaching which offers them a choice. They have very little idea of how to make such a choice and are prone to feel they have been abandoned. They feel little shame at being terrorised intellectually . . . They see only the ruthless force and brutality of its utterances to which they always submit in the end.*

To achieve this effect Hitler sought to convince his audience of the sincerity and strength of his own emotions. 'Men believe', Nietzsche wrote, 'in the truth of all that is seen to be strongly believed in'. Hitler frequently gave the impression of being so carried away by what he said as to be out of control, but learned the orator's and actor's art of stopping just short of incoherence, and of varying the effect by dropping his voice, by employing sarcasm, or by switching from bitter denunciation of the 'criminals' who had betrayed Germany to a glowing declaration of his faith in her capacity to rise again in renewed strength.

In speeches which often lasted two hours or more, he did not make the mistake of haranguing his listeners all the time. He could make them laugh with his mimicry and win their approval by the quick-wittedness with which he answered hecklers. He spent hours practising his gestures and facial expressions in front of a mirror, and studying the shots which the photographer Heinrich Hoffmann took when he was speaking, in order to select those which were most effective, eliminating the rest.

In *Mein Kampf* Hitler insists that to be successful, propaganda must combine simplification with reiteration: 'it must confine itself to a few points and repeat them over and over'. The surviving notes for his early speeches show the care he took in planning the sequence of his themes and finding the most telling phrases. He paid equal attention to the place and time of meetings:

> *There are rooms which refuse steadfastly to allow any favourable atmosphere to be created in them . . . In all these cases one is dealing with the problem of influencing the freedom of the human will . . . In the morning and during the day it seems that the power of the human will*

rebels with its strongest energy against any attempt to impose upon it the will or opinion of another. On the other hand, in the evening it easily succumbs to the domination of a stronger will.

The complement to his preparations, the control by which he constantly revised them, was his sensitivity to the reactions of his audience:

An orator receives continuous guidance from the people before whom he speaks . . . He will always be borne along by the great masses in such a way that from the living emotion of his hearers the very words come to his lips that he needs to speak to their hearts. Should he make even a slight mistake, he has the living correction before him.

This is the explanation for the time Hitler often took to warm up, feeling out an audience's mood until he hit upon the best way to reach it. Though he often experienced difficulty in establishing human relationships with individuals, his rapport with a mass audience was exceptional.

But however strong the impression of spontaneity, however unrestrained the torrent of words which poured out, those who knew him well believed that he was never swept away by the enthusiasm he elicited, but knew very well what he was saying and the effect he meant to produce. What made Hitler dangerous was this combination of fanaticism and calculation. . . .

The interest of *Mein Kampf*, a book which has few rivals in the repulsiveness of its language, its tone and above all its contents, is that it provides insights into Hitler in both roles — into his mind and his views of the world on the one hand, into the way in which he set about organizing a political movement on the other, with the creation of the Hitler myth as the link between the two.

The basis of Hitler's beliefs was a crude Social Darwinism: 'Man has become great through struggle . . . Whatever goal man has reached is due to his originality plus his brutality . . . All life is bound up in three theses: struggle is the father of all things, virtue lies in blood, leadership is primary and decisive.' In *Mein Kampf* he wrote: 'He who wants to live must fight, and he who does not want to fight in this world where eternal struggle is the law of life has no right to exist.'

Hitler was fascinated by history, and like Spengler saw it as a succession of human ages each expressing itself in a distinctive culture of interrelated ideas and institutions: the Graeco-Roman culture of the ancient world, which he professed to admire without showing much knowledge of it; the Middle Ages, the culture of which he saw as 'Germanic', eclipsed at the Renaissance by the modern capitalist society of the West which, again like Spengler, he believed to be sick and in decline. The capacity to create such cultures was confined to the 'Aryan' race, a concept Hitler never defined. 'If we divide mankind into three categories — founders of culture, bearers of culture, destroyers of culture — the Aryan alone can be considered as representing the first category.* It was he who laid the groundwork and erected the walls of every great structure in human culture.'

Each culture or empire had declined for the same reason: miscegenation, which weakened, then destroyed, the power to continue the struggle which is the law of life. 'All the great civilisations of the past became decadent because the originally creative race died out, as a result of contamination of the blood.' Hitler believed that Western civilization was decadent and that the future destiny of the German people was to replace it, just as the Germanic tribes had replaced a Roman empire no longer able to defend itself and gone on to create a vigorous new culture.

To achieve this, the Germans must conquer a new German empire which would dominate the European continent. This pointed to a foreign policy which went far beyond the demands for the revision of the Treaty of Versailles with which Hitler began his career as an agitator. No more than sketched in Volume I of *Mein Kampf*, this became in Volume II a full-blooded policy of acquiring *Lebensraum* ('living space') in Eastern Europe at the expense of Russia. To wage another war for the re-establishment of Germany's 1914 frontiers would be criminal; the only purpose which would justify such action was 'to secure for the German people the soil and territory to which it is entitled on this earth'.

> *And so we National Socialists consciously draw a line beneath the foreign policy of our pre-War period. We take up where we broke off six hundred years ago. We stop the endless German movement to the south and west and turn our gaze towards the land in the east. At long last we break off the colonial and commercial policy of the pre-War period and shift to the territorial policy of the future.*

---

*Hitler mentions the Japanese as an example of the second; the third was represented by the Jews.

> *And if we speak of territory in Europe, we can have in mind
> only Russia and her vassal border states.*

In his *Zweites Buch* Hitler explains that, thanks to the Bolshevik
Revolution, this would be a comparatively simple undertaking: 'The
gigantic empire in the East is ready to collapse.' The Slav masses were
incapable of creating a state for themselves, and the Germanic ruling
group which had dominated them hitherto had now been replaced by
a Jewish Bolshevik leadership which, for reasons to be explained shortly,
could neither organize nor maintain a state. The war with France, which
Hitler had earlier seen as necessary to secure the revision of frontiers,
now became (as it proved to be in 1940–1) the preliminary to the primary objective of a successful attack on Russia. The other prerequisites
were an alliance with Mussolini's Italy (to which Germany should be
ready to surrender the South Tyrol), and with England, with which
Germany should at all costs avoid the rivalry overseas which had proved
fatal to the Kaiser.

The gaps in such a conception are obvious — for example, the
fact that, far from suffering from overpopulation, Germany did not
have the numbers needed to take over and develop the territory in the
East which her armies occupied. But they are less important than the
correspondence between the objectives Hitler set out in the 1920s and
those he sought to accomplish in the 1940s.

Hitler fully shared that belief in the primacy of foreign over domestic policy which was the traditional view of German history. He
had no interest in constitutional and legal or economic and social
policies in themselves, looking upon them, in this period of the 1920s,
as primarily a means of attracting support and securing a place in the
political game. He extended this view to the state itself: 'The State is
only a means to an end. Its end and its purpose is to preserve the existence of the race . . . The State is only the vessel and the race is what it
contains.' So far as the form of the state went, Hitler based everything
on the *Führerprinzip*, the principle of leadership. This visualized the
concentration of power in the hands of a leader, unlimited by any kind
of constitutional or parliamentary control, and with the authority to
direct the state to give priority to foreign policy and rearmament, including the conquest of new living space in the East.

Drawing on the experience he had gained since leaving Vienna
and the period for reflection in Landsberg gaol, Hitler summed up the

art of politics in 1928 as 'carrying out a people's struggle for existence', subordinating both foreign and domestic policy to that end.

> *Foreign policy is the art of safeguarding the momentary, necessary living space, in quantity and quality for a people. Domestic policy is the art of preserving the necessary employment of force for this in the form of race value [Volkswert] and numbers.*

'Race value' needs explanation. 'The source of a people's whole power', Hitler says, 'does not lie in its possession of weapons or in the organisation of its army but in its inner value, that is, its racial value.' To preserve that, it is important for the state to defend its people against contamination by three poisons, each of which he identified with the Jews. These are: internationalism, a predilection for things foreign which springs from an underestimation of one's own cultural values and leads to miscegenation; egalitarianism, democracy and majority rule, which are hostile to individual creativity and leadership, the origin of all human progress; and pacifism, which destroys a people's healthy natural instincts for self-preservation. In a speech at Nuremberg on 21 July 1927, Hitler declared:

> *A people has lost its inner value as soon as it has incorporated into itself these three vices, as it has eliminated its racial value, preached internationalism, given up its self-direction and put in its place majority rule, i.e. incompetence, and has begun to indulge in the brotherhood of mankind.*

I have left to the end the most distinctive feature of Hitler's system, his anti-Semitism, in order to place it in the more general framework of his *Rassenpolitik* (race policy). This extended, on the one hand, to the extermination of the unfit, under the 1933 programme for the prevention of hereditarily diseased offspring, even when born to non-Jewish Germans, and thus to the racial basis of Nazi agrarian policy; and on the other to the exploitation and extermination of non-Jewish Poles and Russians as *Untermenschen* (subhumans). There is no question, however, that the Jews occupied a unique place in his *Weltanschauung*. No personal experience has come to light which could help to explain the intensity of Hitler's hatred of the Jews, although some biographers have pointed to the obscene language in which he habitually wrote and spoken of this as pointing to a sexual origin. It is a disturbing question to consider when was the last occasion on which this man, who was responsible for the death of six million Jews, actually spoke to or met a Jew in person. But 'the Jew' as one encounters him in the pages of *Mein Kampf* and Hitler's ravings bears no resemblance to flesh-and-blood human beings of Jewish descent: he is an invention of Hitler's obsessional fantasy, a Satanic creation, expressing his need to create an object on which he could concentrate his feelings of aggression and hatred.

Hitler rationalized these feelings by declaring that what distinguished the Jews from other races was the fact that they possessed no territory of their own, and so could not participate in that struggle for living space which he saw as the basic pattern of history. Lacking territory, the Jews could not carry out the construction of a state, but had to become parasites (an obsessive metaphor of Hitler's) battening on the creative activities and work of other nations.

> *The ultimate goal of the Jewish struggle for existence is the enslavement of productively active people . . . by the denationalisation, the promiscuous bastardisation of other peoples, the lowering of the racial level of the highest peoples as well as the domination of this racial mishmash through the extirpation of the völkisch intelligentsia and its replacement by members of its own people.*

In international affairs Jewish capitalists sought to divert nations from their true interests and plunge them into wars, gradually establishing their mastery over them with the help of the power of money and propaganda. At the same time, the Jewish leaders of the international Communist revolution had provided themselves with a world headquarters in Moscow from which to spread subversion internally through the propagation by the Marxist parties of internationalism, egalitarianism and pacifism, all of which Hitler identified with the Jews and saw as a threat to Aryan racial values.

Turning the argument the other way, anti-Semitism provided Hitler with further justification for Germany to follow a policy of conquering additional living space in the East at the expense of Bolshevik Russia, which Hitler constantly identified with the 'Jewish world conspiracy'. Not only would this strengthen the racial character of the German people, but it would destroy the base of international Jewry, and cut off the poisonous plant of Marxism at the root.

In Hitler's twisted cosmological vision, the eternal enemy of the Aryans, the race which possessed the power to create, was the Jew, the embodiment of evil, the agent of the racial pollution which had undermined and destroyed one civilization after another.

> *Should the Jew, with the help of his Marxist creed, conquer the nations of this world, his crown will become the funeral wreath of mankind, and once again this planet, empty of mankind, will follow its orbit through the ether as it did millions of years ago . . .*

What Hitler meant by the 'elimination' of the Jewish danger remained undefined, but to a German National Socialist from Bohemia who visited him in prison and asked if he had changed his position about the Jews, he replied:

> *Yes, yes, it is quite right that I have changed my opinion about the methods to fight Jewry. I have realised that up to now I have been much too soft. While working out my book I have come to the realisation that in the future the most severe methods of fighting will have to be used to let us come through successfully. I am convinced that this is a vital question not just for our people, but for all peoples. For Judaism is the plague of the world.*

The twin tenets of Hitler's worldview, his determination to 'root out' the Jews (whatever he meant to suggest by that) and to conquer *Lebensraum* in Eastern Europe, not only remained unchanged but were repeatedly stated, years before he came to power, in *Mein Kampf* and in many speeches and interviews. . . .

As he claimed in *Mein Kampf*: 'In this period there took shape within me a world picture and a philosophy which became the granite foundation of all my acts. In addition to what I then created, I have had to learn little since, and have had to alter nothing.' Hitler wrongly dates this to his years in Vienna before 1914; it was a process which began then but was not complete until he committed it to paper in the mid 1920s. After that, however, he was quite right in saying that his *Weltanschauung* provided a granite foundation to which he added nothing. His was a closed mind impervious to argument or doubt. It was thanks to this, the assurance that he possessed the key to history, and with it could unlock the future as well, that he felt able to exploit tactical opportunities, without any risk of losing sight of his objectives, awaiting his time, believing that it would arrive and that he would then be able to commit the German people to a programme which remained as primitive and brutal as when he spelled it out in *Mein Kampf*. The advantage this gave was already evident in the years up to 1930, when circumstances did not favour him and few outside the party took him seriously, but he nonetheless prepared for a change in his favour which he could not foresee but was confident would come.

Michael Burleigh and Wolfgang Wippermann

Hitler's Racism

It is not certain which racialist works Hitler actually read. There is no 'man who gave Hitler his ideas' in a simplistic teleological sense. However, it is certain that Hitler knew the most important racial-anthropological, racial-hygienic, and racial anti-Semitic theories, and in *Mein Kampf* turned them into a comprehensive, self-contained, if totally insane, racial-political programme. His racial discourse began with the following 'truths':

> *Even the most superficial observation shows that Nature's restricted form of propagation and increase is an almost rigid basic law of all the innumerable forms of expression of her vital urge. Every animal mates only with a member of the same species. The titmouse seeks the titmouse, the finch the finch, the stork the stork, the field mouse the field mouse, the dormouse the dormouse, the wolf the she-wolf, etc.*

On a first reading, these observations seem involuntarily comic. In reality, both this passage and the paragraphs which follow contain three axioms fundamental to racist thought. The first is the claim that only those living things which produce healthy offspring with one another constitute a race — a definition of race which can already be found in the works of Kant. Secondly, Hitler presupposed the existence of 'higher' and 'lesser' races, a notion common to virtually every racial ideologist since the late eighteenth century. Following Gobineau and others, Hitler claimed that the 'Aryans' alone were the 'culture-creating race'. The Chinese and Japanese were merely 'culture-bearing'; the other races, i.e. Blacks and Slavs, of 'lesser value', while the 'Jewish race' was the embodiment of evil. The third axiom was that among humans as well as animals there was, and should be, an 'urge towards racial purity'. Interbreeding between the races would result in 'bastardisation' and a deterioration of racial 'value'. This idea can also be found in the work of reactionary aestheticians from Gobineau onwards, and it is expressed in a 'scientific' guise in the research of men like Eugen Fischer. In 1913 Fischer published a study of the Rehoboter Bastards, or the children of Boers and Hottentots in South-West Africa. Without the slightest evidence, Fischer claimed that the children of so-called mixed marriages were of 'lesser racial quality'. Their intellectual achievements increased or decreased according to the proportion of European blood. However, they would never create their own culture, for they required constant European leadership.

In the course of a chapter devoted to 'Nation and Race', Hitler dwelt upon the need to prevent 'miscegenation' while promoting racial selective breeding. Since there were still 'considerable remnants of unmixed Nordic–Germanic people' in the 'body of the German people', one should 'not only gather together and maintain the most valuable remnants of primeval racial elements, but slowly and surely lead them to a commanding position'. Although Hitler mentioned no names, it is clear that here he was indebted to the ideas of racial-hygienicists. It is not particularly important whether he had actually read the work of scientists such as Haeckel, Schallmayer, and Ploetz, or whether, more probably, he derived his ideas from the sub-scientific undergrowth of tracts produced by Hentschel, Lanz, and Dinter. In a subsequent chapter, entitled 'World View and Party', Hitler summed up his racial–ideological presuppositions. The 'völkisch world view . . . by no means believes in an equality of the races, but along with their difference it recognises their higher or lesser value and feels itself obligated, through this knowledge, to promote the victory of the better and the stronger, and demand the subordination of the inferior and weaker in accordance with the eternal will that dominates this universe'.

How was this 'victory of the better and stronger' to be achieved? In *Mein Kampf*, Hitler outlined a catalogue of measures which can be found in racial-hygienic and eugenicist literature from Galton, Haeckel, and Schallmayer onwards. However, the terminology employed was rather different. Hitler eschewed technical scientific terms like Weissmann's 'germ plasm' or Mendelian 'hereditary properties' in favour of calls for the 'maintenance of the purity of the blood'. Firstly, care should be taken 'to ensure that only those who are healthy produce children'. The 'obstruction of the reproductive capacities of those with syphilis, tuberculosis, the hereditarily burdened, cripples and cretins' was unavoidable. He repeated this last point, which again can be found in the work of Haeckel, Ploetz, and Schallmayer, in countless speeches and writings before 1933. The corollary of these 'negative eugenic' measures involved 'positive' attempts to increase the birthrate. Again,

in both *Mein Kampf* and subsequent speeches and writings, Hitler rec-
ommended a number of measures, which some historians have mis-
takenly regarded as 'modern', or even 'socially revolutionary'. These
measures included the introduction of child allowances, public hous-
ing projects, the promotion of equal education opportunities for
working-class children, and so forth. In reality, all of these projected
measures were motivated by racial considerations, firstly, because both
'alien races' and the 'less valuable elements' of the German population were excluded from the benefits of Nazi 'social policy', and secondly, because all of these social 'improvements' were designed to
encourage the reproduction of certain types of people.

Again, in *Mein Kampf*, Hitler made no secret of this objective. He
advocated the acquisition of 'outlying colonies', which were to be set-
tled by 'bearers of the highest racial purity'. The latter were to be selected by especially constituted 'commissions of racial experts'. Only
those applicants deemed to be 'racially valuable' were to receive an 'at-
testation (of the right) to settle'. Again, Hitler refrained from acknowl-
edging his intellectual debt to those eugenicists and racial-hygienicists
who had argued along precisely these lines for several decades. In contrast to racial-hygienicists, Hitler expected no immediate results from
these measures. The initial object was 'at least to eliminate the germ
of our present physical and intellectual decline'. Only after the 'six-
hundred-year obstruction of the reproductive capacities and possibilities to reproduce of the physically degenerate and the mentally ill',
and through 'the consciously planned promotion of the fertility of the
healthiest bearers of the nation', could a level of recovery be achieved
'which is hardly imaginable today'.

However, 'recovery' would only be possible if victory were achieved
in the 'struggle' against the Jews. This struggle was both absolutely
necessary and indeed willed by God. As Hitler wrote, 'I believe today
that I am acting in the sense of the Almighty Creator: by warding off
the Jews, I am fighting for the Lord's work.' The alternative outcome
was distinctly bleak. For should 'the Jew, with the help of his Marxian
creed . . . conquer the nations of this world, his crown will become
the funeral wreath of humanity, and once again this planet, empty of
mankind, will move through the ether as it did thousands of years
ago'. This plangent, pseudo-eschatological vision reflects the second
and most important element in Hitler's racism, namely racial anti-
Semitism. Virtually everything Hitler thought about the Jews was
contained in this passage. Unlike other anti-Semites, Hitler made no

distinctions between German and foreign, rich and poor, liberal, conservative, socialist, or Zionist, religious or nonreligious, baptised or unbaptised Jews. In his eyes, there was only 'the Jew'. 'The Jew' was striving for mastery of the peoples of the world. His most pernicious weapon was 'Marxism', whereby Hitler made no distinction between its Communist and socialist variants. If 'the Jew' should manage to win this ongoing 'struggle', then the result would be the downfall not only of the Germans, but of all peoples, and indeed of the world as a whole. 'The Jew' represented evil incarnate, performing for Hitler much the same function as the Devil does for many Christians. It was not fortuitous that in this connection Hitler used religious terms like 'creed', or that he employed apocalyptic language to describe the threat represented by 'the Jew'. The latter was the embodiment of absolute evil: the 'struggle' against 'him' was both righteous and good.

According to Hitler, the Jews in Germany and elsewhere were the champions of 'Marxism', the 'dictatorship of the proletariat', 'democracy' and the 'majority principle'. Jews were responsible for the outbreak of the First World War, and for the war's catastrophic outcome, namely Germany's collapse in 1918. They were the 'wire-pullers' behind the German Revolution, and the 'fathers' of the Weimar Constitution. Following the Revolution, they exercised their baleful influence in every political party — excepting the NSDAP — within the bureaucracy, the economy, cultural life, and the mass media. Other countries were either ruled by 'the Jew', like 'Jewish-Bolshevik Russia', or controlled by Jews, through their alleged dominance of 'world finance'. Both of these apparently polar opposites — namely Communism and 'finance' capitalism — were merely instruments designed to further plans for Jewish 'world domination', as essayed in the Protocols of the Elders of Zion. Even the propagation of the 'Jewish universal language' of Esperanto was a device designed to achieve this same end.

There was little in this Jewish conspiracy theory that was new, or which could not be found in the ravings of anti-Semites in other countries. Again, there was little originality in Hitler's coupling of the Jews with the question of prostitution, although in this case one would have to go back to the semi-pornographic tracts of Lanz and Dinter to find the same degree of obsessional and prurient concern with this issue. Hitler devoted twenty pages to this problem in *Mein Kampf*. He regarded prostitution as the 'pace-setter' of syphilis. Indeed, for him, in 1925–6 (!), 'the struggle against syphilis . . . was the task facing the nation', and indeed, humanity as a whole. This 'struggle' was one of the 'touchstones of the racial value' of a nation. The race which failed this 'test' would 'die out, or forfeit its position to healthier or hardier races capable of greater resistance'. In order to prevent this unhappy outcome, Hitler proposed a series of measures, ranging from 'the pitiless isolation' and 'sterilisation of the incurably ill', through the 'iron hardening' of youth in order to eradicate their sexual desires, to the facilitation of 'early marriage', and philogenerative welfare measures. However, these measures would be otiose unless the struggle against 'the Jew' was radicalised. 'The Jew' was responsible for prostitution, the spread of syphilis, and the 'spiritual prostitution' of the German people. Directly and indirectly 'he' sought to achieve the 'racial decomposition', 'bastardisation', and 'poisoning of the blood' of the 'body of the German nation', either through surrogates, notably French colonial troops 'planted' upon the Rhineland, or directly through 'his' own marital or extra-marital relations with 'Aryan' women. Assuming the sexual passivity of the latter, Hitler emulated Dinter's quasi-pornographic and prurient interest in this subject: 'With satanic joy in his face, the black-haired Jewish youth lurks in wait for the unsuspecting girl whom he defiles with his blood, thus stealing her from her people. With every means he tries to destroy the racial foundations of the people he has set out to subjugate.' In this oft-cited but sometimes underrated passage, Hitler both fused and developed the ideologies of anti-Semitism and racism. The Jews were accused not only of trying to 'subjugate' the German nation politically, but now of systematically undermining its 'racial foundations'. Racial-hygienic measures would therefore only be meaningful once the 'Jewish Question' had been 'solved'. What was the point of improving the racial health of the German population, if it was continually liable to subversion by the racial arch-enemy? In other words, Hitler had succeeded in combining and radicalising all previous strains of religious, social, and racial anti-Semitism: 'the Jew' was evil personified, therefore all means were appropriate and necessary in the fight against 'him'. The language used to describe 'the Jew' suggests one of the means he had in mind. They were 'spongers', 'parasites', 'poisonous mushrooms', 'rats', 'leeches', 'bacilli', 'tuberculosis bacilli' and so forth. Although some historians like to imagine that these metaphors were merely used for rhetorical effect, unaccountably ignoring the palpable inner violence of the man using them, the terms employed suggested one possible fate for the Jews, namely extermination.

Ian Kershaw

The Hitler Myth

Few, if any, twentieth-century political leaders have enjoyed greater popularity among their own people than Hitler in the decade or so following his assumption of power on 30 January 1933. It has been suggested that at the peak of his popularity nine Germans in ten were 'Hitler supporters, Führer believers'. Whatever qualification may be needed for such a bald assertion, it can be claimed with certainty that support for the Nazi Party never approached such a level, as Nazi leaders themselves well recognized. Acclaim for Hitler went way beyond those who thought of themselves as Nazis, embracing many who were critical of the institutions, policies, and ideology of the regime. This was a factor of fundamental importance in the functioning of the Third Reich. The adulation of Hitler by millions of Germans who might otherwise have been only marginally committed to Nazism meant that the person of the Führer, as the focal point of basic consensus, formed a crucial integratory force in the Nazi system of rule. Without Hitler's massive personal popularity, the high level of plebiscitary acclamation which the regime could repeatedly call upon — legitimating its actions at home and abroad, defusing opposition, boosting the autonomy of the leadership from the traditional national-conservative élites who had imagined they would keep Hitler in check, and sustaining the frenetic and increasingly dangerous momentum of Nazi rule — is unthinkable. Most important of all, Hitler's huge platform of popularity made his own power position ever more unassailable, providing the foundation for the selective radicalization process in the Third Reich by which his personal ideological obsessions became translated into attainable reality.

Biographical concern with the details of Hitler's life and his bizarre personality — fully explored in numerous publications — falls some way short of explaining the extraordinary magnetism of his popular appeal. Nor can Hitler's obsessive ideological fixations, also well known, satisfactorily account for his remarkable popularity. It would, for example, be easy to exaggerate the drawing power of anti-Semitism as the determining element in winning support for the Nazi Movement (though its functional importance as a unifying idea *within* the Movement is scarcely disputable). And for a population concerned with improving material conditions from the depths of the slump and overwhelmingly frightened of the prospect of another war, the idea of a coming war for *Lebensraum* was unlikely to have a dominant appeal. It has been plausibly suggested, therefore, that deep into the dictatorship itself Hitler's own ideological obsessions had more of a symbolic than concrete meaning for even most Nazi supporters.

What seems necessary is to add to the extensive knowledge of Hitler as a person by turning the focus on to the *image* of Hitler as Führer. . . .

The dual concerns of image-building and image-reception are closely intermeshed. There is not the slightest doubt that the 'Hitler myth' was consciously devised as an integrating force by a regime acutely aware of the need to manufacture consensus. Hitler himself, as is well known, paid the greatest attention to the building of his public image. He gave great care to style and posture during speeches and other public engagements. And he was keen to avoid any hint of human failings, as in his refusal to be seen wearing spectacles or participating in any form of sport or other activity in which he might not excel and which might make him an object of amusement rather than admiration. His celibacy, which Goebbels portrayed as the sacrifice of personal happiness for the welfare of the nation, was also regarded by Hitler as a functional necessity directed at avoiding any loss of popularity among German women, whose support he saw as vital to his electoral success. All this was closely related to Hitler's known views on the 'psychology of the masses', already expounded in *Mein Kampf* and taking a line similar to that in Gustave le Bon's writings on the almost boundless manipulability of the masses. And during the Third Reich itself, Hitler was evidently aware how important his 'omnipotent' image was to his leadership position and to the strength of the regime. To this extent, it has been aptly stated that 'Hitler well understood his own function, the role which he *had* to act out as "Leader" of the Third Reich', that he 'transformed himself into a function, the *function of Führer*'.

The manipulative purpose behind the 'Hitler myth' was, therefore, present from the outset. It was also welcomed and furthered in

quite cynical terms, for the 'stupefying of the masses' and their wean-
ing away from the lure of socialism towards an anti-socialist, counter-
revolutionary mass movement, by those members of the ruling classes
prepared to give active backing to the Nazi Party — though it would
be easy to exaggerate the extent to which the 'Hitler myth' was either
built to serve, or objectively did ultimately serve, the interests of monopoly capitalism. What does seem indisputable is that the constructed
'Hitler myth' was indispensable in its integrative function, firstly as a
counter to the strong centrifugal forces within the Nazi Movement itself, and secondly in establishing a massive basis of consensus among
the German people for those aims and policies identifiable with the
Führer. And the more the objective contradictions in the social aspirations of Nazism's mass base became apparent, the greater was the
functional necessity for the reification and ritualization of the 'Hitler
myth' in order to provide a firm base of affective integration.

Towards the end of 1941, at the height of Nazi power and domination in Europe, Goebbels claimed the creation of the 'Führer myth' as
his greatest propaganda achievement. He had some justification for
his claim. . . . However, it has been rightly pointed out that the 'heroic'
Hitler image was 'as much an image created by the masses as it was
imposed on them'. Propaganda was above all effective where it was
building upon, not countering, already existing values and mentali-
ties. The ready-made terrain of pre-existing beliefs, prejudices, and
phobias forming an important stratum of the German political culture
on to which the 'Hitler myth' could easily be imprinted, provides,
therefore, an equally essential element in explaining how the propaganda image of Hitler as a 'representative individual' upholding the
'true sense of propriety of the German people' could take hold and
flourish.

Necessarily, therefore, we start with the roots of the leadership cult,
which long pre-dated the rise of Nazism, and with its early gestation
within the Nazi Movement before its extension to the mass electorate
between 1930 and 1933. As is well known, in the March election of
1933 — held in a climate of national euphoria on the Right and extreme terroristic repression of the Left — less than one voter in two
supported Hitler's Party. Most Germans were still either hostile to or
unconvinced by their new Chancellor. Yet in the course of the next
three years or so, against the backcloth of an apparently total revital-
ization of German society, Hitler won over that 'majority of the major-

ity' which had not voted for him in 1933. The Führer cult was now firmly established as a mass phenomenon, providing the Nazi regime with the legitimation of an adored leader enjoying an unprecedented degree of adulation and subservience from his people. . . .

No one was more aware of the functional significance of his popularity in binding the masses to him, and hence to the regime, than Hitler himself. He pointed out that the strength of the regime could not depend on 'the laws [!] of the Gestapo alone', and that 'the broad mass [of the population] needs an idol'. On another occasion, he commented that the ruler who was dependent only upon executive power without finding 'the way to the people' was destined to failure. His well-documented fear of loss of personal popularity and the corresponding growth in instability of the regime is further testimony of his awareness of the centrality of the integratory force of his role as Führer. This integration was largely affective, for the most part forging psychological or emotional rather than material bonds. But its reality can scarcely be doubted. And at moments of internal crisis — such as in June 1934 — the regime was stabilized and its leadership given extended room for manœuvrability through the surge in Hitler's popularity and the strengthening of bonds of identity between people and Führer. In his portrayed public image, Hitler was able to offer a positive pole in the Third Reich, transcending sectional interests and grievances through the overriding ideal of national unity, made possible through his necessary aloofness from the 'conflict sphere' of daily politics, separating him from the more unpopular aspects of Nazism.

Hitler recognized that enthusiasm and willingness for self-sacrifice could not be conserved, and were bound to fade when confronted with 'the grey daily routine and the convenience of life'. He saw, therefore, that the masses could be bound to him only through constant psychological mobilization, demanding ever recurring successes. Until the middle of the war, the successes came, and spectacularly so, especially in the arena of foreign policy and military affairs, bringing many Germans who were far from Nazis into close identification with Hitler, revamping sagging morale, forcing open acclaim, prompting active participation — if shallow and largely ritualized — in support of 'his' achievements, disarming potential opponents, making objections to Nazi policy difficult to formulate. This was, for example, undoubtedly the effect of the plebiscites staged in 1933, 1934, 1936, and 1938, in which the massive acclamation, though the product of intense propaganda and coercion and obviously in no sense a true reflection of the state of opinion, nevertheless reflected genuine widespread approval and admiration for Hitler's accomplishments and persuaded waverers to fall in line.

The plebiscitary acclamation which could always be mobilized by Hitler provided him with an unassailable base of popularity, and as such offered the regime legitimation both within Germany and in the eyes of foreign powers, allowing the scope for further mobilization and a gathering momentum of Nazi policy. The massive popularity of Hitler, recognized even by enemies of the regime, formed therefore a decisive element in the structure of Nazi rule in Germany. It goes far towards helping to account not only for the high and growing degree of relative autonomy from non-Nazi élites enjoyed by Hitler and the Nazi leadership, but also — as the counterweight to terror, repression, and intimidation — for the weakness of resistance to the regime. The 'Hitler myth' and terror were in this sense two indispensable sides of the same coin, ensuring political control and mobilization behind the regime. It is no coincidence, therefore, that terroristic repression escalated wildly in the final phase of the waning regime as the binding force of Hitler's popularity weakened and collapsed.

Robert G. L. Waite

Guilt Feelings and Perverted Sexuality

A major problem in dealing with the life of Adolf Hitler is that of determining the extent to which he had confidence in himself as a person and as a political leader. This essay will discuss one aspect of his remarkably complex personality and will show that one of history's

Reprinted without footnotes from *The Journal of Interdisciplinary History*, I (1971), pp. 229–249, with the permission of the editors of *The Journal of Interdisciplinary History* and The MIT Press, Cambridge, Massachusetts. © 1971 by The Massachusetts Institute of Technology and the editors of *The Journal of Interdisciplinary History*.

most ruthless rulers was beset by feelings of guilt and the need for self-punishment.

In public and private speech, Hitler revealed his concern by talking repeatedly about unworthiness, guilt, and conscience. He worried, for example, about his own worthiness in the sight of God and attempted to quiet his doubts in two ways. He protested too much that he really was worthy, saying, typically, "The Great Judge of all time . . . will always give victory to those who are the most worthy [*würdig*]." And again, "I carry my heavy burdens with dutiful thanks to Providence which has deemed me *worthy*. . . ." Another way of silencing his own doubts was to insist that, while he certainly was worthy, others were not. Thus the Jews were unworthy to be citizens of his Reich and must die. By 1945 he reached the conclusion that the entire German people had proved unworthy of him; they too should perish.

Over and over again he showed that he was bothered by conscience and felt the need of dulling its demands:

> *Only when the time comes when the race is no longer overshadowed by the* consciousness of its own guilt *then will it find internal peace.*

> Conscience *is a Jewish invention. It is a blemish like circumcision.* . . .

> *I am freeing men from . . . the* dirty and degrading *modification of a chimera called* conscience and morality.

> *We must distrust the intelligence and the* conscience. . . .

> *We must be ruthless . . . we must regain our* clear conscience *as to ruthlessness. . . . Only thus shall we* purge *our people.*

Hitler was even convinced that dogs suffer from a "bad conscience."

The Führer felt guilty about something. But when a historian attempts to give the precise reasons for those guilt feelings, he is reminded again of Trevelyan's trenchant admonition to those who would try to make of history a science: "in the most important part of its business, history is . . . an imaginative guess."

Aided by the insights of psychoanalysis, let us set forth here our best guesses as to the causes of Hitler's feelings of guilt. One possibility can quickly be eliminated. Hitler felt no remorse whatever over the calculated murder of millions of "racially inferior" people, or the holocaust of war, or the annihilation of the village of Lidice, or the planned destruction of the Fatherland and the burning of Paris, or the squandered lives of young German soldiers. Atrocities did not disturb Hitler. Other guesses are needed.

Hitler seems to have felt unworthy of being the Führer of a racially pure Germany because he suspected that he himself might have been "guilty of having Jewish blood" — as the barbarous expression ran in the Third Reich. He had been so shaken in 1930 when he heard dark hints that his own grandfather might have been a Jew that he sent his personal lawyer, Hans Frank, to investigate. Frank's report was not reassuring. It said that Hitler's father was born out of wedlock to a certain Maria Anna Shicklgruber who had worked as a domestic in Graz, Austria, "in the home of a Jewish family by the name of Frankenberger." That Frank's investigations may have been in error does not alter the crucial fact that Hitler *believed that they might be correct* and was haunted by the fear that he himself might be "part Jewish." He testified to this fear in various ways. He took special pains to dictate the precise language of the Nuremberg Racial Laws of 1935 and gave orders that not one word should be changed. The wording of Article 3 is particularly interesting. Of all the civil disabilities for Jews he might have ordered, he set forth this one: "Jews may not employ female household servants of German or related blood who are under 45 years of age." Hitler's own grandmother had been forty-two when she gave birth to Hitler's father.

Anxiety about a Jewish grandfather was also shown when he projected his own fears onto Matthias Erzberger, a leader of the Center party whom Hitler accused of betraying Germany by accepting the Versailles treaty: "Matthias Erzberger . . . *the illegitimate son of a servant girl and a Jewish employer,* was the German negotiator who set his name to the document which had the deliberate intention of bringing about the destruction of Germany." The servant girl in a Jewish household was still on his mind years later. In one of his nightly monologues during 1942 he told his entourage about "a country girl who had a place in Nuremberg in the household of Herr Hirsch," who had raped her.

Hitler projected guilt feelings about the impurity of his own blood in another way. He sought to lessen his personal anxiety by universalizing the guilt, saying that all Germans were at fault. Thus he insisted that "*All of us* are suffering from . . . mixed, corrupted blood. How can we purify ourselves and make atonement?"

There is further evidence that Hitler suspected his own blood was tainted. Just two months after taking over Austria in March 1938,

Hitler had a survey made of the lovely little farming village of Döllersheim — the village where his father had been born and his grandmother buried. The purpose of the survey was to determine the suitability of the area for an artillery range for the German army. The commanding general of Wehrkreis XVII was given orders directly from Hitler to make the area ready "as soon as possible" for that purpose. The inhabitants were evacuated, the village was demolished by artillery fire, and the graves of the cemetery were rendered unrecognizable. Why? There are thousands of empty acres in this part of Lower Austria. Hitler must have chosen this particular village as an artillery range because he felt a great compulsion to wipe out — quite literally — the suspicion of his own Jewish blood by obliterating the birthplace of his father and the grave of his grandmother whom he considered guilty of contaminating him.

In the so-called "Gestapo Reports" of the Main Archives of the party, there are records of several separate investigations of Hitler's own family background. The most thorough of these inquiries was made in 1942 — just prior to the onset of the massacres which killed about 6 million Jews. Why were these special investigations undertaken? Hitler rarely talked about his own family. Why then did he have this remarkable concern about his ancestors unless he was anxiously hoping to prove that he was a "pure Aryan" — or at least as Aryan as his own racial laws required?

Hitler also manifested his concern about "racial contamination" in both his public and private life. Racial purity was, of course, absolutely basic to the whole theory of National Socialism, and in public speeches he often spoke about "blood baths," "the blood order," and "the bloodflag." But his concern about blood went beyond that. He worried about his own blood and seems to have been convinced that there was something wrong with it. He became a vegetarian partly because he thought that a vegetable diet would purify his blood. And he regularly got rid of his blood by letting leeches suck it from him. Later, his quack doctor, Theodor Morell, drew it from him, and preserved it in test tubes, so that Hitler could gaze at it apprehensively.

The feeling that his own blood was impure contributed to his sense of unworthiness and inadequacy in performing the role of mighty Führer of a racially pure Reich. Hence he often looked anxiously into a mirror and asked his valet for assurance, saying, "I really do look like the Führer. Don't I, Linge?" As a young man he had been teased about looking Jewish, and the suggestion continued to bother him.

Hitler also seems to have felt guilty about incestuous desires. His relations with both his mother and his niece were very close indeed, and the word incest was often on his mind. Whether or not he actually acted out his incestuous feelings is not very important psychologically. As Freud showed us long ago, fantasies can be as psychically formative as realities.

It is also possible that acute feelings of unworthiness, guilt, and self-loathing were a consequence of a massively masochistic sexual perversion. Hitler gained sexual satisfaction by having a young woman — as much younger than he as his mother was younger than his father — squat over him to urinate or defecate on his head.

When confronted with data such as these, a biographer of Adolf Hitler has at least three options. He can ignore such evidence as sensational, embarrassing, and quite beneath the dignity of a serious historian. He can use some of the data selectively as unusual sidelights, showing the eccentricities of his subject. Or he can try to show how a discussion of Hitler's psychological abnormalities had historical consequences and can help in a fuller understanding of him as a person. With appropriate trepidation — and trepidation is certainly appropriate here — let us suggest some historical results in Hitler's personal feelings of guilt and unworthiness.

Most obviously, he sought relief from his burden of guilt by an elaborate system of defenses. Indeed he displayed virtually all the major mechanisms Anna Freud has described in her classical work on the subject. He relied heavily, for example, upon reaction formation. Thus his perversion and voyeurism were masked behind ostentatiously prudish behavior. He appeared a moral and ascetic person who forbade the telling of off-color stories in his presence, who did not swear, who denied himself alcohol and tobacco, and who objected when women wore lipstick. He complained that it was manufactured from French urine. He showed that he was disturbed by the filth of his perversion in the number of times the words urine, filth, and dirt were on his mind, saying, typically, that he would free men from "the dirty and degrading" aspects of conscience, or that Jews were "filthy," "unclean," "like a maggot in a rotting corpse." His reaction formation against filth was appropriately extreme and took the form of excessive cleanliness. He washed his hair at least once a day, bathed and changed his underwear twice daily, and scrubbed his hands frequently. He was greatly concerned about his body odors. One of the reasons he became a vegetarian was because — like Benjamin Franklin — he believed that eating meat increased the objectionable odor of flatulation, a chronic complaint of Hitler's which he sought to alleviate by taking enormous quantities of "Dr. Köster's Antigas Pills." These efforts to make his body odors less objectionable were linked to his fear that he might be part Jewish. Jews, he insisted, had a peculiar and objectionable odor.

Hitler also sought to lessen his feelings of guilt through self-punishment — hence his abstentious habits and the masochism of his perversion. It is even conceivable that he actually punished himself physically to the point of partial self-castration. And time and again he promised to commit suicide, the ultimate masochistic dissolution. Among the many childish games he played was a form of substitute suicide. Hitler disliked tying his own necktie and ordered his valet to do it for him. He would hold his breath during the process and count slowly to ten. If Linge could finish the knot before Hitler had finished counting, the Führer was greatly relieved.

Adolf Hitler also indulged in a form of self-punishment which may have had important historical consequences. As McRandle was first to suggest, Hitler punished himself by unconscious desires for failure and defeat. Of course, his life can be seen quite differently, as a remarkable success story, with an unlikely hero played by a neurotic dropout of Linz and Vienna who had failed in all his undertakings and been jailed at the start of his political career, but who, within a decade, became the master of Germany and then arbiter of Europe. Historians are clearly justified in dwelling on Hitler's extraordinary gifts and brilliant victories. And yet there is a curious pattern of behavior that also needs to be noted in attempting to understand this very complex personality. Throughout his life, Adolf Hitler flirted with failure and involved himself unnecessarily in situations that were fraught with danger to himself and his movement.

During his first years in elementary school, Adolf had had an excellent record, but he failed to get a diploma from Realschule and ran away to Vienna. He failed his first examination for the academy of art, and, when given a second chance, he did not apply himself and failed a second time. His first bid for power in 1923 shows a similar pattern of choosing the alternatives least likely to succeed. Throughout the summer of 1923 he made no plans for seizing political power. He gratuitously insulted the leading military figures of Bavaria and Germany,

Generals Franz Ritter von Epp, Otto von Lossow, and Hans von Seeckt — men whose support or neutrality was indispensable to him if he planned a coup. Having failed to make preparations, he suddenly called forth a great national revolution which had no chance of success, loudly promising either total victory or suicide. Instead, he ran away and hid in the summer home of a Harvard graduate, "Putzi" Hanfstaengl. Arrested and confronted by political disaster, he extricated himself by brilliant demogoguery.

Hitler's record during the "seizure of power" in 1920–1933 is usually considered brilliant, perhaps because it was successful. And surely there were signs of both enormous energy and political acumen. But there is also evidence of political mistakes so glaring as to suggest an unconscious desire for failure. He went out of his way, for example, to alienate the one great political force he needed to mollify, and ran for the presidency against President Field-Marshal Paul von Hindenburg. Hitler's success in 1933 was due at least as much to the stupidities and failures of Weimar's political leaders as it was to his own efforts.

Similarly, however one interprets his foreign policy, it can be viewed as an invitation to disaster. Three differing interpretations may be considered. First, if A. J. P. Taylor is right in insisting that all Hitler really wanted was a negotiated revision of Versailles, then the methods he employed to attain that end were indeed "singularly inappropriate." Second, if we are to suppose that Hitler wanted only a limited war against Poland to gain Danzig and the corridor, certainly his bellicose speeches against the Western powers, his atrocities against the Jews and other minorities, and his broken promises to Chamberlain show him proceeding in ways unlikely to isolate Poland and most likely to assure his victim of strong allies. Finally, let us suppose he really plotted the great war of European conquest that he had promised in *Mein Kampf*, again in 1925, in his second book of 1928, and in a dozen speeches. If so, he made inadequate preparations for fighting such a war. He got himself involved in a general conflict against the Western powers and still promised total victory or total destruction. Once more, largely through intuition, skill, and luck, he was victorious in the West. Then he decided to attack Russia at the very time that it was trying desperately to appease him by shipping Germany thousands of tons of supplies. While his offensive against the USSR faltered and failed, Hitler suddenly declared war on the United States, the greatest industrial power on earth. Thus it was Hitler who took the initiative in bringing about the kind of global war he could not conceivably win. And during those titanic years from 1941–1944 Hitler dawdled and dithered over the crucial question of a war economy for Germany. Economic mobilization was not really declared until the autumn of 1944, that is, until well after "Fortress Europa" had been breached from the West and Russia was counterattacking along a thousand miles of the Eastern front. Only then, when it was much too late, did Hitler hesitatingly move in the direction of full economic mobilization. But he could never bring himself to give clear orders for a complete war economy.

In the end, as he had done so often in his life, he ran away and hid, this time in his air-raid shelter in Berlin. He killed himself by taking poison and having his bride perform the coup de grâce.

Throughout his career, Hitler seldom contemplated a line of action without thinking of defeat. The disjunctives which characterized his thought almost invariably included the possibility of failure and of suicide. Typically, in the midst of the Beer Hall Putsch, he turned to Gustav von Kahr, Lossow, and Hans von Seisser and said, "You must be victorious with me or die with me. If things go wrong, I have four bullets in my pistol: three for my fellow workers if they desert me, the last bullet is for me." He contemplated failure and suicide on many other occasions: while hiding at the Hanfstaengl summer home in 1923; upon his arrival in 1924 at Landsberg; in 1931 after the suicide of his niece, "Geli" Raubal; in 1932 if he were not appointed chancellor; in 1936 if the occupation of the Rhineland failed; and on many other occasions.

Even at the very height of prewar success he was concerned about failure. On November 10, 1938, for example, he addressed the German press in what should have been a moment of triumph. His first big pogrom against the Jews in the *Kristallnacht* had been executed with the acquiescence of the German people. During the preceding months he had enjoyed a series of other victories: the reintroduction of universal military training; the reoccupation of the Rhineland; the highly successful plebiscite approving his withdrawal from the League of Nations; Anschluss with Austria; and most recently the triumph of the Munich agreement. And yet his speech of November 10 is studded with foreboding. The words *Angst, Rückschlag, Niederlage,* and *Misserfolg* were very much on his mind:

> *I must tell you that I often have one single* misgiving . . . *I become almost* anxious. . . . . *I have had nothing but successes, but what would*

happen if I were to suffer a failure? Yes, Gentlemen, even that can happen. . . . How would [the masses] act if we ever had a failure? Formerly, Gentlemen, it was my greatest pride that I built up a party that even in time of defeat stood behind me. . . .

Certainly in sending first his lawyer and then the Gestapo to investigate the racial purity of his own family he was taking an enormous risk. Psychologically he had based his very identity as a person on the projection of his own feelings of guilt, inadequacy, failure, and perversion onto the Jews; politically, he had staked his entire career on the principle of Aryan superiority and the terrible threat of the "Jewish Peril" from which he was defending Western civilization. If his investigators had found that Hitler's own grandfather had been a Jew, he could have been ruined by this disaster to both his psyche and his life work.

Incidents surrounding the launching of World War II also suggest preoccupation with prospects of failure. Albert Speer recalls that on the night of August 24, 1939, when Hitler's pact with Stalin — which gave him a free hand to attack the West — was announced, the Führer met with a small group of intimates at his "Eagle's Nest" overlooking Berchtesgaden. The group stood out on the balcony to watch a spectacular display of northern lights as they pulsated and throbbed above the Bavarian Alps. The dominant color was red, and the skies and mountains and the faces and hands of the watchers were washed in scarlet. Hitler saw an omen in the eery and foreboding light. He turned apprehensively to his military aide and said: "This time *we won't make it* without using force."

The complexities and contradictions of Hitler's personality are shown clearly in his conduct of the war. He displayed a great capacity for innovation in his use of armor and airpower; and his military campaigns against Poland and the West were smashing triumphs. Further, Hitler's successes as a tactician were, in the early years of the war, matched by remarkable strategic insight. Indeed, a distinguished British military analyst has concluded that "no strategist in history has been more clever in playing on the minds of his opponents — which is the supreme art of strategy."

All this is true. Hitler, it bears repeating, could act with devastating effectiveness, and his military abilities and victories should not be disparaged. Yet here too are suggestions that his remarkable career was beset by unconscious desires to punish himself in the very midst of success. There was the curious refusal to press his advantage at

Dunkirk. There was the long hesitation and inaction after the fall of France — a time when "the wave of conquest broke on the shoals of delay and indecision." Month after month during the critical summer of 1940, Hitler continued to violate the cardinal principle of Clausewitz, an authority he had studied so avidly: "Once the great victory is gained there should be no talk of rest, of getting breath, or of consolidation, etc., but only of pursuit . . . of attacking. . . ."

Instead of concentrating his forces against his only remaining enemy, an isolated and desperately wounded England, Hitler turned to court his Nemesis. He sent his armies — without winter issue — marching into Russia. That he set the date for invasion in 1941 on the precise anniversary of Napoleon's ill-fated campaign (June 22) is perhaps coincidental, but why did he choose the code name of "Barbarossa"? It is true that Hitler saw himself, like Frederick Barbarossa, as a crusader whose mission it was to destroy an infidel Eastern enemy; but, as an avid reader of history, Hitler knew that the most notable thing about Barbarossa was that he was a failure. He had failed in five campaigns against the Lombard towns; he had failed to centralize the Holy Roman Empire; he had failed to obtain his objectives during the Third Crusade. And he had died by drowning. Adolf Hitler was pathologically afraid of the water, and had nightmares about loss of breath and strangulation. Moreover, the words Hitler used in announcing the invasion of Russia are worth remembering. "The world," he said, "will hold its breath." When Adolf Hitler held his breath and counted to ten while his valet tied his tie, he was symbolically enacting suicide and self-destruction.

Hitler also sought to dull his feelings of guilt by a kind of "introjection" in which he took upon himself the role of a great moral and religious leader. He saw himself as a messiah who was establishing a new religion and leading a great crusade against the cosmic forces of evil, that is, the incarnate evil of "the international Jewish conspiracy." It is not surprising, therefore, to find Hitler very seriously comparing himself to Jesus. He said on one occasion, as he lashed about him with a whip, "In driving out the Jews I remind myself of Jesus in the temple"; and on another, "Like Christ, I have a duty to my own people. . . ." He considered himself betrayed by Ernst Röhm in 1934 and drew the analogy to the betrayal of Jesus, saying, "Among the twelve apostles, there was also a Judas. . . ."

That he saw himself as the special agent of God and identified with Him was made manifest on many occasions:

> *I go the way that Providence dictates for me with all the assurance of a sleepwalker.*

> *God has created this people and it has grown according to His will. And according to our will* [nach unserem Willen] *it shall remain and never shall it pass away.*

> *I believe that it was God's will that from her* [Austria] *a boy was sent into the Reich and that he grew up to become the Leader of the nation.*

> *By warding off the Jews, I am fighting for the Lord's work.*

Hitler patterned the organization of his party and his Reich after the Roman Catholic church, which had impressed him so much as a young boy. He saw himself as a political pope with an apostolic succession when he announced to a closed meeting of the faithful in the Brown House during 1930, "I hereby set forth for myself and my successors in the leadership of the National Socialist Democratic Party the claim of political infallibility. I hope the world will grow as accustomed to that claim as it has to the claim of the Holy Father." The oath of direct obedience to the Führer was strikingly reminiscent of the special oath the Jesuits swore to the pope, and Hitler spoke of his elite SS, who wore the sacred ⚡ and dressed in black, as a Society of Jesus, from which, he said, he had learned so much.

The bolts of excommunication and anathema which Hitler hurled against nonbelievers and heretics were not unlike those of a Gregory VII:

> *Woe to them who do not believe. These people have sinned . . . against all of life. . . . It is a miracle of faith that Germany has been saved. Today more than ever it is the duty of the Party to remember this National Socialist Confession of Faith* [Glaubensbekenntnis] *and to bear it forward as our holy* [heiliges] *sign of our battle and our victory.*

Hitler chose a cross as the symbol and sign of his movement.

The Nazis, like the Catholics, had their prophets, saints, and martyrs. Hitler's followers who fell during the Beer Hall Putsch were sanctified by Hitler when he said, in dedicating their memorial, that their death would bring forth "a true belief in the Resurrection of their people . . . the blood that they shed has become the baptismal water of the

Third Reich." The annual Nazi march on November 9 from the Bürgerbraükeller to the Feldherrnhalle was a studied reenactment of the stations of the cross combined with the Passion Play. The analogy was made clear by the stress on "the blood that was shed for the redemption of the Fatherland."

Hitler's holy reliquary was the Brown House which contained the sacred Blood Flag which had been born by the martyrs of November 9. It was Hitler and Hitler alone who could perform the priestly ritual of touching the Blood Flag to the standards of the Brownshirts.

Hitler substituted Nazi high holy days for traditional religious holidays. They included January 30, the day Hitler came to power in the year he referred to as "the Holy Year of our Lord, 1933," and April 20, the leader's own birthday and the day when the Hitler Youth were confirmed in the faith. The holiest day, however, and one which served as a kind of Nazi Good Friday was November 9, celebrated as the Blood Witness [*Blutzeugen*] of the movement.

Religions require devils. For National Socialism, the Jewish people played that part, and Hitler insisted that the German people could achieve salvation only after they had destroyed the Jew who was, in Hitler's words, "*the personification of the Devil*" and the "symbol of all evil." The concept was made unmistakably vivid in the childish rhyme:

> *Wer kennt den Jude*
> *Kennt den Teufel.*

Hitler also provided a sacred book for his new religion, and *Mein Kampf* replaced the Bible as the traditional wedding present given to all young Aryans. The close parallel between Christian commitment to God and the sacred oath of allegiance to Hitler is best seen in a description of public oath-taking recorded in the Nazi newspaper, *Westdeutscher Beobachter:* "Yesterday witnessed the profession of the Religion of the Blood in all its imposing reality. . . . Whoever has sworn his oath of allegiance to Hitler has pledged himself unto death to this sublime idea."

It is true that Hitler sometimes told his intimates that he did not wish to be deified, but he did little to stop his followers from exalting him as savior and messiah. Indeed, he directly approved the patent paganism and Führer worship of the Warthegau church as a model for the church he planned after the war. And he did not object to the following version of the Lord's Prayer which was recited by the League of German Girls:

Adolf Hitler, you are our great leader
Thy name makes the enemy tremble.
Thy Third Reich comes, thy will alone is law
upon earth. Let us hear daily thy voice and
order us by thy leadership, for we will obey
to the end, even with our lives.
We praise thee! Heil Hitler!

It is to be noted that prayers were given not only for the Führer, but to him as a deity.

In speeches and soliloquies, and in ways he may not have been aware, Hitler himself spoke in the very words of Christ and the scriptures — thereby revealing a considerable knowledge of the Bible. A few examples will suffice here: in dedicating the House of German Art in Munich he observed, "Man does not live by bread alone." In talking to the Brownshirts on January 30, 1936, he echoed the words of Jesus to his disciples as recorded in St. John's Gospel, saying, "I have come to know thee. Who thou art, thou art through me, and all I am, I am through thee." He reminded one of his disciples that "I have not come to Germany to bring peace but a sword." In a public speech in Graz in 1938 he announced, "God Almighty has created the Nation. And what the Lord has joined together let not Man set asunder."

He was particularly prone to Biblical quotations when talking to the Hitler Youth. On September 5, 1934, he told them, "You are flesh of our flesh and blood of our blood." In 1932 he advised them either to be "hot or cold, but the lukewarm should be damned and spewed from your mouth." The phrasing is too close to the New Testament to be coincidental. The Revelation of St. John reads: "I know thy works, that thou art neither cold nor hot; I would thou wert cold or hot. So then, because thou art lukewarm, and neither cold nor hot, I will spew thee out of my mouth."

During one of the last suppers with his followers, Hitler invited them to eat of their leader's body, asking them if they would like some blood sausage made from his own blood. In effect he was saying, "Take, eat: this is my body, which is broken for you. . . ."

The defense mechanism used by Adolf Hitler that had the greatest historical consequence was that of projection. Hitler made his own feelings of guilt more bearable by shifting the finger of guilt away from himself and pointing it at Jews. Allport has given a succinct description of the process and has shown the connection between guilt and self-hatred with the need for projection:

> *The hated scapegoat is merely a disguise for persistent and unrecognized self-hatred. A vicious circle is established. The more the sufferer hates himself, the more he hates the scapegoat, the less sure he is of his . . . innocence; hence the more guilt he has to project.*

It needs to be emphasized that in Hitler's case both the degree of self-hatred and the corresponding amount of projected hatred were of truly monumental proportions. He hated Jews for many reasons and accused them of every conceivable crime. But never did he become "so emotional, so arbitrary and so absurd" as when he fulminated against Jewish sex crimes, incest, and perversion — precisely those sexual aberrations about which he felt personally so guilty. The direct projection onto the Jews of guilt felt as the result of his own perversions is shown in an incident in 1938 involving the dismissal of General Werner von Blomberg as minister of defense. Hitler expressed outraged shock at the disclosure that the general had married a former prostitute. He used the scandal as an excuse for dismissing an uncooperative general, and had the Gestapo collect incriminating evidence against Frau General Blomberg. They supplied him with photographs which showed her plying her profession by participating in various forms of deviate sexual activity. A man who has seen the photographs says that they were of "the most shocking depravity." What concerns us here is Hitler's instinctive reaction upon first seeing the pictures. He said at once that the male partner in the photographs "*must have been*" of Jewish extraction." He then became "absolutely convulsed by the wildest anti-Semitic outpouring he had ever given vent to in his entire life."

Thus did the Jews become the hated personal enemy of Hitler and his Reich. In destroying the Jewish people, Adolf Hitler was not only "doing the work of the Lord." He was destroying the evil thing which he felt within himself. This would seem to be the meaning of the curious comment he once made to Rauschning: "The Jew is always within us" [*Der Jude sitzt immer in uns*].

The historical importance of this projection is clear: the racial anti-Semitism which lay at the very core of German fascism and which produced the greatest mass horror of history was, among other things, a direct consequence of Adolf Hitler's personal feelings of guilt and self-hatred.

The Industrial Might of the Third Reich. A remilitarized Germany pays homage to Hitler on his 47th birthday, as the Reichsführer drives between lines of troops and armored cars in Berlin. (UPI/Corbis-Bettmann)

The Crucial Role of German Elites

Variety of Opinion

Quite contrary to the widespread impression that Hitler gained power in January 1933 with strong backing from big business, his appointment to the chancellorship came just when relations between his movement and the business community had reached the lowest point.

Henry Ashby Turner, Jr.

Hitler never doubted for one moment that recovery must be masterminded by the experienced men running German industry and not by party zealots.

William Carr

The papacy and members of the German hierarchy in the pre-war years had at times denounced the cult of racism, of blood and soil. But there were no clarion protests against the anti-Semitic policy of the Nazi rulers then or during the war years.

Ernst Christian Helmreich

This strategy constituted a form of cultural eugenics, simultaneously nourishing the "healthy" and weeding out the "unhealthy."

Alan E. Steinweis

> *The most suitable arm for a revolt was also the most conservative and nationalist force in society. . . . Without the Army, the prospects for the Resistance were poor indeed.*
>
> Peter Hoffmann

In January 1933 Adolf Hitler became the chancellor of Germany. He was not yet the dictator. First he had to gain the allegiance of the people and, above all, the elites. Once the political system, the courts, and the police were firmly in hand, the Nazi party could persuade business, religious, cultural, and military leaders to support a national effort to restore law and order, as well as to regain Germany's rightful place among the states of Europe.

Henry Ashby Turner, Jr., *denies that German business moguls were instrumental either in the collapse of the Weimar Republic or in the rise of the Nazi party. In his economic objectives before 1933 Hitler remained deliberately ambiguous and, accordingly, the business community was puzzled about his true intentions. Turner allows that there was some flirtation between them, but little more, as Hitler wooed industrial capitalists with vague promises. Hitler's final surge to power was therefore not financed by the leaders of big business, who mostly preferred their fellow elites and felt they had reason to distrust an outsider who was not one of their kind.*

William Carr *examines Nazi economic policies after 1933. Once in control, Hitler thwarted the German labor movement and made open appeals to the business community. He was soon able to negotiate an arrangement by offering tax breaks, wage controls, and lucrative military contracts. The Führer's bid for respectability with business and banking interests was aided by his financial adviser, Hjalmar Schacht. Their partnership survived until 1936, when Hitler decided to drop his mask and moved to implement a four-year plan that was frankly geared toward war. Under these conditions, it was appropriate that Schacht be replaced by Hermann Goering. Although the ambitions of business did not push Germany to war, Carr believes, they did become part of a Nazi dynamism in which political, economic, and military considerations became impossible to disaggregate.*

Ernst Christian Helmreich *discusses one of Hitler's most delicate problems: gaining the cooperation of the Christian churches. Fortunately for Hitler, both Protestants and Catholics could be counted on to remain staunch German patriots. Especially vexing for religious leaders, however, was the Nazi persecution of the Jews. On this issue, controversy has ordinarily focused on (but not been confined to) the Catholic hierarchy and the Roman papacy. Paradoxically, as Helmreich shows, pressure exerted by the Nazi state on religious organizations was eased as Germany's military fortunes worsened in the war. Yet by then there was little that the Catholic clergy could do without a clear condemnation from the Vatican of Nazi racial policy. That was not forthcoming.*

Alan E. Steinweis *outlines the reorganization of German cultural life at the behest of Hitler's minister of propaganda, Joseph Goebbels. Former elite groups were abolished, and artists were subjected to the authority of a central Chamber of Culture. This measure served both to impose state discipline on the arts and to exclude Jews, Gypsies, Communists, and homosexuals. Who was elite would henceforth be determined by the Nazi party.*

Peter Hoffmann *recounts the story of Hitler's generals, who finally made a belated and disastrously unsuccessful effort to assassinate him in July 1944. After the mid-1930s only the army leaders had any realistic chance to mount an effective resistance to Nazi rule. Rumors of plots against the Führer's life abounded, and a few were actually attempted. But all those failures paled in comparison to Count von Stauffenberg's ill-fated plan to plant a bomb at Hitler's military headquarters and bring the Third Reich to an abrupt end. Instead, a final purge of elites followed, and the war ground on toward its miserable conclusion.*

In these pages we gain a sense of why Hitler could not have succeeded alone, nor solely with the assistance of his old political cronies. He needed the complicity of Germany's traditional figures of authority, whose commanding presence and expertise so well complemented the fervor and muscle of the Nazi party. Elites added a veneer of respectability to raw enthusiasm and terror, thereby discouraging overt resistance to the regime. Thus many decent Germans no doubt responded at first to the idealism of a new day, only to watch helplessly thereafter as their hopes were perverted beyond recognition or retrieval.

Henry Ashby Turner, Jr.

The Legend of Capitalist Support

Only through gross distortion can big business be accorded a crucial, or even major, role in the downfall of the Republic. The business community displayed, to be sure, little enthusiasm for the new democratic state, and very few major executives could be termed democrats by conviction. Particularly at the outset of the republican period they felt jeopardized by a political system that assigned ultimate authority over national policy to a mass electorate. They also deplored many republican policies, especially the rapid expansion of *Sozialpolitik* — welfare state legislation — and direct governmental intervention in labor-management relations. But once the difficulties of the Republic's first five years had been overcome and a measure of prosperity restored, most men of big business reconciled themselves to the new state, if not always to its policies. So long as the country prospered, they saw little chance for a change of regime. Most remained frustrated politically, having discovered that economic potency did not translate readily into political effectiveness in a democratic polity, where ballots weighed more than money and where blocs of disciplined interest-group voters counted for more than did financial contributions.

Big businessmen did, to be sure, play a part in causing the crisis that eventuated in the paralysis of the Republic's parliamentary system in 1930. The insistence by some sectors of big business on curtailment of the capstone of republican *Sozialpolitik*, the national unemployment insurance program, helped at that time to precipitate what in retrospect emerges as one of the earliest of the now familiar fiscal crises of twentieth-century capitalist welfare states. The outcome of that crisis was, however, determined not by the business community but rather by the political spokesmen of organized labor. Also, the resulting parliamentary deadlock did not in itself put an end to Weimar democracy. That stalemate assumed fateful proportions only because it triggered a fundamental shift of authority to the presidency through use of the emergency powers assigned to that office by the constitution. Behind that move stood not Germany's capitalists but rather its military leadership. Generals, not corporation executives, effected the establishment of presidential rule in 1930. As a consequence of that development — which initially made some of the leading figures in the business community very uneasy because of their concern about the reaction of credit markets abroad — they and their compeers found themselves with even less political influence than they had enjoyed earlier. As long as the parliamentary system functioned, the politically active elements of big business had frequently managed to combine their small parliamentary bloc with other interest groups through horse trading of the usual sort so as to influence the shape of legislation. The links between big business and those bourgeois parties that regularly received subsidies from it had enabled its political spokesmen to exert pressure, if not always successfully, on government policies when those parties participated in ruling coalitions. Under the governmental system that began to take shape in 1930, however, the wishes of the business community carried little or no weight with the decisive source of authority, President Hindenburg, or with the military men who served as his counselors. During the period of presidential rule, men chosen by those counselors, men not beholden to big business, determined national policy. And it was those men — Brüning, Papen, and Schleicher — and not Germany's capitalists who set the disastrous political and economic course that destroyed what remained of the Weimar Republic and fostered the growth of the Nazi Party.

If the role of big business in the disintegration of the Republic has been exaggerated, such is even more true of its role in the rise of Hitler. While a significant part of the business community contributed materially — if less than wholly voluntarily — to the consolidation of Hitler's regime after he had become chancellor, he and his party had previously received relatively little support from that quarter. The early growth of the NSDAP took place without any significant aid from the circles of large-scale enterprise. Centered in industrially underdeveloped Bavaria, tainted with illegality as a consequence of the failed beer hall putsch of 1923, saddled with a program containing disturbingly anti-capitalist planks, and amounting only to a raucous splinter group politically, the NSDAP languished in disrepute in the eyes of most men of big business throughout the latter part of the 1920s. The major executives of Germany proved, with rare exception, resistant to the blandishments of Nazis, including Hitler himself, who sought to reassure the business community about their party's intentions. Only the Nazi electoral breakthrough of 1930, achieved without aid from big business, drew attention to it from that quarter. Those businessmen who attempted to assess the suddenly formidable new movement encountered a baffling riddle. The closer they scrutinized the NSDAP, the more difficult it became to determine whether it supported or opposed capitalism and, more specifically, the large-scale, organized enterprise to which capitalism had given rise in Germany. That riddle was not a chance occurrence. Hitler wanted things just that way. By cultivating a strategy of calculated ambiguity on economic matters, he sought to enable the appeals of his party to transcend the deep-seated social divisions in the country. That strategy led to puzzlement and wariness among the politically active components of big business, who wanted above all to establish the NSDAP's position on the economic issues that preoccupied them and assumed ever more urgency as the Great Depression deepened.

For nearly two years — from the autumn of 1930 until the summer of 1932 — elements within or close to big business engaged in flirtations of varying intensity and duration with National Socialism. Some saw in Nazism a potential ally against the political left and organized labor, which many in the business community blamed for much of the country's misfortune, including the depression. Some of those who harbored such hopes set out, often with the help of opportunistic intermediaries, to cultivate prominent figures in the leadership ranks of the NSDAP. On the Nazi side, Hitler and certain of his lieutenants appear to have operated initially on the same assumption that colored leftist analyses, namely, that capitalists amounted to an important factor in politics. But whereas the parties of the left sought to mobilize mass support against big business in order to break the alleged control of the capitalists over the state, Hitler and his accomplices set out merely to neutralize the business community politically in order to keep Germany's capitalists from obstructing the Nazis' grasp for power.

Hitler and other Nazi spokesmen therefore sought repeatedly to convince those capitalists whose ears they could gain that there was no need to fear socialism from National Socialism. In a strict sense that was true, since the Nazis did not seek government ownership of the means of production. But Hitler and other Nazi emissaries revealed only highly selective versions of their movement's aims to members of the business community. They omitted mention of the aspirations of many Nazis, including Hitler himself, for far-reaching changes in German social and economic relationships that would, among other things, have drastically impinged on the position of capitalists. Nor did they, as has often been alleged, promise to dissolve the trade unions, hold out the prospect of lucrative armaments contracts, or project a war of exploitative conquest. The Nazi leaders may have secretly harbored such aims, but to divulge them at a time when the NSDAP was striving to attract voters from all possible quarters and gain admission to the national government would have been out of keeping with their opportunistic tactics. Instead, most portrayed Nazism to the business community as primarily a patriotic movement that would undercut the political left by wooing the wage earners of Germany back into the "national" political camp. Ignoring the concrete economic issues that preoccupied businessmen, Hitler held out to those with whom he came into contact the prospect of a political panacea that would sweep away Germany's mundane problems by unifying it domestically and strengthening it internationally. He also soft-pedaled or left altogether unmentioned his anti-Semitism when speaking to men of big business, having recognized its unpopularity in those circles. Such reassuring versions of the NSDAP's goals generally produced skeptical reactions among members of the business community, however, for those reassurances were offset by clamorous anti-capitalist rhetoric on the part of other Nazis and by the NSDAP's frequent alignment with the political left on concrete socio-economic issues. Right down to Hitler's installation in the chancellorship, Nazism spoke with a forked tongue and behaved duplicitously in the eyes of most capitalist magnates. As a consequence, only rarely did relations between the NSDAP and big business progress beyond the level of flirtation prior to the Nazi takeover. Despite repeated blandishments from Hitler himself and some members of his entourage, most politically active figures in the business community remained confused by the contradictory utterances about economic matters emanating from the NSDAP and uneasy about what direction that party would finally take. Aside from a few minor executives who belonged, for the most part, to the younger generation of Germans so strongly attracted to the Nazi movement, only one capitalist of note, Fritz Thyssen, became a loyal adherent of Nazism before 1933. . . .

Quite contrary to the widespread impression that Hitler gained power in January 1933 with strong backing from big business, his appointment to the chancellorship came just when relations between his movement and the big business community had reached the lowest point since the NSDAP's election gains of 1930 had forced it upon the attention of the politically engaged men of big business. Germany's leading capitalists remained passive, ill-informed bystanders during the backroom intrigues in the circles around President Hindenburg that resulted in Hitler's installation as chancellor. By that time the business community was recovering from its initial apprehensions about the cabinet of Kurt von Schleicher. His government had failed to follow the leftward course many had initially feared it would; to the relief of the business community, Schleicher upheld most of the Papen cabinet's policies. While few of the country's capitalists harbored any real enthusiasm for the enigmatic general who stood at the head of the government, an inclination to prefer his continuation in office prevailed in late January 1933. The alternative of still another cabinet crises would, most of the political leadership of big business feared, once more give rise to the uncertainties about economic policy that they believed had thwarted recovery during the politically turbulent year just past. Rather than risk a disruption of the economic upturn widely detected since late 1932, it seemed preferable to hope for a period of stability under the general. When the most prominent industrial association, the Reichsverband, broke with previous practice and attempted to intervene with President Hindenburg as the final cabinet crisis of Weimar Germany broke out at the end of January 1933, it did so to warn against according Adolf Hitler a prominent place in a new, provocatively rightist cabinet. However, that effort to wield the influence of the business community for political purposes proved, like so many undertaken during the Weimar period, in vain.

Contrary to another long-standing misapprehension, spokesmen of the business community did not collude with those of agriculture in agitating for Hitler's installation as chancellor in January 1933. By that time relations between those two interest groups had deteriorated to the breaking point because of increasingly irreconcilable and acrimonious disagreements over trade policy. Whatever took place in early 1933 by way of a recrudescence, in support of Hitler's appointment, of the alliance between traditional elites of the Empire, one important element — big business — was conspicuous by its absence. The often-invoked continuity between the imperial and Nazi regimes thus suffers from a crucial gap.

If big business did not, as is so often maintained, help boost Hitler into the chancellorship by throwing its influence behind him, how much effect did the political money have that flowed from the business community to various Nazis? How much help to Hitler and his party in their quest for power were the contributions and subsidies accounted for here, as well as similar ones that presumably went undocumented? That question can obviously not be answered definitively since the evidence remains incomplete. Some observations can be made, however, on the basis of patterns of behavior that have emerged from this study. First of all, the multi-million-mark contributions from big business that allegedly fueled the Nazi juggernaut existed only in the imaginations of certain contemporary observers and, later, of some writers of history. Those firms and organizations that regularly engaged in large-scale political funding continued — right down to the last election prior to Hitler's appointment as chancellor — to bestow the bulk of their funds on opponents or rivals of the Nazis. The few sizeable contributions that appear to have reached the Nazis from big business sources shrink in significance when compared to the amounts that went to the bourgeois parties and to the campaign to re-elect President Hindenburg. With rare exceptions such contributions to Nazis were not given primarily for the purpose of strengthening the NSDAP or boosting it into power but rather in pursuit of a variety of essentially defensive strategies. They usually went to individual Nazis, not to the party as such. Some of the donors looked upon financial support for prominent Nazis as insurance premiums designed to assure them friends in power if the new movement should succeed in capturing control of the state. Others, who felt that their firms had special grounds to fear the NSDAP if it should come to power, paid out what can only be characterized as protection money to potential rulers. Still others sought to reshape Nazism in line with their wishes by strengthening, through financial subsidies, the position within the party of individual Nazis they regarded as exponents of "moderate" or "reasonable" economic policies. A portion of the subsidies doled out to individual Nazis by men of big business for such reasons may have been used by the recipients for party purposes, but from all indications a considerable share went toward enhancing their personal living standards.

Discussion of financial assistance to the Nazis from big business have usually been based on a false assumption, namely, that the NSDAP, like the bourgeois parties of the Weimar Republic, depended on subsidies from large contributors. This simply was not the case. Just as the Nazi leaders proudly proclaimed at the time, their party financed itself quite handsomely through its own efforts, at least down to the autumn of 1932. The NSDAP proved, in fact, an unprecedentedly effective forerunner of those highly organized fund-raising associations that have since become familiar features of liberal, democratic societies. In contrast to the bourgeois parties of the Republic, whose top echelons solicited large contributions and then distributed funds to the lower echelons, money flowed upward within the NSDAP from the grass roots, through the regional organizations, and to the national leadership in Munich. Compared to the sustained intake of money raised by membership dues and other contributions of the Nazi rank and file, the funds that reached the NSDAP from the side of big business assume at best a marginal significance. As the relations between leading Nazis and members of the business community abundantly reveal, the former rarely adopted the pose of supplicants seeking material aid, at least not until their party experienced its first serious financial difficulties during the autumn of 1932. By that time, however, deteriorating relations had made members of the business community less disposed than ever to contribute to the NSDAP. The Nazis themselves, not Germany's capitalists, provided the decisive financing for Hitler's rise to power. . . .

If the political record of big business is sadly lacking in political acumen, it is even more sorely devoid of public morality and civil courage. Most of the leaders of the business community were never tempted to become Nazis. The NSDAP's promise to destroy the existing elite and impose a new one in its place held little allure for men already at the top of their society. Its plebeian tone offended their taste. So did its anti-Semitism, for whatever other prejudices the leading men of German big business harbored, that form of bigotry was rare in their ranks. Most also found disturbing Nazism's demand for total power and its voluble strain of anti-capitalism, which focused predominantly on large-scale enterprise. Almost as alarming were the unorthodox fis-

cal and monetary schemes put forward by prominent Nazis as reme-
dies for the depression. Still, most men of big business viewed Nazism
myopically and opportunistically. Like many other Germans whose
national pride had been wounded by the unexpected loss of the war
and by a humiliating peace treaty, they admired Nazism's defiant nationalism and hoped it could be used to help reassert what they regarded
as their country's rightful place among the great powers. Preoccupied
as they were with domestic economic issues, they also hoped Nazism
could be used against their long-standing adversaries, the socialist parties and the trade union movement. That hope waxed and waned as
the Nazis shifted their political tactics. During the last half year preceding Hitler's appointment as chancellor, it subsided to low ebb. But
few spokesmen of big business spoke out publicly against the NSDAP.
Viewing it in terms of narrow self-interest, most failed to perceive the
threat it posed to the very foundations of civilized life. Therein lay
their heaviest guilt, one they shared, however, with a large part of the
German elite.

William Carr

The Cooperation
of Big Business

Hitler has often been dismissed as a complete ignoramus in economic
matters, a blundering amateur who understood nothing of the intrica-
cies of the subject and cared even less. This is to seriously underesti-
mate him. While it is true that he had no formal training in economics
and was certainly not as interested in it as in foreign affairs and military strategy, nevertheless it was an area of public affairs that forced itself on his attention again and again. And because he was alert to the
political consequences — or to what he thought were the political

William Carr, *Hitler: A Study in Personality and Politics.* Copyright © 1978 by William
Carr. Reprinted by permission of Edward Arnold (Publishers), Limited. Footnotes
omitted.

consequences of economic decisions — he was able to exert a not inconsiderable influence on broad economic strategy.

Political realism governed Hitler's attitude, and that of other Nazi leaders, to the problem of economic recovery, the most serious challenge facing the new regime. Hitler never doubted for one moment that recovery must be masterminded by the experienced men running German industry and not by party zealots. No sense of gratitude of the intervention of agrarian-industrial axis on his behalf dictated this choice. Ever since 1927 he had been seeking contact with big business and fighting "socialist" elements in the party likely to scare off middle-class support. The nearer he came to the chancellery, the more he called unruly elements to order and affirmed his belief in the virtues of (non-Jewish) private enterprise. For a man pathologically suspicious of "bourgeois" professional people, all his life he had a touching regard for the plain bluff entrepreneur whose preeminence in industry he attributed not to inherited wealth and privilege but to the unerring operation of the principle of Social Darwinism.

Hesitation in coming out openly on the side of large-scale industry was due not to lingering doubts about its fitness to effect the recovery or of its rightness to do so, but simply to the exigencies of the confused political situation. Hitler was not master in his own house in the early months of 1933. Many rank-and-file Nazis were agitating for economic change to benefit small retailers and businessmen; party officials bullied employers whenever they could; and middle-class organizations such as NS Hago, the retailer's association, and the Kampfbund für den gewerblichen Mittelstand, or League of Defence for the Commercial Middle Class, were stage-managing noisy campaigns against department stores and consumer cooperatives. Not until the end of May, after the destruction of the trade union movement, did Hitler feel strong enough to come out openly in favour of the traditional masters of German industry. After a meeting with leading industrialists, Hitler readily secured cabinet approval of a most reactionary package deal confirming the blatant class policies of preceding regimes: wages were to be held down to the 1932 levels; industry was promised tax concessions, a reduction in the burden of social payments, and large state contracts; NS Hago and the Kampfbund were called to order; and Wilhelm Keppler, the friend of large-scale industry, replaced Otto Wagener, advocate of the corporate state, as Hitler's party adviser on economic affairs.

In two respects Hitler's personal intervention probably had at least marginal influence on the direction of economic policy in 1933. In the first place, he made it crystal clear from the very beginning that economic recovery must be closely geared to military expansion. This was important for, despite what has been said about the growth of a political "consensus" in favour of a facist dictatorship, it would be quite wrong to suggest that there was complete identity of viewpoint about the appropriate measures for overcoming the crisis. When Hitler persuaded the cabinet on 8 February to endorse the proposition that the highest priority in any future recovery programme must be given to rearmament for the next five years, he was in effect preparing the way — possibly more quickly than might otherwise have been the case — for a working partnership between heavy industry, army and party, all three of which had an interest in expanding the armed forces as speedily as possible.

Secondly, Hitler's appointment of Schacht as president of the Reichsbank in place of Luther was probably a step of equal importance. Luther was unwilling to provide the massive credits Hitler demanded for the recovery-cum-rearmament programme. Personal preferences apart, Luther's hands were tied because the Reichsbank was effectively controlled by the Bank of International Settlement, set up in 1930 to supervise the payment of reparations under the Young Plan. It was Schacht, a fervent admirer of Hitler and his chief financial adviser since 1931, who solved the problem. Thanks to his international standing, Schacht was able to persuade the bank to allow the Reichsbank to deal in securities again. Of course, although Schacht employed the Keynesian instrument of deficit financing to revive the economy, one need scarcely point out that the object of economic expansion was not the improvement of the living standards of the German people but the thoroughly illiberal one of creating a powerful army to enslave other peoples.

The economic crisis of 1936 and Hitler's intervention in it have been variously interpreted. The reader is reminded that as the demand for raw materials grew to keep pace with the increasing tempo of rearmament, a shortage of foreign exchange developed. In March the insistence of Russia and Roumania on hard cash for their oil precipitated a serious fuel crisis, revealing the precarious nature of the balance of payments. Those sections of industry still interested in export markets together with Schacht's ministry of economics began to express some concern about the direction of the economy. Voices were even raised in favour of retrenchment and some slowdown in the pace of rearmament. Against this background Hitler wrote the celebrated memorandum of August 1936 in which he firmly relegated economic considerations to second place and insisted that, whatever the cost, the highest priority must continue to be given to armaments to ensure that Germany was ready for war by 1940. To obtain the necessary raw materials for this purpose Germany would have to rely less on international trade and rather more on her own autarkical efforts, until such time as she could expand her territory and solve her economic problems at a stroke.

Was this a decisive moment when the dictator's influence changed the course of events? Hardly that. What he was saying in the memorandum simply reflected a significant realignment of forces which took place in the winter of 1935–6. It has been argued that the tacit understanding between party, army command, ministry of economics and heavy industry on which German recovery rested from 1933 onwards, ended in 1936 when the party established its ascendancy over all its rivals forcing them into a policy of accelerated armament, autarky and expansion. This is a somewhat unsatisfactory analysis. A factor of crucial importance overlooked in these interpretations is the decision of army command, taken in the winter of 1935–6 with Hitler's approval, to move on from the construction of a defensive army (not scheduled for completion before 1938) to the creation of an offensive army, which, as originally planned, would not have been ready before 1942. At the same time existing balance of industrial power was breaking up with the emergence of I. G. Farben as the leading industrial concern in Germany. And I. G. Farben, which had a long-standing interest in the production of synthetic fuel, was strategically placed through close contacts with the air ministry to play a leading role in Goering's attempts to establish autarky. Indeed, the hysterical outbursts in Hitler's memorandum against the cautious orthodoxy of the ministry of economics — where Schacht, though a believer in autarky up to a point, was opposed to a further reduction of Germany's international ties — betrayed some misunderstanding on the Führer's part of the inescapable commitment of much of German industry to continued rearmament. The fact was that by 1936 industry had become so dependent on internal markets that a return to world markets as an alternative to further rearmament was no longer an attractive proposition even if the world economy had been in a healthier state. And more fundamentally the *raison d'être* of the dictatorship would have been destroyed had the Nazis subordinated armaments to the demands of a consumer-goods oriented economy devoted to the raising of the living standards of working people.

It was the coincidence of army plans for rapid expansion with the objective needs of a large part of industry as well as with the vaguely expansionist mood of the party that determined the new course. The first fruits of the refurbished partnership was the Four Year Plan, an exercise in limited autarky. It was announced by Hitler to party comrades at the party rally; it was deeply influenced by the strategic thinking of the Wehrwirtschaftsstab, or military economics staff, of Colonel Thomas; and it was planned by the staff of I. G. Farben. One must conclude, therefore, that Hitler did not take an unexpected initiative in 1936 that changed the course of events, but simply came out on the side of a new alignment of forces which happened to support the option he personally favoured and had pressed for — the creation of an offensive army in the shortest possible time. . . .

It cannot be doubted any more, in the light of recent research, that the economic situation was rapidly deteriorating in 1939. Shortages of raw materials and skilled labour had become critical while government expenditure (chiefly on armaments) continued to grow, thereby creating dangerous inflationary pressures. Publicly, Hitler obstinately refused to accept the facts of economic life. To keep on insisting on the highest priority for armaments seemed to show no appreciation of the harsh choice that would have to be made sooner or later to avert economic collapse. On the other hand, it may well be that his sensitive antennae detected with uncanny accuracy the unavoidable political consequences of a steadily deteriorating situation. As he told the Reichstag in January 1939: "In the final instance the economy of the Reich today is bound up with its external security. It is better to see that while there is still time as when it is too late." In his address to the commanding generals on 22 August, he was brutally frank about the interdependence of economic policy and foreign policy: "We have nothing to lose, only to gain. As a result of restrictions our economic situation is such that we can only hold out for a few years. Goering can confirm that. There is nothing else for it, we have to act." In other words, Hitler probably realized that the maintenance of the mobilization capacity of German industry at its present high level for an indefinite period was virtually impossible once the peace-time needs of the armed forces were met. If large-scale arms exports were impossible and if the economic and social disruption consequent upon a switch to the production of other goods was unacceptable, then Germany was left with a clear choice — either to continue to endure mounting inflation to defray the astronomical costs of further rearmament or to create a fresh demand for armaments by waging war.

Having said this, one must also admit quite frankly that there is far too little positive evidence to permit us to determine with any degree of accuracy the importance of such considerations in Hitler's decision for war. Serious though the internal situation was in 1939, one cannot say with absolute certainty that it was impossible for Germany to wait any longer before going to war. One cannot discount the possibility that the steadily deteriorating situation — of which Hitler was kept informed — may have done little more than confirm his own pessimistic long-term diagnosis of Germany's ills and strengthen the case for a war of conquest which he deemed necessary in any case on politico-ideological grounds. It may well be that within a year or two economic pressures would have forced Hitler's hand. What we do not have is sufficient evidence that this was the case in 1939.

It is even more difficult to determine the role of the great industrial combines in setting Germany on the road to war and in nudging Hitler towards expansion. It seems fairly clear that because industry retained, broadly speaking, the essentials of economic independence at a time of rapid industrial concentration, firms such as the Mannesmann-Konzern, the Reichswerke Hermann Goering and I. G. Farben, all closely associated with rearmament, and leading banks, especially the Dresden and Deutsche Banken, were in a position to develop their own expansionist plans for the domination of central and southeastern European markets. Of course these plans did not necessitate the forcible absorption of surrounding territories in the Reich for their realization. Industrial imperialism and territorial imperialism were distinctive plants. Nevertheless, they were nurtured in the same soil and each was closely affected by the other's growth. Domination of central and southeastern Europe was also a Nazi objective both to attain economic self-sufficiency (the *Grossraumwirtschaft*) and to serve as a base for a future *Drang nach Osten* or Thrust to the East. On this practical foundation a working partnership came into being. There is evidence of this partnership in action both in Austria and Czechoslovakia where certain industrial corporations were able to secure a dominant position in the

economics of these countries in 1938–9. To establish more precisely
what the relationship was between the forward thrust of the great industrial combines controlling the German economy and the expansionist policies of the Nazi hierarchy in 1938–9 we need much more
information than we have at present about the policies of individual
firms. Provisionally, all that one can say is that economic imperialism
on its own would not necessarily have led to war — and did not do so
in other capitalist economies. It was only in conjunction with the territorial imperialism of the Nazis that economic imperialism developed "a particularly explosive power."

Ernst Christian Helmreich

The Ambiguity of Religious Leaders

Neither the Protestant nor the Catholic church broke with their heritage from the past during the Weimar Republic. But this is not to say
that they remained static. Changes were made which largely continued trends that had already been developing under the Empire. Although the Weimar Constitution boldly proclaimed, "There is no state
church," this did not mean that the close relations between the state
and church were broken. While the churches became more self-
governing, their self-rule was administered under the supervision of
the state. The Land churches and the Catholic church, as well as a growing number of the Free churches, were public corporations, and by
their very status were subject to some state regulations.

The Protestant churches had, during the Weimar period, given
themselves new governing bodies, and laws, orders, and regulations
had multiplied, as had the bureaucracy which administered them. It is
easy to decry this extensive legalism and emphasize its stultifying effect on church life, but it did mean that the churches on the whole were

Reprinted from *The German Churches under Hitler: Background, Struggle, and Epi-
logue*, by Ernst Christian Helmreich. Reprinted by permission of Wayne State University Press. Copyright © 1979 by Ernst C. Helmreich.

well run, and that their rights and privileges were founded in law. This legal foundation was very valuable when the Nazis tried arbitrarily to bend the churches to their will. The courts, particularly in the early years of Hitler's rule, decided many appealed cases in favor of churchmen on the basis of law and established procedures. And it was not only the courts which at times stayed Nazi hands. The often maligned bureaucrats, the civil servants who staffed the various state departments and bureaus in charge of religious and cultural affairs, often continued to run things in customary ways to the benefit of the churches. Accustomed to carrying on an orderly procedure, they opposed the irregular innovations of newly installed Nazi officials. The penchant for order and law did not disappear at once in Germany, not even among the Nazis.

But there is more to a church than its organization and the administration of its institutional affairs, important as these matters are in large church bodies. Churches are made up of people; they are a part of society and are beset by all the problems which confront a nation. The Catholic church, through its close ties with the Center party and the Bavarian People's party, had been forced more than ever to share and bear political responsibilities. A government party throughout most of the days of the republic, the Center party nevertheless had many supporters, especially in the church hierarchy, who looked back to monarchical days with a certain longing. In Protestant church circles many were conservatively inclined and ready to discard existing parliamentary political forms and practices. To point this out is to say nothing more than that the churches were composed of Germans not yet firmly attached to their new form of government. The hardships, the sins of the times, were all too easily blamed on the government which, many Germans felt, needed to be changed and set on new paths.

But if the government needed reform, and there were few Germans no matter what their political allegiance who doubted it, so too did the churches. Within the Catholic church, hierarchically led and true to Rome, the demand for regeneration was not pronounced among the laity, nor could it easily make itself felt. The hierarchy, by no means complacent, were aware that there was much to be done to strengthen the church, and they were all too willing to seek government support in this task. Catholics as a whole were eager to manifest their loyalty to Germany. When the Nazis found increasing acceptance of their claim to be the true repository of patriotism, many rank-and-

Hitler and the Church. Throughout the war, the Nazi State was able to maintain good relations with the Catholic hierarchy in Rome. Here Hitler greets Alberto Vassallo di Torregrossa, the Papal Nuncio, in Munich. (Ullstein Bilderdienst)

file Catholics felt their loyalty to state and nation was being jeopardized by the church's continued support of the Catholic parties and their denunciations of national socialism. The patriotic desire not to stand aside while Germany was being rebuilt was probably the factor most influential in bringing about the initial peaceful relations between both Catholic and Protestant churches and national socialism when Hitler became chancellor.

The papacy and members of the German hierarchy in the pre-war years had at times denounced the cult of racism, of blood and soil. But there were no clarion protests against the anti-Semitic policy of the Nazi rulers then or during the war years. When the government began to treat Christians who were racial Jews in the same way as full Jews, the Catholic church leaders — concerned about safeguarding their own, began to take more notice. In general their reaction was similar to that of the Protestant leaders, but there were some noteworthy Catholic reactions. For example, the decree of September 1, 1941, which required all Jews to wear a Star of David, prompted Cardinal Bertram to send advice to his fellow bishops. Guenther Lewy has summarized it admirably.

> *His council was to avoid "rash measures that could hurt the feelings of the Jewish Catholics, as the introduction of special Jewish benches, separation when administering the sacraments, introduction of special services in specific churches or private houses." The segregation of the Catholic non-Aryans would violate Christian principles, and, therefore, should be avoided as long as possible. The priests, Bertram suggested, might however advise the Jewish Catholics to attend the early mass whenever possible. An admonishment to the faithful to exercise brotherly love toward the non-Aryans similarly should be postponed until disturbances resulted. "Only when substantial difficulties result from attendance at church by the non-Aryan Catholics," the Archbishop of Breslau continued, "(like staying away of officials, Party members and others, demonstrative leaving of divine services), should the Catholic non-Aryans be consulted about the holding of special services." In case a reminder to the faithful to treat the Jewish Catholics with love should become necessary, Bertram suggested a statement that included St. Paul's admonishments to the Romans and Galatians not to forget that among those believing in Christ there is neither Jew nor Greek, for all are one in Jesus Christ (Romans 10:12, Galatians 3:28).*

Bertram was certainly not recommending a courageous policy but one of servile accommodation: the presence of officials and party members was more desirable than that of a hard-pressed Christian of non-Aryan descent seeking solace and redemption in God's word. In much the same vein, Bishops Berning and Wienken tried to obtain permission for Jewish Catholics not to wear the star when they went to church; apparently they were not very concerned about other times. The Gestapo, as on other occasions, operated with an even hand — even if it was a damnable one — and refused to make any alterations in their general edict. Actually the people in the churches caused no difficulties, although Jewish Christians often did refrain from attending church.

In the end the problem of racial segregation never became acute in the churches, partly because so many Christian Jews were deported. On the other hand, both Catholic and Protestant churches (no doubt unwilling but without strong protest) did succumb to the government's extreme racial segregation measures against the Poles.

In 1942 the government began considering a plan to force the dissolution of racially mixed marriages. This compulsory divorce policy would affect a large number of Catholics and challenged one of the most important doctrines of the church. Cardinal Bertram addressed letters of protest to the ministers of justice, the interior, and ecclesiastical affairs. Bishop Wurm and other Protestant leaders also protested. The compulsory divorce law was never issued, perhaps because of ecclesiastical protest, but perhaps also because some hundreds of Aryan wives demonstrated in Berlin when their non-Aryan husbands were about to be transported "to the East."

The most compelling factor in easing policies towards the churches was the disastrous course of the war. On February 2, 1943, Stalingrad surrendered, the beginning of May brought German defeat in North Africa, July 10 the invasion of Sicily, July 25 the fall of Mussolini, September 3 the invasion of southern Italy, and five days later the announcement of the Italian armistice. On September 10 German troops took over the occupation of Rome. Such sledgehammer blows clearly called for a united home front, and measures were taken to decrease internal tensions.

On January 13, 1943, Hitler had issued an ordinance, "The Employment of Men and Women in Tasks of National Defense." It specifically exempted clergymen and monastic priests, others who were in the service of churches forty-eight hours a week, and nurses or members of monastic orders fully employed in agriculture. On April 26, 1943, Bormann issued a special directive on dealing with political-confessional matters. Nothing was to be done to cause confessional difficulties or unrest among the people. "Every little pinprick policy must be stopped." On May 9, Bormann expressly forbade any agitation against the churches in the Labor Service: "One must carefully avoid injuring true religious conceptions. Such actions simply antagonize the best persons. . . . It is entirely wrong — and therefore fundamentally forbidden in the National Labor Service — to enter upon any polemic against church institutions and dogmas." The Labor Service was not a church but a state service, whose duty it was to unify, not divide, the people.

In February, 1939, Heydrich as head of the security service had prepared a long memorandum on Catholic higher schools for the training of priests in which he proposed cuts in state support. The memorandum was considered again on July 19, 1943, when it was decided that nothing should be done about it.

At this time German cities were being subjected to heavy bombing; Hamburg was virtually destroyed at the end of July, with a death toll estimated at around 40,000. This bombing led the minister of education, with Bormann's approval, to issue a directive on August 25, 1943, concerning confessional religious instruction at schools which had been evacuated. It was most favorable to the traditional demands of the churches. Confessional instruction was to be given to the same extent as before, and teachers were to be moved with the school if possible. If no religion teachers were available, local clergymen were to be asked to give confessional instruction in local church rooms and to issue certificates to pupils. If local regulations permitted, religious instruction could be given in other rooms as well, if they were not more than four kilometers from the place to which the school had been moved. His intention to conciliate the churches is clearly shown in his closing plea: "Please take care that in administering this directive you observe a generous line of action."

Going easy on the churches was on the whole the policy during the rest of the war. As the ring was drawn more tightly around Germany and collapse threatened, the churches also tended to make as few difficulties as possible for the state. It is clear that the hierarchy were aware of the deportation of Jews and what it meant. Yet the German bishops never spoke out as Dutch, Belgian, or French bishops did when Jews were being transported from their countries. The nearest the hierarchy came to a joint protest was the Fulda pastoral letter of September 12, 1943, "Ten Commandments as Laws of Life for Nations." In the introduction the bishops recognized the critical situation the Reich was facing and spoke words of tribute and encouragement to the Catholic faithful. By way of commentary on the individual commandments they could make many pointed statements without directly attacking the government. Cardinal Bertram objected, but it was nevertheless read in Catholic pulpits. It was the last joint pastoral letter issued by the German bishops during the Hitler era. The police summary on the letter lacked the customary sharp denunciations and concluded: "in no other pastoral letter was the span of its possible effects between positive and negative so great as in this case." The bishops clearly had done a remarkable job of tightrope walking.

The statement on the Fifth Commandment, "Thou shall not kill," while it was directed against the gas ovens and the killing of Jews, nevertheless was not worded openly and fearlessly. There was no indication of the magnitude of the Nazi extermination policy, although the hierarchy must have had some knowledge of what was going on. The bishops, as well as the government, were concerned about maintaining "internal unity" during the war. After commenting that no one had the right arbitrarily to interfere with God's power over life and death, the bishops declared:

> *Killing is bad in itself, even when it is done in the interest of the common welfare: against innocent and defenseless mentally ill and other sick; against incurable invalids and fatally injured, against those with inherited disabilities and children with serious birth defects, against innocent hostages and disarmed war and other prisoners; against people of alien race and descent. Even the government can and is permitted to punish with the death penalty only those who are truly death-deserving criminals.*

Here the bishops made no distinction between Christian Jews and other Jews. However, the former were always their chief concern, as they were when the Vatican came to protesting the deportation of Hungarian Jews in 1944. There were a few who took a broader view. Foremost among them was Provost Bernhard Lichtenberg in Berlin, who spoke up against anti-Semitism and daily said a prayer for all Jews, not only the baptized ones. He was arrested in 1941 and died while being transported to Dachau in 1943. Others sought to protect and help various individual Jews. No one, however, has successfully contradicted Lewy's conclusion: "In sharp contrast to the countries of western Europe, in Germany only a handful of Jews were hidden by the [Catholic] clergy or otherwise helped by them in their hour of distress." The churchmen, as probably most of their congregations (and as 99 percent of all postwar Germans aver), did not approve of the government's rabid policy, but they were inclined to play it safe and not do much about it. The cannonball of anti-Semitism had started rolling down the hill many years in the past, no one bothered to stay its momentum after 1933, and when the war came it dragged Germany with increasing acceleration into a moral abyss.

Catholicism always involves not only the laity and the hierarchy, with its leadership of the local churches, but also the papacy. And papal policy was not very different from that of the German people or the German hierarchy. The pope too played it safe. His very international position forced him into a policy of neutrality and impartiality at the start of the war. He had sought to prevent the hostilities, and then his attention was bent on restoring peace. His was not an enviable position, and the involvement of the Soviet Union and later the United States made it no easier. Whatever he said and did in public would be held against him by one side or another. He naturally fell back on diplomatic procedures, on confidential negotiations with the responsible governments, in which he had long years of practice. He instructed his nuncio to raise constant protests in Germany about wartime policies; he sought to alleviate the suffering caused by the war. In his efforts to achieve peace he even went so far as to offer his good offices (1939–40) to German resistance leaders in their approach to British authorities. He did seek to prevent the deportation of Jews in Italy, Hungary, and other countries. In the realm of diplomacy, in his efforts to achieve things from behind the public scene, the pope did not remain silent or inactive. On the other hand, he was indeed circumspect in his public utterances in his efforts to maintain official impartiality. The history of World War I also showed that it was easy to be misled as to what was propaganda and what was reality. Unfortunately, the war atrocities were true this time, and the pope never issued a solemn public indictment. There were many other things he might have denounced, such as saturation bombing by both sides and the killing of thousands of defenseless men, women, and children. Perhaps such a protest might have been effective, but perhaps Hitler, and other wartime leaders as well, would have raised the same question Stalin was reputed to have asked: "How many divisions does he [the Pope] have?"

That a ringing denunciation of Hitler's policies would have made the situation of the Catholics in general, and of the Catholic church in particular, more difficult in Germany is doubtful, considering the plans Hitler had in mind for the future of the churches anyway. Yet the possibility of evoking immediate harsh retaliatory measures was always taken into consideration at the Vatican. That a public papal plea for the Jews would have led to an effective upsurge of Catholic opposition to the National Socialist regime seems most unlikely. That it would have led to a worldwide crusade against Hitler's tyranny is improbable and in fact inconsequential, for the mass of the available manpower of the world was already enrolled under the banner of the United Nations. What would have happened had the pope spoken out more openly than he did, is speculative; speculation may be interesting, but it is hardly historical. However, some things are historically clear. The pope and the German hierarchy worked closely together in the war years as they had in former periods of German history; the hierarchy did not beseech the pope to speak out during the war as they did in August, 1936, and at the time of the encyclical *Mit brennender Sorge* (1937). Neither hierarchy nor pope ran away, none succumbed, none won crowns of martyrdom; all lived on to fight for their faith another day.

Alan E. Steinweis

The Control of Cultural Life

In September 1933, the Nazi-controlled cabinet of the German Reich, acting on the initiative of the propaganda minister, Joseph Goebbels, created the Reich Chamber of Culture (Reichskulturkammer). Under Goebbel's supervision, the chamber served until 1945 as the exclusive, officially recognized, compulsory professional corporation for the arts, entertainment, and the media. Divided into subchambers for music, theater, the visual arts, literature, film, radio, and the press, this organization encompassed several hundred thousand professionals, influenced the activities of millions of amateur artists and musicians, and made a profound impact on millions of Germans who in one way or another were consumers of culture.

Goebbels designed the chamber system according to corporatist principles that had attained broad currency in interwar Germany (indeed in interwar Europe) during the crisis of liberalism. The occupational interests of German artists were now to be served by a single

From Alan Steinweis, "Cultural Eugenics: Social Policy, Economic Reforms and the Purge of Jews from German Cultural Life," in Glenn R. Cuomo (ed.) *National Socialist Cultural Policy.* Copyright © Glenn R. Cuomo. From *National Socialist Cultural Policy* edited by Glenn R. Cuomo. Reprinted with permission of St. Martin's Press, Inc.: New York, 1995.

state-acknowledged mass organization, rather than by a multiplicity of interest groups. Hence, the numerous cultural unions and occupational associations active in the Weimar era were forcibly integrated into the new chamber system during 1933 and 1934. The fractiousness and adversarialism characteristic of these old organizations had supposedly reflected the decay of the liberal order; they were now forced to merge into an "organic whole." German artists were to become an "estate" (*Stand*).

The chamber's stated mission was to "promote German culture on behalf of the German Volk and Reich" and to "regulate the economic and social affairs of the culture professions." The strategy pursued was two-pronged: It entailed both the "promotion of creative and productive forces" as well as the "eradication of unworthy and dangerous elements." In essence, this strategy constituted a form of cultural eugenics, simultaneously nourishing the "healthy" and weeding out the "unhealthy." Most research on the chamber relates to the latter function, which assumed the form of massive racial-political purges and an intrusive artistic-intellectual censorship. However, the economic, social, and professional dimensions of chamber policy — the so-called promotion of ideologically acceptable persons, aesthetics, and values — has received little attention from historians. In the areas of work creation, professional education, certification, wage and benefits policy, and social insurance, the chamber system formulated numerous measures designed to alleviate poverty, unemployment, and underemployment among its members.

The creation of the Chamber of Culture arose from the convergence of several factors. First, the National Socialist regime required a mechanism to regulate access to participation in the nation's cultural life. The chamber's membership guidelines, as they evolved up to the outbreak of war in 1939, allowed it to decline membership to Jews, Communists, homosexuals, Gypsies, and members of other "racial," political, or social groups condemned to ostracism by the dictates of Nazi ideology. Yet it would be simplistic to conceive of the chamber exclusively as a tool employed by a totalitarian state to enforce a sinister ideology and to terrorize powerless artists and entertainers. Rather, the creation of the chamber also reflected an attempt by the new regime to ingratiate itself with artists and entertainers who for years had been calling for a major overhaul in the structure of their professions.

Indeed, the professional, economic, and social agenda of the chamber during most of its 11-year existence stemmed from a widely accepted diagnosis of the disastrous financial conditions prevailing in the German cultural establishment during the Weimar Republic. The Depression and resultant government austerity measures had severely undermined the financial position of artists. This is not to imply, however, that the situation had been entirely satisfactory during the so-called Golden Years of the Weimar Republic before 1930. On the contrary, the Depression had merely exacerbated a bad situation, reinforcing a commonly held conviction that fundamental structural reform of the arts would be necessary.

Many experts attributed the troubles of German artists to the liberal structure of German cultural life. They claimed that the cultural marketplace was simply too free for its own good. The problem ostensibly stemmed from inadequate provisions for cultural activity in the Reich Commercial Code and from the historical failure of artists to professionalize as aggressively as did members of other occupations. Fundamental to this critique was the absence of a central authority capable of enforcing an equitable, socially responsible distribution of income. Left to the vicissitudes of a free market, theaters, orchestras, and other cultural institutions competed among themselves for talent, resulting in a "star system" — the polarization of artists into a large proletariat and a small cadre of high-salaried stars. The system's inability to prevent the unqualified and the untalented from entering the employment pool further aggravated the situation. The unqualified dilettantes who populated the cultural proletariat kept salaries and wages low even for the genuinely talented and often deprived truly deserving artists of work altogether. A further structural deficiency exacerbated the problems connected with this so-called dilettantism: The arts lacked central leadership in matters of education and training. It was often alleged that inferior academies, poor teachers, and charlatans were churning out too many inferior artists and performers.

Unsatisfactory professional structures were also widely blamed for the absence of an adequate pension system for artists. The fact that thousands of artists and performers lived in indigent retirement did not speak well for Germany's reputation as a land of culture. Experts on the economics of culture had attributed the absence of a satisfactory pension system to two factors: the decentralized structure of the art profession, and the highly skewed distribution of wealth among artists. Widespread poverty, on the one hand, and the inability to compel subscription by the financially comfortable, on the other, had combined to prevent the formation of a pension insurance pool that could pass actuarial muster. Furthermore, theater people and musicians employed by public companies and orchestras, who generally were well paid, had already been integrated into local or provincial pension systems for civil servants. Support from philanthropic foundations, such as the Schiller Foundation, made old age more comfortable for some who fell through this system's numerous cracks, but philanthropy could hardly begin to address the broader, systemic problem. Especially after the onset of the Depression, Nazis and others on the right wing tended increasingly to merge the foregoing structural analysis with xenophobic, anti-Semitic views. They bemoaned the supposed flooding of the German cultural marketplace with Jews and foreigners. Their critique was internally coherent, in that it perceived artistic-cultural renewal and structural deliberation as two sides of the same coin. "Non-Germans" were depriving "Germans" of jobs, and the "alien" influences on German culture were scaring audiences away from galleries, theaters, and concert halls. A genuine economic crisis facing the German art world was explained in terms that made sense to Germans who eschewed cultural modernism and who were predisposed to subscribe to notions about Jewish conspiracies.

Hence, from the Nazi point of view, the Chamber of Culture was designed to address a set of interrelated cultural and structural problems. In 1933, Nazis and their sympathizers could doubly applaud the advent of the Chamber of Culture, first, as a blow against economic liberalism, and second, as a mechanism for ridding the German theater of the "Jewish-Bolshevist virus," which supposedly thrived in liberal host environments. Many who did not subscribe to the Nazi assessment of the situation in its entirety nevertheless sympathized with the need for an activist official policy toward the arts. Richard Strauss, then the greatest living luminary of German music, exemplified this attitude. After accepting the presidency of the new Chamber of Music, he publicly praised the Nazi regime, claiming that "the new Germany is unwilling to let artistic matters slide, as it did more or less up to now." The point here is not that Strauss and many others who looked to the state for solutions to the financial-structural crisis of German culture were Nazis; most were not. Rather, a significant common ground existed between the Nazi movement and non-Nazi advocates of structural reform of German cultural life. Both favored centralization, deliberalization, and professionalization of the arts. During the crucial founding phase of Nazi rule, this common ground proved sufficient to win legitimacy (if not popularity) for the regime in broad segments of the German cultural establishment.

Peter Hoffmann

Generals and the German Resistance

Whereas the Resistance was representative of all German society in sociological, economic, and political terms, it was not representative in quantitative terms, like an unofficial parliament. Broad support, actual or potential, among the population was lacking for the actions of the Resistance as well as for its ideas.

There were three main reasons for the lack of broad support for the Resistance. First, most Germans accepted Hitler's government as duly constituted and properly legal. They shared this position with the Vatican; the governments of Britain, France, Italy, the United States, and the Soviet Union; the organizers of the 1936 Olympic Games; the chairmen of foreign veterans' organizations; members of the British royal family; internationally famous explorers and scholars; and other prominent private and semiofficial persons. In 1938, during the Sudeten crisis, Prime Minister Neville Chamberlain refused to accede to secret requests from the German Resistance to refuse Hitler's demands so that the dictator might be overthrown for irresponsibly starting a new war. Chamberlain explained his refusal by comparing the German opposition with the supporters of James II who had been driven out of England in the Glorious

Reprinted by permission of the publisher from *German Resistance to Hitler* by Peter Hoffman, Cambridge, Mass.: Harvard University Press. Copyright © 1988 by the President and Fellows of Harvard College.

Revolution of 1688 — those "Jacobites" had wanted to overthrow William III of Orange and to put James II on the English throne.

Another reason for the lack of widespread support for the Resistance was the success of Hitler's government. It had restored order, overcome unemployment, restored a credible defensive capacity, and achieved large territorial revisions of the Treaty of Versailles. Later, Hitler's government also appeared to be having success in a war that was regarded by great numbers of Germans as having been forced upon Germany. Setbacks in that war did not begin to unfold on any significant scale until 1942. Even in 1943 and 1944, these setbacks did not seem irreversible. When the government's control began to break down in 1944 and 1945, the loyalty of the population to their political and military leadership still suffered only marginally. The general population felt threatened not so much by the policies of the regime as by the Allied air raids, the advance of the Allied armies in the east and west, and the prospect of an Allied military occupation. The government's campaign of murder against the Poles, Jews, Soviet prisoners-of-war, Jehovah's Witnesses, Gypsies, and other persecuted groups were very secret and little known, and what was known of them did not seem to threaten individuals at large if they did not belong to one of the persecuted categories.

The final reason for the absence of broad-based support for the Resistance was the feeling that the Nazi police state and its instruments were ubiquitous. In addition to the Gestapo and the SD, there were innumerable agents, agencies, and informers of the party, on the provincial level (Gau), the district level (Kreis), the precinct level (Bezirk), and the block level.

The "natural" opposition to the Nazis, composed of the trade unions, the Social Democrats, and the Communists, were more at odds with each other than with the Nazis before Hitler's appointment as Chancellor, and even afterward. A coalition of left-wing opponents, or a "popular front," became possible only when the Communists received directives to this effect and when the Soviet Union and France formed an alliance in 1935. The disarray of the left-wing opposition, as well as their conspiratorial methods, made it relatively easy for the Gestapo to infiltrate and control them.

The Army and its officer corps, however, were largely immune to Gestapo surveillance and penetration and to the influence of the Nazi Party. The social fabric of the Army officer corps and its code of ethics left little room for informers, even if such persons had not tended naturally rather to congregate in police organizations. Notwithstanding Hitler's laments after the coup d'état of 20 July 1944 about disloyalty in the Army officer corps, the officer corps was loyal and useful to the dictator. At the same time, the insulation of the officer corps from the Nazi police state made it a haven for many who were threatened for political or "racial" reasons and who chose to go into "internal emigration" through service in the Wehrmacht. This situation was true also, to a smaller degree, of the Navy and the Air Force. The Navy, however, was concerned to live down a revolutionary image dating from 1918. The Air Force was for the most part a new service developed under the aegis of Göring. Given the necessity of an organized armed force for the overthrow of the Nazi state and given the Wehrmacht's exceptional insulation, elements of the Army had to be regarded as the instrument particularly suited for being the arm of a revolt. It remained to find methods of gaining control of sufficient Army elements for this purpose. The greatest obstacle here was the system of military obedience and the oath of loyalty. The most suitable arm for a revolt was also the most conservative and nationalist force in society. No major government has been overthrown in the twentieth century as long as it retained the loyalty of the Army; without the Army, the prospects for the Resistance were poor indeed. . . .

Year after year, police authorities in Germany learned of assassination plots against the Reich Chancellor and other persons prominent in the government. In many cases, the alleged assassins belonged to categories of persons who were subject to persecution by the Nazi regime: Communists, Jews, and Catholics. In 1935, for example, a Jewish medical student living in Bern, Felix Frankfurter, wished to attack Hitler, but he could not get near him and shot instead the Swiss Nazi leader Wilhelm Gustloff. In December 1936, a Jewish student called Helmut Hirsch went from Prague to Germany to assassinate a high-ranking Nazi, possibly Hitler; he was arrested by the Gestapo before he could act.

On 9 November 1938, a Swiss Catholic theology student, Maurice Bavaud, attempted to assassinate Hitler in Munich. Bavaud, who had stalked Hitler for weeks intended to use the opportunity of the annual march on 9 November commemorating Hitler's abortive 1923 putsch. Hitler regularly marched at the head of the column, which wound through the streets of Munich along the route of the original march. Bavaud pretended he was a reporter for a Swiss paper and obtained a front-row seat on one of the reviewing stands along the route. He had a loaded pistol in his overcoat pocket. At Hitler's approach, the SA troops who were lined up in front of the stand raised their right arms for the salute. Bavaud could not get a shot off. He hoped to try again later, but he was forced to leave Germany when he ran out of money. He was apprehended by the police with an invalid railway ticket on a westbound train. During interrogation, he revealed his intentions. He was tried, convicted, and executed.

On the same occasion at which Bavaud was unsuccessful, a south German cabinetmaker, Georg Elser, explored opportunities for an assassination attempt of his own on Hitler. Elser was a disaffected laborer with socialist sympathies. On the eve of the commemorative march in Munich, Hitler always spoke to a gathering of party faithfuls in the beer hall, as he had done in 1923. The speech always lasted well over an hour.

In the following year, Elser managed to slip into the beer hall over a series of nights some two months before the commemorative gathering. He installed a powerful explosive device with an accurate timer in a pillar before which Hitler always stood during his speech. On the night of the speech, 8 November 1939, Hitler spoke briefly and left early because, unlike the other occasions, he wanted to be back in Berlin by the next morning. A morning flight from Munich to Berlin could not be guaranteed because of the morning fogs in November, so that Hitler had to catch his personal train. Departure times could not be set on short notice because the run had to be fitted into time slots for maximum speed. After Hitler had left, the explosive device went off as timed and killed several party men. It would almost certainly have killed Hitler had he still been standing at the rostrum. Elser was apprehended as he tried to cross the border into Switzerland. He was shot on Hitler's order at Dachau Concentration Camp in April 1945.

Both the Bavaud and the Elser incidents led to increased security measures. Hitler's bodyguard command had been slow to react. Bavaud was arrested in the same month in which he had made his assassination attempt, but security was still lax in the Bürgerbräu beer hall in October and November 1939. The commemorative march, however, was never held again, partly as a precaution against the possibility of an air raid eliminating the Nazi leadership all at once. Hitler's rare public appearances were protected by vast security operations, particularly when they could be anticipated by the public.

The new security measures helped to frustrate an assassination plot in Berlin in November 1939 by Erich Kordt, a Foreign Office official working immediately under Foreign Minister von Ribbentrop. Also in 1939, the British Military Attaché in Berlin, Colonel Mason-Macfarlane, suggested to his government that Hitler could be shot from a window of the attaché's apartment which looked out on a reviewing stand that Hitler used frequently. But His Majesty's Government took a poor view of this unorthodox proposal.

There were numerous other plans and plots to kill Hitler. The Chief of the General Staff of the Army, General Halder, at least thought about shooting Hitler in the fall of 1939, when the military leaders believed Hitler's plan to attack France could only lead to disaster. During his conferences with Hitler, Halder carried a loaded pistol in his pocket. After Hitler's victory over France in June 1940, one of the dictator's most ruthless enemies, Vice-President of Police in Berlin Fritz-Dietlof Graf von der Schulenburg, prepared an assassination plan for Hitler's victory parade which had been scheduled for 27 July in Paris. But the parade was called off because of the danger of British air raids and larger considerations of policy. There was also a proposal by the Director of Home Operations in the British Air Ministry, D. F. Stevenson, to bomb the parade and kill Hitler. This plan, submitted to the Deputy Chief of Air Staff on 13 July, was abandoned even before cancellation of the parade. Stevenson had changed his mind after considering the probable strength of German air defenses, explaining: "The triumphal march through Paris is in accordance with military custom — we did the same thing ourselves after the battle of Waterloo."

As the war continued, Hitler became ever less accessible. For a successful assassination to take place, a willing and able assassin with access to Hitler was required. Furthermore, the conspirators were convinced that an assassination must be coupled with a thoroughgoing coup d'état. They believed that Hitler's elimination alone would merely transfer power to another Nazi leader, probably Göring or Himmler. A Resistance government would have to take several immediate measures: remove the Nazi Party and SS criminals from government, the judicial system, and other offices at the national, state, and municipal levels; dissolve the concentration camps; release political prisoners; and at the same time keep the military machine intact until an armistice could be negotiated. . . .

In July 1944 Colonel Claus Count von Stauffenberg [Chief of Staff of the Commander of the Home Army] made at least three attempts of his own to assassinate Hitler. On 6 July he traveled to Hitler's Berghof retreat, carrying with him a quantity of plastic explosive. He apparently still hoped that the tasks of coup leader and assassin could be divided, to improve the chances of success for the combined operation. He must have hoped that Major-General Helmuth Stieff, another conspirator, would agree to carry out the assassination on 7 July, on the occasion of the uniform and equipment demonstration at which Stieff would be present. After Stieff's refusal, Stauffenberg had to abandon this plan.

Because of this failure and the other ones in the ten months since Stauffenberg had joined the conspiracy, he came to the conclusion that, if the attack was to be carried out at all, he must become both coup leader and assassin. The date of Stauffenberg's final decision to assassinate Hitler must have been after Stieff's refusal. For Stauffenberg himself to act as assassin, certain factors had to be taken into consideration. First, he was severely handicapped. He was therefore unable to use a pistol in an assassination attack. Colonel Henning von Tresckow, another conspirator, had in any case long since decided that the odds were not good enough for an attack with a pistol. In a crowded conference room, an assassin might not be able to fire a shot before his movement was foiled by Hitler's SS adjutants and bodyguards. If an assassin could shoot at all, he had to aim for Hitler's head and kill him at once. The odds were poor even for a fully competent marksman in the briefing room. A pistol would have to be carried in a trouser pocket, for belts were not worn in the briefing room. The conspirators believed that hidden x-ray equipment might reveal a concealed pistol. Moreover, it was widely believed that Hitler wore a bullet-proof vest.

The second factor of importance to the success of the coup was that Stauffenberg had to survive and return to Berlin. He was indispensable for managing the coup d'état that was to follow the assassination. This meant that he could not blow himself up with Hitler, using a short or simultaneous fuse that would enable him to choose the moment of detonation. He therefore had to use enough explosive to kill everyone in the briefing room, since he could not know where Hitler would be in relation to the bomb when it exploded. Stauffenberg had to use a time-delay fuse. He must activate it in private, deposit his briefcase containing the bomb, ascertain that it had gone off, and escape from the headquarters compound. There was in this method very little that could be assumed with certainty. Headquarters security measures provided for the immediate blocking of all exits in case of an explosion. Anyone trying to leave the inner compound where Hitler's briefings were held had to pass through three checkpoints in succession. These measures were intended for cases of sabotage by construction workers or infiltrators, commando raids, the detonation of mines within the security parameters, or aerial bombing, but the alarm would also certainly be set off by the explosion of Stauffenberg's bomb. In that case the odds against Stauffenberg's escape, which was essential to the success of the plot, were extraordinarily poor.

Stauffenberg was back at the Berghof retreat on 11 July 1944, to report to Hitler on the raising of new combat units to throw into the breach caused by the collapse of the Army Group Center in Russia. This time Stauffenberg did not attempt to assassinate Hitler, because some of the senior conspirators had insisted that the two most powerful men after Hitler, Himmler and Göring, must be killed along with him in order to eliminate any chance for the regime to continue functioning. Neither Himmler nor Göring was present at this meeting, although it had not been unreasonable to expect at least Himmler to be there, because the SS was to train the new units.

Stauffenberg went to Hitler's headquarters again on 15 July. By this time, Hitler had moved his headquarters to Wolfschanze near Rastenburg in East Prussia because of the serious situation at the Russian front. When both Himmler and Göring did not turn up, Stauffenberg wanted to set off the bomb regardless, but found no opportunity to start the fuse. He decided that next time he would proceed whether Himmler and Göring were there or not.

Early in the morning of 20 July 1944 Stauffenberg again flew the more than 300 miles from Berlin to Wolfschanze. He had been summoned to report on the "blocking divisions" that the Home Army was raising to shore up the eastern front. Stauffenberg was to give his report during Hitler's daily situation briefing. Again he brought with him the explosive charge with its delay fuses set.

Because Stauffenberg was indispensable to the success of the coup after the assassination, the plan was for him to leave the briefing room before the explosion. Immediately afterward, the Chief of Signal Troops,

General Erich Fellgiebel, who was a co-conspirator, would telephone the news of Hitler's death to Berlin. Upon receiving news of the assassination, General Olbricht, with his new Chief of Staff, Colonel Albrecht Mertz von Quirnheim, and other plotters in Berlin, would immediately set in train a series of moves to seize executive power. The conspirators in the Home Army command would issue prepared orders under the codeword "Valkyrie." Communications between Hitler's headquarters and all territories under German control would be discontinued by Fellgiebel's orders. The coup leaders would use the military teletype system to inform the Armed Forces, and the national radio to inform the public, that "the Führer is dead," that a clique of Nazi Party bosses was trying to stab the fighting front in the back, and that the Army was taking over executive power to maintain order.

Several problems were connected with this plan. General Fritz Fromm, Commander of the Home Army, knew of the plot. He had made no effort to stop it; it was fair to assume he would not challenge the proceedings. But he was not likely to participate unless success was assured. In case of failure, he would probably be on the opposing side. In this case, even if Fromm was prevented from interfering, his neutralization would leave any inquiring military district commanders without confirmation of the Valkyrie orders from their Commander in Chief. They might not carry out the extraordinary orders if they detected confusion and irregularity.

If the attack failed, and if this did not become known for some time, owing to an effective communications blackout, Stauffenberg's presence in Berlin immediately after the assassination attack could have improved the situation. But in the long term the Chief of Staff could replace the Commander only if he could convince subordinate officers that the Commander had been incapacitated through bonafide causes. If the fact of the failed assassination attack was known at the same time that Stauffenberg sought to initiate operation Valkyrie, the chances of its succeeding were practically nil. The military district commanders would see no reason to obey the orders from the Home Army if they were so obviously based on a false premise, namely Hitler's death at the hands of Nazi plotters. Stauffenberg's absence for two to three hours en route from Wolfschanze to Berlin after the attack therefore added a weakness to the existing ones.

Other factors compounded these difficulties. The Valkyrie orders for the mobilization of the Home Army units were signed by Olbricht and Colonel Mertz von Quirnheim. Upon inquiries from the military districts, Fromm would not confirm the orders unless he had convinced himself the coup was succeeding and unless he had joined it. Stauffenberg could not confirm the orders before his return to Berlin. But if they had not been issued by then and if the communications blackout did not hold, the orders could be countermanded from Hitler's headquarters, whether the Führer had survived or not.

On the morning of 20 July, Stauffenberg and his aide, Lieutenant Werner von Haeften, arrived at the Wolfschanze airfield at approximately 10 A.M. They were taken to the headquarters commandant's commissariat for breakfast. From 11 A.M. onward, Stauffenberg had conferences with officers of Hitler's staff in preparation for the midday briefing at which he was to report. The last preliminary briefing was presided over by Fieldmarshal Keitel in his office hut. The bunker in which Hitler stayed and Hitler's briefing hut were in another small fenced and guarded compound, a little over 1,300 feet west of Keitel's hut. Keitel's briefing ended just as Hitler's was scheduled to begin, and Keitel was always anxious to be on time.

As the officers at Keitel's briefing rose, Stauffenberg said to Keitel's adjutant that he would like to wash up and change his shirt. He was shown into a lounge but emerged again quickly, looking for his aide. Changing a shirt would plausibly explain a one-handed man's need for a few minutes' privacy with his aide. Haeften, meanwhile, who was in a nervous state, had almost betrayed himself. He was holding the explosive while Stauffenberg conferred, but he left it unattended for a few moments in a conspicuous place, whereupon an orderly asked questions about it. Haeften said only that Colonel von Stauffenberg "needed this for the Führer's situation briefing."

Finally the two conspirators joined each other in the lounge. Stauffenberg was to set the fuse on two packages of explosive while Haeften held each package in turn. The two packages contained about two pounds of explosive each, an amount considered sufficient to kill everyone in the briefing room.

In the meantime, Keitel, his adjutant, and several other officers stood outside the front door of Keitel's hut, waiting for Stauffenberg before going to Hitler's briefing hut. Keitel wanted to go, and his adjutant sent a sergeant, the same one who had asked Haeften about the mysterious parcel, to tell Stauffenberg to come along. The sergeant went to the lounge, opened the door, found Stauffenberg and Haeften standing there whispering and manipulating an object, and reported the Fieldmarshal's request for Stauffenberg to hurry. Stauffenberg answered abruptly that he was on his way. At the same moment, Keitel's adjutant called from the front door, "Stauffenberg, do come along!" The sergeant stood at the lounge's door, watching Stauffenberg and Haeften, until Stauffenberg came out with his briefcase in his left hand.

Because Stauffenberg and Haeften had been interrupted in the complicated process of setting the fuses, Stauffenberg went off with only one bomb in his briefcase, or only half the explosive he had at his disposal. The explosives expert in the later investigation, as well as the conspirators themselves, believed that the entire amount, or four pounds, would have killed everyone in the briefing room. This was the conspirators' objective. The sergeant's interruption had prevented Stauffenberg from using all of the explosive. Stauffenberg must have felt that the sergeant would see what he was doing. Stauffenberg's lingering was also annoying Keitel and his adjutant. These factors made Stauffenberg's situation seem awkward and conspicuous. He must have concluded that it was too dangerous to continue the preparations. He may also have had the misconception that he needed to set the fuse in both explosive packages, whereas in reality the speed and heat of the explosion of one charge would have been enough to detonate the other practically simultaneously, thus multiplying the explosive force.

From here on, the course of events was irreversible. When Stauffenberg emerged from Keitel's hut, Keitel had gone ahead, but two other officers were still waiting. One of them, Keitel's adjutant, glowered angrily at Stauffenberg, who returned his black look, and tried to seize Stauffenberg's briefcase in order to carry it for him. The one-armed colonel would not have it, jerking the briefcase out of the adjutant's reach. The adjutant and his orderly later remembered admiring Stauffenberg's energy.

The 1,300 feet between Keitel's hut and Hitler's briefing hut could be covered in about four minutes. While walking toward Hitler's hut, Stauffenberg conversed with the other officer, a general who had also been at Keitel's briefing. The three officers went through the gate of Hitler's inner compound. Inside, the briefing hut was a few paces beyond the guest bunker, where Hitler had been living temporarily since 14 July 1944 while his own larger bunker was under reconstruction for reinforcement with yet another layer of steel and concrete. The midday situation briefings were not normally held in Hitler's bunker, either before or after this date. While Hitler had been residing in his own bunker, up to 20 March 1944, the midday conferences were held in a wooden annex. While he was residing in the guest bunker, after 14 July, they were held in the briefing hut. The briefing hut had masonry walls and steel window-shutters to protect it against shrapnel and shell fragments. These may have suggested a bunker-like reinforcement to Stauffenberg, who had attended a briefing there on 15 July, and he therefore may have expected the explosion to be more powerful as a result of compression. But all five windows were open on this summer day, and there was a hollow space under the floorboards which was noticeable as one walked. The environment thus required a greater explosive charge than a bunker would have needed. Stauffenberg had prepared himself adequately, but the sergeant's intervention had foiled him.

As the three officers reached the briefing hut, Stauffenberg handed his briefcase over to Keitel's adjutant and asked the officer to place him with the briefcase near Hitler so that he might catch what was said before making his own report. He explained that his hearing was impaired from his injuries.

The briefing was in progress when Stauffenberg and the others entered the room. Everyone except Hitler was standing around a heavy, oblong map table; Hitler was sitting on a stool at the center of the table. Lieutenant-General Adolf Heusinger, filling in for the indisposed Chief of the General Staff, was giving a report on the eastern front, while Heusinger's assistant operations officer put maps on the table as needed. There were now twenty-four persons in the room, including the late arrivals. Ordinarily the officer giving a report, who in this case was Heusinger, stood on Hitler's right, while the assistant stood on the reporting officer's right. Keitel's adjutant obliged Stauffenberg by placing him behind and between Heusinger and his assistant, putting the briefcase on the floor in front of Stauffenberg. Hitler acknowledged Stauffenberg's arrival. Heusinger's report continued.

After a minute or so, Stauffenberg mumbled about a telephone call and signaled to Keitel's adjutant. They left the room together. Stauffenberg asked to be connected with General Fellgiebel. The adjutant ordered a sergeant to do it and went back in. Stauffenberg picked up the receiver, put it down, and left the hut. He walked about 800 feet to a bunker where Haeften and Fellgiebel were waiting for him. A car with a driver was waiting, too. After a minute or so, there was a tremendous explosion in the briefing hut. Stauffenberg and Haeften got into the car and ordered the driver to take them to the airfield.

Stauffenberg had little difficulty bluffing his way through the first checkpoint. He growled concerning "Führer's orders" and was waved on. The second checkpoint was equally unproblematical. But at the third, obstacles had been placed in the road, and the noncommissioned officer in charge refused to let anyone pass. Stauffenberg used the telephone, reached an officer in the commandant's staff with whom he had breakfasted in the morning, and got him to order the guard to let him pass. The rest of the narrow cobbled road to the airfield, through a leafy forest, was covered without further delay. At some point en route Haeften threw out of the car the other two-pound package of explosive, which was later recovered. At the air field Stauffenberg boarded a He 111 airplane, provided by General Eduard Wagner, the Quartermaster General, who was also in the plot.

During his flight of around two hours to Berlin, Stauffenberg must have been convinced, judging by his sparse utterances later in the day, that he had killed Hitler. On his way out of Wolfschanze he had passed the briefing hut at a distance of not much more than 100 feet and had gained an impression of tremendous destruction. The air was filled with smoke and debris; uniformed men were running up; cars were moving in the direction of the hut. This was the scene as Stauffenberg and Haeften passed. It looked, in Stauffenberg's words, as if a 15-centimeter shell had hit the hut. No one could have survived.

The bomb went off in the briefing room with a blinding flash and deafening noise at approximately 12:50 P.M. Everyone in the room was thrown to the ground or against a wall. All were burned and bruised. Some were injured severely, cut by flying pieces of wood. Almost everyone's eardrums were pierced. Everyone's hair stood on end from the suction and heat of the explosion. Pockets and boots were full of glass. A stenographer died on the same afternoon; two more participants died on 22 July, and another on 1 October.

Hitler had been leaning on his elbow on the map table when the explosion propelled the table top upward and gave him a tremendous jar. His eardrums were pierced. He had cuts and bruises. His trouser legs hung down in shreds. But apart from slightly impaired hearing and a badly bruised right elbow, Hitler emerged unhurt. After washing and changing, he received Mussolini, whose visit had been scheduled.

Hitler showed his awed fellow dictator the ruins of the briefing room. During tea, when it became clear that a coup d'état was being launched in Berlin, Hitler ordered immediate countermeasures. . . .

By midnight the revolt had collapsed everywhere. In the Home Army Command, General Fromm regained liberty and authority long enough during the night to order four of the leaders shot immediately — Stauffenberg, Haeften, Mertz von Quirnheim, and Olbricht. Within the hour Fromm was himself summoned to Goebbels' Propaganda Ministry and arrested on suspicion of being in the plot. He was tried, convicted of cowardice, and shot on 12 March 1945.

Most of the remaining plotters in the Home Army Command were arrested around midnight. Hundreds of arrests followed as the Gestapo destroyed the German Resistance movement. A "People's Court" tried and convicted about two hundred people who were involved in the 20 July plot. Most of them were executed within two hours of sentencing; appeals were a farce. The condemned men were strangled slowly with thin wire. The first few dozen executions were filmed for Hitler to watch.

The survivors. These starving men, survivors of the German concentration camp at Nordhausen, were among the tiny minority of those who entered the camps and lived to tell the tale of mass extermination. Their eyes tell of the horror they have seen. (UPI/Corbis-Bettmann)

The Social Impact of Nazism

Variety of Opinion

> *It was in the hundreds of localities like Northeim all over Germany that the revolution was made actual.*
>
> William Sheridan Allen

> *The full weight of the intricate machinery of state was brought directly and suddenly to bear upon the working population.*
>
> Timothy W. Mason

> *These alternative forms of social behavior within the Third Reich show that considerable sections of the younger generation held themselves aloof from National Socialism.*
>
> Detlev Peukert

> *The male chauvinist mentality of the NSDAP's men ensured that women who were attracted to the Party were condemned to "separate development."*
>
> Jill Stephenson

> *Far from being helpless or even innocent, women made possible a murderous state in the name of concerns they defined as motherly.*
>
> Claudia Koonz

Nazi violence and illegality after Hitler became chancellor were widely condemned.

Sarah Gordon

Perceived as a struggle of all-or-nothing, the war in the East called for complete spiritual commitment, absolute obedience, unremitting destruction of the enemy.

Omer Bartov

Our final problem concerns the coordination (Gleichschaltung) *of German society under the Nazi regime. This term connotes an effort by the state to penetrate all aspects of public life and to leave private as little as possible. Every organization and every individual were to march to the same beat. Those who seemed reluctant would be goaded; those who refused would be eliminated. In reality, as we shall see, such far-reaching intentions were not totally realized, but they are nonetheless frightening to contemplate.*

William Sheridan Allen *takes us to a small town of twenty thousand inhabitants in the vicinity of Hannover. Because Northeim was a rail junction and an administrative center with a large number of state employees, it was admittedly atypical in its vulnerability to Nazism. Yet it illustrates the sheer vitality of local Nazi organizations, to which the town's broad middle class tended. Allen first explains the irrational nature of that fateful attraction and then analyzes the dire consequences. Traditional allegiances and activities soon vanished, and the swastika alone flew from the mast.*

Timothy W. Mason *picks up the story of the German labor movement following the abolition of trade unions in May 1933, just four months after Hitler's seizure of power. The replacement of the unions by the unified German Labor Front under Robert Ley was an indication that the Nazi party needed the cooperation of German workers if industry were to fulfill the task of preparing the nation for a possible war. The Labor Front thereupon undertook a massive job of persuasion, encouraging workers to find "Strength through Joy." This slogan meant, among other things, more organized holidays, sports, folk dances, and theater presentations — all under the watchful eye of the party. But with the advent of war, many workers were mobilized, production quotas were increased, and the strain of the workplace began to tell. The inevitable result, as Mason demonstrates, was a harsh militarization of the labor force. The full meaning of dictatorship became painfully evident, and the joy was soon gone.*

Detlev Peukert *chronicles the fate of young people in the Third Reich. Initially the Hitler Youth and its female counterpart, the Bund Deutscher Mädel, seemed to be just a peculiarly German form of scouting, with an emphasis on camping, games, and harmless fun. But in time these organizations became bureaucratized and militarized, thereby imposing a tough discipline that was not to the liking of every adolescent. Dissatisfaction with officially sponsored groups thus produced a youthful protest movement not unlike the gangs of American inner cities. Peukert identifies two of them: the Edelweiss Pirates and the Swing Youth. Although different in style, they shared a disdain for the frantic patriotism and puritan morality of their do-gooding peers. Even in a Nazi state, it appears, the impatience and sex drive of the young were irrepressible.*

Jill Stephenson *provides the first of two readings on women. Thousands of German females began to enter the labor force before the First World War. By abandoning or altering their traditional social functions as homemakers and mothers, they invited an archcriticism that they were damaging the quality of the race. This, at any rate, was the Nazi view, which Stephenson characterizes as blatant male chauvinism. Not all women, she shows, were quite pleased with a place on the pedestal or in the kitchen. Female dissenters responded in a variety of ways: Many stubbornly resisted Nazi blandishments, some sought refuge in their church, and others simply became indifferent.*

Claudia Koonz *sets a different accent. Even when women seemed to be excluded from the masculine cliques inside the Nazi movement, she contends, they willingly formed a cadre of compliant helpmates. Women voted in large numbers for the Nazi party, then provided it with gracious services that offset the frequent crudeness and cruelty of their menfolk. Thus the woman's place in the Nazi universe was separate, unequal, and contaminated. Only a small minority resisted. Those whom Koonz frankly calls "Nazi women" tended to predominate, and their role proved to be as reprehensible as it was conspicuous.*

Sarah Gordon *stresses the high degree of integration by German Jews before 1933. Even Hitler found that anti-Semitism was not unduly popular in the 1920s, and he was forced to tone down that aspect of his political propaganda. Blaming Jews for all the ills of society nevertheless remained essential to the theory and practice of Nazism; once in power, Hitler proved it. A process of disassimilation began: first exclusion, then expulsion, and finally extermination. Gordon doubts that the majority of the German people supported such drastic measures and considers that the infamous "Night of the Broken Glass" (Kristallnacht) — the first concerted violence against the German Jews in 1938 — was actually a failure on the part of the Nazis. Yet no vigorous and widespread protest was evident, and the future was bleak.*

Omer Bartov, a young Israeli historian, has the final word. Like Sarah Gordon, he observes that most Germans shrank from public violence and were unenthusiastic about the opening of war in 1939. But they went along. Whether from conviction, ignorance, or just a blind sense of duty, they were thereby implicated in the vast destruction and genocide of the war years, which reached a climax during the bitter struggle between Nazi Germany and the Soviet Union on the eastern front. Here, Bartov reminds us, perished not only hopes and dreams but millions of victims whose fate must not be forgotten.

By its sprawling and untidy nature, the social history of the Nazi years cannot easily be contained within a brief space. Nor does it fit any simple theory. But, at the least, this group of essays recalls that the complex historical record is full of contradictions and subtle distinctions. Whatever our moral or ideological stance, surely uninformed prejudice has no place in the study of Nazism.

William Sheridan Allen

The Nazification of a Town

Northeim is not now, and never was, a "typical" German town. The composition of Northeim in Weimar and Nazi days was not the same as the rest of Germany. There were an inordinate number of civil servants and the town was dominated economically by the railroad. Few places in Germany began the Third Reich with a two-thirds vote for

From *The Nazi Seizure of Power: The Experience of a Single German Town, 1922–1945*, rev. ed., William Sheridan Allen. Copyright © 1965, 1984 by William Sheridan Allen. Reprinted with permission of Franklin Watts, Inc.

the NSDAP, the national average being on the order of two-fifths. On the other hand, there were many places in Germany that saw more violence than Northeim in the early days of the Third Reich.

What, then, is to be learned from Northeim's experience in the Nazi years?

In the first place, it is clear that an essential arena in the Nazi electoral surge and the seizure of power was on the local level, and that the critical figures were the local Nazi leaders. Northeim's Nazis created their own image by their own initiative, vigor, and propaganda. They knew exactly what needed to be done to effect the transfer of power to themselves in the spring of 1933, and they did it without more than generalized directives from above. Exactly how much was initiated locally and how much was promoted by the example of other Nazi groups in other towns or by the District and national Nazi leadership cannot yet be fully determined. Certainly there were no written orders from above, though there may have been verbal ones. But the major initiative clearly came from local leaders. It would be extremely interesting to know exactly what means were used by the NSDAP to instill the sense of purposefulness and initiative into its local groups, which were then used by the movement as a whole. It would be useful to know in explicit detail how coordination was combined with flexibility in this authoritarian instrument. The material available for this study of Northeim did not supply complete answers to these questions. It has, however, made clear that there would have been no Nazi revolution in Northeim, at least not of the totality that has been described here, without an active and effective local organization. Hitler, Goebbels, and the other Nazi leaders provided the political decisions, ideology, national propaganda, and, later, the control over the government that made the revolution possible. Hitler also gave his followers a simple goal that no other party shared: the idea of taking total and exclusive power at the first chance. But it was in the hundreds of localities like Northeim all over Germany that the revolution was made actual. They formed the foundation of the Third Reich.

As for the reasons behind the particular experience in Northeim, the most important factor in the victory of Nazism was the active division of the town along class lines. Though there was cohesion in Northeim before the Nazis began their campaigns leading to the seizure of power, the cohesion existed within the middle class or within the working class and did not extend to the town as a whole. The victory of

Nazism can be explained to a large extent by the desire on the part of Northeim's middle class to suppress the lower class and especially its political representatives, the Social Democratic party. Nazism was the first effective instrument for this.

This is why Northeimers rejoiced in the gains of the Nazis and this is why they applauded the institution of the dictatorship. The antipathy of the middle class was not directed toward individual members of the SPD, but only toward the organization itself; not toward the working class as such, but only toward its political and social aspirations; not, finally, toward the reality of the SPD, but mainly toward a myth that they nurtured about the SPD. For a variety of reasons, Northeim's middle class was so intent on dealing a blow to the Social Democrats that it could not see that the instrument it chose would one day be turned against itself.

Exactly why Northeimers were so bitterly opposed to the Socialists cannot be answered on the basis of a study of this town alone; the answer lies in the history and social structure of Imperial and Weimar Germany, and possibly can be given only by a social psychologist. Nevertheless it seems clear that the nature of the SPD had something to do with the burghers' attitudes. Northeim's Socialists maintained slogans and methods which had little correspondence with reality. They maintained the façade of a revolutionary party when they were no longer prepared to lead a revolution. They never seriously attempted to mend fences with the middle class and frequently offended bourgeois sensibilities by their shortsightedness and shallow aggressiveness.

Yet it would be wholly incorrect to place all the blame upon Northeim's Social Democracy. The middle class responded to the existence of the SPD in ways which were almost paranoid. Its members insisted upon viewing the SPD as a "Marxist" party at a time when this was no longer so. They were determined to turn the clock back to a period when the organized working class was forcibly kept from exerting influence. They felt threatened by the very existence of this organization. This view of the SPD was not in accord with reality, since by any objective standard the goal of the SPD in Northeim was to maintain the kind of town that Northeim's middle class itself wanted.

What was needed in Northeim to stop the Nazis was a political coalition of the decent people, regardless of party, to recognize that — whatever it promised — Nazism was an indecent thing. That such a coalition never developed was the main reason the Nazis got into power. But it was the middle class that gave them their chance.

Perhaps the behavior of the good burghers of Northeim becomes more understandable when one realizes the extent to which they were committed to nationalism. The excess of patriotic feeling in the town during the pre-Hitler period was the great moral wedge for Nazism. In many ways the actions and beliefs of Northeimers during the last years of the Weimar era were the same as if World War I had never ended. It was in this sort of atmosphere that the SPD might seem treasonable and the Nazi reasonable.

A similar effect was wrought by the depression. While Northeim's middle class was not decisively affected by the economic crisis, the burghers were made desperate through fear and through an obsession with the effects of the depression, especially the sight of the unemployed. As for the effect of the depression upon the lower classes, it was equally large. There is no doubt that the progressive despair of the jobless, as reflected in the longer and longer periods of unemployment, weakened the forces of democracy in the town. It may be that this sapped the SPD's will to fight and led it into ritualistic responses to Nazism. It was hard for Socialists to bend all their efforts to combating Nazism when this involved defending a system that could produce this sort of economic misery. Had the SPD seriously undertaken to introduce democratic socialism in response to the depression, it seems likely they would have found new sources of strength among their own followers, and very likely might have won the votes of the many Northeimers who cast ballots for the NSDAP simply because the Nazis promised to end the depression. In short, intelligent and credible radicalism was a response the depression called for, but the Socialists did not offer it.

The depression exposed Northeim's Socialists in other ways, too. The use of economic pressure at the sugar factory and at the railroad deprived the SPD of much of its prestige and power. If it could not even defend its own people when the chips were down, how could it defend democracy, and how could it bring about the socialist society? The success of management's action at the railroad yards no doubt opened up several possibilities for the Nazis. It was there that they learned how economically vulnerable the workers were; it was there that they learned essentially that the SPD would not fight.

But the main effect of the depression was to radicalize the town. In the face of the mounting economic crisis, Northeimers were willing to tolerate approaches that would have left them indignant or indifferent under other circumstances. Thus the disgusting and debilitating party acrimony and violence mushroomed in the years before the dictatorship. The extent of the violence in Northeim was an expression of the radical situation, but it also added to it by making violence normal and acceptable. Along with the growing nationalism and increasing impatience over the depression, violence and political tension were significant factors in preparing the town for the Nazi takeover.

All these factors were exploited with considerable astuteness by Nazi propaganda. In the face of the senseless round of political squabbling and fecklessness, the Nazis presented the appearance of a unified, purposeful, and vigorous alternative. Their propaganda played upon all the needs and fears of the town and directed itself to almost every potential group of adherents. This was largely because the Nazis were willing to be programmatically flexible in their propaganda and because they had a simple feedback system to measure and adjust the effectiveness of their propaganda. By their own energy, adaptability, and effort Northeim's Nazis captured the allegiance of the town's confused and troubled middle class.

This set the stage for the actual seizure of power, but the revolution itself was also conducted in such a way as to insure success. The fact that this was, in the words of Konrad Heiden, a *"coup d'état* by installments"* kept *Reichsbanner* from responding decisively at any one point. By the time the SPD had been broken, the terror system had been inaugurated, largely through social reinforcement.

The single biggest factor in this process was the destruction of formal society in Northeim. What social cohesion there was in the town existed in the club life, and this was destroyed in the early months of Nazi rule. With their social organizations gone and with terror a reality, Northeimers were largely isolated from one another. This was true of the middle class but even more true of the workers, since by the destruction of the SPD and the unions the whole complex of social ties created by this super-club was effaced. By reducing the people of Northeim to unconnected social atoms, the Nazis could move the resulting mass in whatever direction they wished. The process was probably easier in Northeim than in most other places, since the town

contained so many government employees. By virtue of their dependence on the government the civil servants were in an exposed position and had no choice but to work with the Nazis if they valued their
livelihood. Especially Northeim's teachers — who formed the social
and cultural elite of the town — found themselves drawn into support
of the NSDAP almost immediately. As other Northeimers flocked to
the Nazi bandwagon in the spring of 1933, and as terror and distrust became apparent, there was practically no possibility of resistance to Hitler.

Timothy W. Mason

Workers in the German Labor Front

The months after the physical destruction of the Trade Unions on 2 May
1933 were marked by chaos and confusion in the social and economic
life of Germany, and, in the minds of all ruling groups — industrialists, civil servants and Party leaders alike — by the greatest uncertainty
about the shape of the new social order. Gradually, in consequence of
the terror and of bitter factional disputes among the ruling groups, the
lines of development hardened: the verbose theorists of a "corporative
social order" succumbed to the practitioners of Party supremacy; and
the deep yearning of the rank and file Nazis to do away with large-
scale industry altogether soon proved to be incompatible with the more
pressing task of doing away with the Treaty of Versailles. Two new institutions and one old one emerged into an uneasy and mutually suspicious equilibrium to preserve, exhort and exploit the mutilated body
of the German working classes.

The task of preservation was allotted to the state. Deprived of
the protection of the independent trade unions and of the workshop

World Copyright: The Past and Present Society, 175 Banbury Road, Oxford, England.
This article is reprinted with the permission of the Society and the author from *Past and
Present: A Journal of Historical Studies*, no. 33 (April 1966).

councils, workers — especially those in smaller undertakings — were being forced in the spring and early summer of 1933 to agree to further wage reductions: there was a reserve labour army of seven million unemployed, and where the impersonal terror of starvation did not suffice, the SA had rawhide whips and rubber truncheons for the enlightenment of "marxists" who failed to recognize that 30 January had brought a new spirit of national and social unity. But the further immiseration of the working classes was not to the advantage of the new régime. In contrast to his straightforwardly reactionary supporters, Hitler recognized that he could not simply preside over the working population in an aloof, bureaucratic manner; the logic of mass politics demanded that he seek their active support. He claimed that he had liberated the working classes from the tyranny of their corrupt marxist "Bonzen", restored the dignity of manual labour and emancipated it from the deprecating glance of the brain-worker. Translated into material terms, these sentiments demanded the retention of existing minimum wage levels; to this end the new official post of Trustee of Labour was created. The Trustees were responsible to the Ministry of Labour for enforcing old, and issuing new minimum wage regulations within a defined geographical area.

The task of exhortation fell to the German Labour Front, a misshapen child of hectic improvization. It was called into existence to defeat the ambitions of Nazi trade unionists in the Party's Factory Cell Organization, who threatened to outgrow the political tutelage of the Party and establish monolithic and radical workers' unions; the new Labour Front was to be tied much more closely to the party leadership. Hitler's most slavish follower, Robert Ley, who had commanded the Action Committee for the destruction of the Free Trade Unions, became *both* supreme organizational manager of the party *and* leader of the Labour Front. Ley was at first surprised by his new appointment, but soon recognized that the one was a mere extension of the other, that it was but a small step from managing the affairs of the party to managing the minds of the working population. The link should ensure that the mass management of minds would be conducted on the basis of orthodox ideological principles. Ley's dual function symbolized the new unity of the German people, a unity embodied only in the organization of the NSDAP: independent working class organizations of any political persuasion were both dangerous and superfluous. But the original conception of the Labour Front demanded that the mass management of minds be its *sole* task. Influential employers were scarcely less frightened by the potential power of an organization, membership of which was in practice compulsory for all industrial workers, than they were by the brutal populism of the Factory Cell Organization. With the full support of the Ministries of Economics and Labour, the employers wrung from Ley in November 1933 a declaration that the Labour Front "would *not* be the organ through which the material questions of workaday life would be decided, *not* the organ within which the natural differences of interest inside the productive community would be resolved". Ley, fighting simultaneously against authoritarian and populist critics of his new rôle, and lacking at this stage a clear picture of the future shape of his organization, had no option but to agree. The employers then dissolved their own class organizations and joined the Labour Front, which became therewith the official bearer of the doctrine that class conflict had been abolished. In its place was to grow that deep and genuine affective harmony of German working people from all walks of life which had so long been latent in society, but the realization of which had so long been frustrated by the machinations of paid agents of Moscow. Affective harmony was good for productivity, and high productivity was both the proof and the goal of "German socialism". The social history of the next six years is the story of the bankruptcy of this ideal, at once cynical and sentimental, archaic and dilettantish. . . .

The German countryside and German culture were translated by a gigantic feat of organization into commodities to which all Germans should have equal access: symphony orchestras played in the factories during the lunch-hour, and firms were given cheap block-bookings for the civic theatres at night; factory libraries were expanded (and purged), sport was nationally organized, encouraged and subsidized so that even the poorest unskilled worker was able to sail or play tennis; and folk-culture groups revived and performed traditional rural songs and dances. Early in 1934 the loudspeakers in the Berlin factories blared out the news of the arrival of the first train-load of "Strength through Joy" holiday-makers in Bavaria. The expansion was swift, and within months the press was carrying photographs of happy German tourists in Madeira and Lisbon and in the Norwegian fjords, transported in passenger ships converted to double the number of available berths. National Socialism had achieved one of the great aims of the International and had laid Europe at the feet of the German worker. Lest he abuse the

"Worker—Vote for Front Line Soldier Hitler!" This National Socialist election poster urges German workers to vote for their friend and ally, Adolf Hitler. (Library of Congress)

privilege, the German worker was accompanied on his foreign tours by well-deserving old Gestapo officers, who saw that he did not contact subversive exile organizations.

If Joy could be produced by economies of scale in the tourist industry it was not for its own sake, nor even for the greater glory of the Third Reich. Joy was an essential condition for recuperating from the trials and strains of industrial labour, for re-conditioning the mind and the body for yet more intensive efforts in the battle for production. But many remained oblivious of this higher purpose of the political fun-palace, and gave themselves over hopelessly to the simple pursuit of pleasure. In 1938 Ley had to remind passengers on a "Strength through Joy" cruise that the organization did not exist to lay on orgies, and in the country at large it was whispered ironically that many a girl had lost her strength through a surfeit of joy. . . .

The first signs of crisis in the labour market came in the summer of 1935, when the spate of military and civil building in North Germany made it very difficult for employers to find the necessary workers; worst affected were building sites in rural areas, where autobahns and barracks were being built. Wage rates were calculated according to a cost of living index, and in rural areas food was much cheaper and wages appreciably lower. The Ministry of Labour at once proposed a measure of equalization, whereby rural wage rates should be increased and inflated urban rates reduced. At the insistence of Party officials, notably Gauleiter Kaufmann of Hamburg, the proposal was vetoed by Hitler, on the grounds that it was impossible to *reduce any* wage rate so soon after the great unemployment, *and* to hope to make progress with the task of gaining the political loyalty of the working class. A fateful pattern was taking shape: the régime needed the political approval of the working classes and their full co-operation in the armaments drive, but the fewer unemployed there were, the less necessary it became for the working classes to give their full co-operation; and this political weakness of the régime for a long time inhibited measures which could have remedied the economic weakness. Hitler constantly asserted the primacy of politics over economics; by March 1942 this meant the primacy of terror. What it was politically impossible, but economically essential to demand of the German working classes, could be demanded without scruple of sub-human slave labour, transported in cattle trucks into the Reich from Eastern Europe.

In the summer of 1935 this fulfillment was a long way off, but in the following twelve months the cycle advanced by several steps.

When Goering was charged by Hitler in September 1936 to carry out a Four Year Plan which should make the German economy ready for war by the time of its completion, he found signs of strain throughout the labour market. . . .

The process of the full militarization of the labour force thus began slowly and uncertainly; and the old logic of the plebiscitarian system was not yet quite played out. In the late summer of 1938, shop assistants in North Germany flatly defied orders from the Ministry of Economics, and instituted early closing on Saturdays, oblivious to appeals that they should show solidarity with their overworked comrades in the armaments plants. The Labour Front weakly offered its retroactive blessing on this increase in the beauty and joy of the lives of the shop assistants; two months later, Goering vented his rage and frustration with the intractable economic problems on the Labour Front, threatening to clap its officials in gaol if they persisted in forcing employers to build swimming baths for their retinues.

The winter of 1938–9 brought no relief; the shortage of labour grew more intense and came to cover all degrees of skill in all trades. Firms had to be prevented by the government from depopulating Austria and the Sudetenland after the acquisition of those territories by the Reich, and unsuccessful attempts were made to mobilize young women for work in agriculture. In February 1939 a new Decree on the Duty of Service was necessary; that of June 1938 had promised to conscript only unmarried men, to pay them at least the same wages as they were already earning, and to conscript them for a limited period of time. No such promises were made by the new decree. In the following month, the controls over the hiring of building workers were extended to cover the hiring and firing of all workers in all major industries: agriculture, chemicals, building materials, iron, steel, metal-working and mining. The prior consent of the labour exchange had to be obtained in every case. A general and complete direction of labour was begun, designed to ensure that the priority tasks of rearmament could be carried out. But the social and economic reality still proved recalcitrant. No clear system of economic priorities was worked out in peacetime; the priority list was supplemented by a super-priority list, which was in turn made obsolete by the internecine rivalry among the armaments firms and among the three branches of the armed forces. Scarcity turned the ideology of ruthless struggle into a set of maxims of prudence for the conduct of everyday life in the Third Reich. Of equal importance for the operation of the latter decree was the fact that the labour exchanges, themselves short of trained staff, could not really cope with their new duties. Clear and generally applicable criteria for deciding whether a request to change jobs was justified or not, were extremely difficult to establish; decisions were erratic and varied from town to town. When applications from workers were refused, only the Gestapo could deal with those who showed their resentment at the decision by slacking — and the Gestapo could not *replace* these workers. The factory community, still invoked by the labour lawyers and the managers of minds, had become a brutal parody of the grim charade it once had been.

On the day the German army marched into Poland, the hiring and firing of all workers was made dependent upon the approval of the labour exchanges; offenders against this decree could be fined and/or imprisoned. For male workers over eighteen years of age, all legislation limiting hours of work was annulled, and the limitations on the hours of work of women and young persons were greatly loosened. Three days later, on 4 September 1939, a War Economy Decree empowered the Trustees of Labour to fix maximum wages *and working conditions* in all branches of industry: the piracy of skilled workers through the offer of generous fringe benefits now became illegal. Higher rates of pay for overtime work, Sunday-, holiday- and night-work were abolished: until the invasion of Poland it was standard practice in German industry for workers to receive time-and-a-quarter for hours worked in excess of eight per day: now, in order that retinues should not think their leaders to be profiting unduly from the war, and in order that the burden of war finance for the government be eased, employers had to pay to the tax offices the difference between the standard and the overtime wage rates. Thus an eleven-hour day at a standard rate of I Rm. per hour brought the worker II Rm., and the tax office 75 Pf. It was, as Goebbels insisted, a people's war. And all regulations granting statutory holidays were suspended. The Trustees were exempted from having to prosecute offenders in the courts, and gained the power to fine them on the spot. The establishment of maximum wages and working conditions for the whole economy evidently proved much too cumbersome a task, and on 12 October, all wages were simply frozen. The suspension of holidays excepted, there is no indication that these desperate measures were considered temporary; the full weight of the intricate machinery of state was brought directly and suddenly to bear upon the working population.

Detlev Peukert

Obedient and Dissident Youth

National Socialist youth policy aimed to secure the younger generation's total loyalty to the regime and their willingness to fight in the war that lay ahead. All competitors had to be eliminated and Nazi forms of organisation and militaristic education developed. These tasks were to be achieved with the distinctively Nazi combination of compulsion and prohibitions on the one hand and incentives and enticements on the other.

In practice, contradictions arose between these objectives of youth policy, and particularly between the different methods of realising them: contradictions which fragmented and obstructed what appeared at first sight to be a uniform programme of totalitarian assimilation. For example, military conscription robbed the Hitler Youth of many badly needed older youth leaders. Competition between the rival authorities of school and the Hitler Youth gave rise to areas of conflict in which young people could play the one off against the other. And, not least, the ideological content of National Socialism remained much too vague. Fragmentary notions of racial and national arrogance were mixed up with traditional pedagogic humanism: the model of the front-line soldier mixed up with the idea that there was an especially profound and valuable "German" culture; backward-looking agrarian Romanticism mixed up with enthusiasm for modern technology.

The life stories of young people under the swastika often contain the most contradictory impressions. If there was any common denominator, it was an education in the reckless, ruthless pursuit of genuine or inculcated interests. The following extract hints at how this came about:

> *No one in our class ever read* Mein Kampf. *I myself only took quotations from the book. On the whole we didn't know much about Nazi*

ideology. Even anti-Semitism was brought in rather marginally at school — for example via Richard Wagner's essay 'The Jews in Music' — and outside school the display copies of Der Stürmer *made the idea questionable, if anything. . . . Nevertheless, we were politically programmed: to obey orders, to cultivate the soldierly "virtue" of standing to attention and saying "Yes, Sir," and to stop thinking when the magic word 'Fatherland' was uttered and Germany's honour and greatness were mentioned.*

War seemed "normal"; violence seemed "legitimate." Hitler's foreign policy achievements between 1936 and 1939 had accustomed the Germans to regard the combination of violent posturing, assertion of their "legal right" to wipe out the "shame of Versailles," and risk-taking as a recipe for success.

The main arm of National Socialist youth policy was the Hitler Youth. By the end of 1933 all youth organisations, apart from the Catholic ones (which for the time being remained protected owing to the Nazi government's Concordat with the Vatican), had been either banned (like the socialist youth movement) or "co-ordinated" more or less voluntarily and integrated into the Hitler Youth (like the non-political *bündisch* youth movement and, in late 1933/early 1934, the Protestant organisations).

By the end of 1933, therefore, the Hitler Youth already contained 47 per cent of boys aged between ten and fourteen (in the *Deutsches Jungvolk*) and 38 per cent of boys between fourteen and eighteen (in the Hitler Youth proper). However, only 15 per cent of girls between ten and fourteen were organised (in the *Jungmädelbund* and only 8 per cent of those between fifteen and twenty-one (in the *Bund Deutscher Mädel*). The Hitler Youth Law of December 1st, 1936, called for the incorporation of all German youth, and this was backed up with growing pressure on those remaining outside to enroll "voluntarily" — until two executive orders ancillary to the Hitler Youth Law, issued on March 25th, 1939, made "youth service" compulsory.

In the years immediately following 1933, many did not regard membership in the Hitler Youth as compulsory. The Hitler Youth built upon many practices of the youth organisations of the Weimar period, offered a wide range of leisure activities, and, at the lower levels (which in the everyday running of things were the most important), was led not infrequently by people who had had previous experience in other youth organisations. In addition, the Hitler Youth uniform often provided the chance to engage, sometimes quite aggressively, in conflict with traditional figures of authority: the teacher, the father, the foreman, the local clergyman.

For many young people in the provinces, where the youth movement was not widespread before 1933, the arrival of the Hitler Youth often meant the first access to the leisure activities in a youth organisation, the impetus to build a youth club or sports field, or the opportunity to go on weekend or holiday trips away from one's narrow home environment.

The emancipatory openings for girls were even greater. In the *Bund Deutscher Mädel* girls could escape from the female role-model centered around family and children — a role-model which, for that matter, was also propagated by the National Socialists. They could pursue activities which were otherwise reserved for boys; and if they worked as functionaries for the *Bund Deutscher Mädel* they might even approach the classic "masculine" type of the political organiser who was never at home. Such opportunities remained limited, however, and were withdrawn increasingly owing to the Nazis' general discrimination against women. Yet these groups undoubtedly proved, in many practical day-to-day respects, to be a modernising force.

With the consolidation of the Hitler Youth as a large-scale bureaucratic organisation, and with the gradual ageing of its leadership cadres in the course of the 1930s, the movement's attraction to the young people began to decline. Political campaigns within the Hitler Youth against those who had been leaders in the Weimar youth movement and against styles and behavior allegedly associated with that organisation led to the disciplining and purging of units. The campaign to bring everyone into the Hitler Youth ranks brought in those who previously had proclaimed their antipathy simply by their absence. Disciplinary and surveillance measures to enforce "youth service" made even harmless everyday pleasures such as meetings of friends and cliques criminal offences. Above all, the claim of legal power by Hitler Youth patrols, whose members were scarcely older than the young people they were keeping track of, provoked general indignation. And in addition, even before the outbreak of war, the Hitler Youth concentrated increasingly on premilitary drill.

The belief that the Hitler Youth successfully mobilised young people is only half the story. The more the Hitler Youth arrogated state powers to itself and the more completely it drew young people into its organisation, the more obvious became the examples of deviant behaviour among adolescents. By the end of the 1930s thousands of young people were turning away from the leisure activities of the Hitler Youth and finding their own unregimented style in independent gangs. Indeed, they defended their independence all the more insistently as Hitler Youth patrols and the Gestapo increased their pressure. In 1942 the Reich Youth Leadership had to admit:

> *The formation of cliques, i.e. groupings of young people outside the Hitler Youth, has been on the increase before and, particularly, during the war to such a degree that one must speak of a serious risk of the political, moral and criminal subversion of youth.*

The leadership could not now make the excuse that the people involved had been conditioned by the Weimar "system": by "Marxism," "clericalism" or the old youth movements. The adolescents who made up this opposition in the late 1930s and early 1940s were the very generation on whom Adolf Hitler's system had operated unhindered.

Amidst the wealth of evidence of unaccommodating behaviour, two groups stand out particularly clearly, groups which shared a rejection of the Hitler Youth but which differed in their styles, backgrounds and actions: the "Edelweiss Pirates" (*Edelweisspiraten*) and the "Swing Youth" (*Swing-Jugend*).

The first Edelweiss Pirates appeared at the end of the 1930s in western Germany. The names of the individual groups, their badges (metal edelweiss flowers worn on the collar, the skull and crossbones, pins with coloured heads), their dress (usually a checked shirt, dark short trousers, white socks) and their activities all varied, but were based upon a single underlying model. "Roving Dudes" from Essen, "Kittelbach Pirates" from Oberhausen or Düsseldorf (named after a stream in the north of Düsseldorf) and "Navajos" from Cologne all regarded themselves as "Edelweiss Pirate" groups. This agreement took on real meaning during weekends trips into the surrounding countryside, where groups from the whole region met up, pitched tents, sang, talked, and together "bashed" Hitler Youth patrols doing their rounds.

The opposition — the Hitler Youth, Gestapo and the law — also soon categorised the groups under a single heading, having first wavered in case the "youth movement" (*bündisch*) label would save them the bother of having to analyse new, spontaneous forms of oppositional activity and construct corresponding new sets of prohibitions. It soon became clear, however, that although it was possible to spot precursor groups and so-called "wild" *bündisch* organisations in

Hitler Youth on Parade. The Hitler youth and its female counterpart, the Bund Deutscher Mädel, were part of the National Socialists' effort to secure the loyalty of the younger generation. (UPI/Corbis-Bettmann)

the early 1930s, there was no continuity of personnel (the "delin-
quents" of 1935–7 long since had been conscripted to the front) and
there was no direct ideological line of descent.

The Edelweiss Pirate groups arose spontaneously, as young people aged between fourteen and eighteen got together to make the most
of their free time away from the control of the Hitler Youth. The age
composition of the group, with a clustering around it of younger children and older war-wounded men and women in reserved occupations,
was not fortuitous: boys of seventeen and eighteen were conscripted
into the National Labour Service and then into the Wehrmacht, while
at fourteen boys reached the school-leaving age and could thus escape
from the immediate, day-to-day sphere of Hitler Youth control. They
were taking their first steps into work — as apprentices or, thanks to
the shortage of manpower caused by the war, increasingly as relatively
well-paid unskilled workers. To an increased sense of self-esteem and
independence the continuing obligation of Hitler Youth service up to
the age of eighteen could contribute very little. The war reduced the
Hitler Youth's leisure attractions: instead there was repeated paramili-
tary drill with pointless exercises in obedience, which were all the more
irksome for being supervised by Hitler Youth leaders scarcely any older
than the rank and file, yet who often stood out by the virtue of their
grammar or secondary-school background. "It's the Hitler Youth's own
fault," one Edelweiss Pirate from Düsseldorf said, explaining his group's
slogan "Eternal war on the Hitler Youth": "every order I was given contained a threat."

The self-confidence of the Edelweiss Pirates and their image
among their peers were unmistakable, as an Oberhausen mining instructor found in the case of his trainees in 1941:

> *Every child knows who the KP [common abbreviation for Kittelbach Pi-
> rates] are. They are everywhere; there are more of them than there are
> Hitler Youth. And they all know each other, they stick close together . . .
> They beat up the patrols, because there are so many of them. They don't
> agree with anything. They don't go to work either, they're always down
> by the canal, at the lock.*

The overriding factor common to these groups was the territorial
principle: they belonged together because they lived or worked together; and a gang usually consisted of about a dozen boys and a few
girls. The fact that girls were involved at all distinguished these oppositional groups from the strictly segregated Bund Deutscher Mädel and

Hitler Youth. The presence of girls at the evening get-togethers and on the weekend trips into the countryside gave the adolescents a relatively unrestricted opportunity to have sexual experiences. In this respect they were much less prudish than their parents' generation, particularly the representatives of Nazi organisations with their almost obsessive fixation on the repression of sexuality. Nevertheless, sexual life in these groups was no doubt much less orgiastic than contemporary authors of official reports believed, or wanted others to believe, when they sought to construct a trinity of delinquency out of (sexual and criminal) degeneracy, (anti-organisational and anti-authoritarian) rebellion, and (political) opposition.

The high point of the pirates' free time was the weekend, when the young people could go off on hikes. Armed with rucksacks, sheath knives and bread-and-butter rations, sleeping in tents or barns, they spent a carefree time with like-minded young people from other towns — although always on the watch for Hitler Youth patrols, whom they, prudently calculating their own strength, either sought to avoid or taunted and fell upon with relish.

An important reason for this need to get as much space as possible as often as possible between themselves and their everyday conditions was the wish to avoid the 'educative' incursions of adults and the daily experiences of denunciations, spying, orders and punishments by National Socialist institutions that were directly bound up with these incursions. The youth movement's old reason for hiking — to withdraw from the pressures of the adult world — was intensified and given a political dimension in the Third Reich. . . .

A quite different form of popular culture developed among young people from the upper middle class: the "Swing" movement. Its adherents took every opportunity to avoid *völkische* music and the "moon-in-June" triviality of German hit tunes in order to listen to jazz and swing numbers, either on records or with live bands. Initially some of these events were allowed to take place in public; then, when Hitler Youth officials took offence at them, they were banned. In one internal Hitler Youth report about a swing festival in Hamburg in February 1940, which was attended by 500–600 adolescents, one can hear all the leitmotifs that pervade the lamentations of authorities faced by the jazz and rock cultures of the twentieth century:

> *The dance music was all English and American. Only swing dancing and jitterbugging took place. At the entrance to the hall stood a notice on which the words "Swing prohibited" had been altered to "Swing*

*requested." Without exception the participants accompanied the dances
and songs by singing the English lyrics. Indeed, throughout the evening
they attempted to speak only English; and some tables even French.*

*The dancers made an appalling sight. None of the couples
danced normally; there was only swing of the worst sort. Sometimes
two boys danced with one girl; sometimes several couples formed a
circle, linking arms and jumping, slapping hands, even rubbing the
backs of their heads together; and then, bent double, with the top
half of the body hanging loosely down, long hair flopping into the
face, they dragged themselves round practically on their knees. When
the band played a rumba, the dancers went into wild ecstasy. They
all leaped around and mumbled the chorus in English. The band
played wilder and wilder numbers; none of the players was sitting
any longer, they all "jitterbugged" on the stage like wild animals.
Frequently boys could be observed dancing together, without exception with two cigarettes in the mouth, one in each corner . . .*

With the ban on public functions, the swing movement shifted to
informal groupings where, naturally, its character became more sharply
defined. Swing clubs sprang up particularly in big cities: Hamburg,
Kiel, Berlin, Stuttgart, Frankfurt, Dresden, Halle and Karlsruhe. Their
members were predominantly middle-class adolescents with enough
schooling to be able to use the English lyrics and bits of foreign slang.
Like the Edelweiss Pirates, who had used German-language hits against
the National Socialists, so the *Swing-Jugend* picked up mainstream
jazz that was quite permissible in variety shows and dances and radicalised it: they made it into an emblem of a youth culture that rejected
the Hitler-Youth ideals, stripped it of its domesticated dance-floor
character and favoured hotter varieties of what in Nazi parlance was
termed "negro music." Dance music gave way to hot jazz; steps as
learned in dancing classes gave way to free, spontaneous rhythmic
movement, erect posture and tidy dress gave way to "jitterbugging,"
hair "down to the collar" (to quote the same Hitler-Youth report) and a
cult of "slovenliness" and "sleaziness."

The characteristics of the swing scene reflected the difference in social background between the offspring of the urban middle class and the
working-class Edelweiss Pirates. The latter met on street corners and in
parks, outside the confines of the parental home yet within a neighbour-
hood territory. The swing boys and girls had the money, clothes and status to be seen at bourgeois city-centre night clubs, as well as homes that

were large enough for them to indulge in their "jitterbugging" and "sleaziness" when their elders were out. They had gramophone records; they could get hold of chic English-looking clothes.

A relaxed regime in their parents' houses, or lack of nighttime supervision offered ample opportunity for gaining sexual experience. Reporting about the swing groups, the Nazi authorities stressed the incidence of promiscuity, group sex, sexual intercourse involving minors and, above all, unabashed pleasure in sexuality which was denounced as moral degeneracy. The wording and tone of such internal reports as a rule said more about their authors and readers than about the actual behaviour of the adolescents. Things were taken too literally that perhaps were only bragging; isolated "incidents" were generalised. Even this caveat, however, does not alter the fact that the sexual behaviour of these adolescents clearly deviated from National Socialist acceptability.

The swing youth were not anti-fascist in a political sense — their behaviour was indeed emphatically anti-political — but both Nazi slogans and traditional nationalism were of profound indifference to them. They sought their counter-identity in what they saw as the "slovenly" culture of the wartime enemies, England and America. They accepted Jews and "half-Jews" into their groups — another outrage for the Nazis — and gave ovations to visiting bands from Belgium and Holland.

The very disgust shown by the authors of the Nazi reports and their dramatisation of events indicate that Nazi officialdom felt attacked at the heart of its concept of itself and of the State. This is the only way, too, to explain the reaction of Heinrich Himmler, who wanted to put the "ringleaders" of the swing movement into concentration camps for at least two or three years of beatings, punitive drill and forced labour.

These alternative forms of social behavior within the Third Reich show that considerable sections of the younger generation held themselves aloof from National Socialism. When the Hitler Youth seemed to have established itself officially, with compulsory membership, it met with apathy and rejection on the part of many adolescents, who were constantly to be found along the border line between passive and active insubordination. Despite various forms of repression, opposition groups seem also to have been attractive to many adolescents who did not actually join them.

Furthermore, the everyday experience of National Socialism, for both working-class and middle-class youth, and their need to give expression to their identity, ran so contrary to what National Socialist ideology and its encrusted organisational structures had to offer, that the creation by young people of their own cultural identity and alternative styles naturally made itself apparent above all in the realm that was important for their age group: namely, leisure. These subcultures demonstrated that National Socialism, even after years in power, still did not have a complete grip on German society: indeed, sections of society slipped increasingly from its grasp the more it was able to perfect its formal means of organisation and repression.

The two central projects of National Socialist social policy — the abolition of class division through feelings of belonging to a "racial community" (*Volksgemeinschaft*) and the smashing of the perceived threat to traditional values from modernity and internationalism — seem to have run aground even before the end of the Third Reich loomed ahead with military defeat.

National Socialism unintentionally paved the way for these manifestations of modern youth culture. Its power was sufficient largely to destroy the traditional forms of working-class and middle-class cultures. In their places, however, National Socialism could offer only military discipline, an anachronistic ideology, and a stifling bureaucracy. The National Socialist blueprint for a future order failed to shape society in its image.

Jill Stephenson

The Wary Response of Women

The paradoxical character of the NSDAP, as a revolutionary force pledged to restore Germany to a mythical past from which it could develop towards an ideal present and future, attracted to it from 1919 those who wanted to return to the point where, they felt, Germany had taken a wrong turning. Unification in 1871 had been part of the

From *The Nazi Organization of Women*, by Jill Stephenson. Copyright © 1981 by Croom Helm, London. Reprinted by permission of the publisher and the author.

"correct" development, as far as it had gone, but the ensuring rapid in-dustrialisation had brought urbanisation and the politicisation of the working class by Marxist Social Democrats. It had also, by its insatiable demand for cheap and docile labour, brought large numbers of women into exhausting, dirty and even dangerous work which threatened the healthy development of the "race" by damaging and debilitating Ger-many's mothers. The massive increase in women's employment out-side the home in the thirty or so years before the First World War had also, by this analysis, threatened family life in other ways, by diverting housewives and mothers from their essential duties in the home for much of their life. Women were too busy or too tired to learn how to run a home in an orderly way, to protect their own health as childbear-ers, and to care adequately for their children. Improved methods of birth control from the later nineteenth century had led women to try to mitigate their problems by restricting the size of their family — yet again, in the Nazi view, endangering the future of the "race." The quality of German life, too, was under threat, with women, "the guardians of German culture," distracted by work, political agitation and the growth of a consumer society from their alleged age-old func-tion of cherishing the nation's distinctive songs, dances, costumes and crafts.

The Nazi revolution would restore women to the idyllic destiny from which they had been diverted before the First World War and which was, said the Nazis, deliberately derided by the Marxists, inter-nationalists, liberals and feminists who seemed, in the post-war period, to have emerged as the victors from Germany's pre-war political and social conflicts. And if women had been deflected from their destiny — which was only the fulfillment of the instinctive aspirations of the fe-male nature, it was said — even before the war, the experience of the war and the trauma of the revolutionary upheavals in a number of Ger-many's cities in 1918–19 convinced increasing numbers of men and women that the circumstances of post-war Germany would only inten-sify the distortion. The kind of changes that could be achieved to counteract modern evils through the new parliamentary system would do no more than tinker with the symptoms, for example, the "filth" that was given free rein in literature and drama by the lifting of censor-ship. Nothing less radical than a revolution — a *national* revolution, not a Marxist one — could bring Germany back to the path of "cor-rect" development. This was what the Nazi Party was fighting for in the *Kampfzeit* (time of struggle, up to 1933). Axiomatically, women could not participate actively in the struggle, since allowing them to do so would be simply to follow the false example set by the Nazis' adversaries. One of the spectres that remained with Nazi activists for years was the horror of women's participation in the attempted revolution of 1918–19, and Rosa Luxemburg — although she was a victim rather than a perpetrator of violence — became a symbol of the evils threatening German society. Years later, she and others were remembered with fear and loathing as an example of what National Socialism was pledged to prevent.

These sentiments contributed to the development of what may cautiously be called the Nazi view of women's role in the nation and in the Party. As Hans Frank was to say, there were "as many 'National Socialisms' as there were leaders," and the variations on the theme of women's place were legion. But it is generally safe to say that in the Nazi view women were to be "wives, mothers and homemakers"; they were to play no part in public life, in the legislature, the executive, the judiciary or the armed forces. Hitler himself frequently expressed opposition to women's participation in politics, claiming that it sullied and demeaned the female nature, as he saw it. It was partly Hitler's personal attachment to the image of women as "mothers of the nation" which delayed and then vitiated the introduction of labour conscription for women during the Second World War, although in his *Götterdämmerung* mentality early in 1945 he was prepared to see women enlisted as soldiers and sent to the front. While leading Nazis differed about the extent to which women should be employed outside the home and to which they could usefully contribute to the Party's campaigns, they generally accepted that from earliest childhood girls should be brought up to accept motherhood as their "natural calling," and that all other roles they might assume or functions they might exercise should be consistent with childbearing and childrearing. Again, this preoccupation derived largely from increasing anxiety in Nazi and non-Nazi circles alike in the 1920s about Germany's falling birth-rate.

While growing numbers of men were drawn to National Socialism in the 1920s because of these ideas among others, there were women, too, who found the Nazis' traditionalist approach to women's role attractive. For them, it was enough to sympathise with and support the Party's "fighting menfolk," and although small numbers of women joined the new local branches of the NSDAP which sprang up all over the country from the mid-1920s, most pro-Nazi women regarded it as inconsistent with their own and the Party's view of women's role to join a political party. But there were, almost paradoxically, a number of women with distinctly feminist views who gravitated to National Socialism because of its anti-Marxism, its ultra-nationalist and racist aspect, or for local or family reasons. It is clear that they either ignored the Party's pronouncements about women's role or else refused to take them seriously. In the critical years between 1930 and 1933 the Party gave them plenty of encouragement in their self-delusion at a time when its leadership was hoping to make a favourable impact on the female voter in its bid for power the legal way. Gregor Strasser, the Party's organisational chief at this time until his unexpected resignation in December 1932, particularly seemed to welcome and encourage women's participation in election campaigns. And so women supporters of National Socialism in the 1920s, up to 1933, might or might not wholeheartedly support the Party's general view of women's place in society, and might or might not be members of the NSDAP.

Women's group activity developed something of a split personality because it embraced these different kinds of women. It also started and grew spontaneously and in a variety of forms because the inherent male chauvinism of the movement led to exclusive concentration on the men's struggle against the Weimar "system." Often enough, a woman whose husband or brother was a Party member would join in giving *ad hoc* support to the men in the area, providing food, making and mending uniforms, or, as in Hanover in 1922, for example, making a flag bearing the Party's symbol. These activists set the tone for what would throughout the rest of the Nazi era be known as "womanly work," the kind of mundane, practical assistance which women, as homemakers, could readily provide, and which men really could not be asked to contemplate. This division of labour reflected the Party's general view of women's functions and underlined its insistence on the segregation of the sexes at work and at play. Women's talents and capacities were different from men's, and, like men's, they should be utilised to the full and not squandered in vain attempts by women to take over men's work or emulate men's achievements. Because of initial neglect of women's contribution to the Party's work, which led to its growth independently of male control, this segregationist policy led perhaps not to "secondary racism," but certainly to organisational apartheid. The male chauvinist mentality of the NSDAP's men ensured that women who were attracted to the Party were condemned to "separate development," which allowed them to work out their role in the Party's service to a great degree as they chose.

The evolution of Nazi women's groups of different kinds caused problems for the Party once it belatedly acknowledged their existence and assistance, in the later 1920s. To solve these, Gregor Strasser ordered the dissolution of all existing women's groups in 1931 and created, in their stead, the *NS-Frauenschaft* (NSF — Nazi Women's Group), the first official Nazi women's organisation under central Party control. Strasser's role here and in the subsequent development of the NSF casts interesting light on his character and methods. Unlike many leading Nazis he clearly felt that the women's organisation could contribute usefully to the Party's work; this was no doubt why he was at pains to create a uniform, harmonious organisation out of the diverse warring factions which had evolved in the 1920s. Others, too, valued the "women's work." The SA depended on women's soup kitchens to feed its members when they were on duty, especially if they were unemployed, and for a time the SA welcomed the rudimentary first-aid service provided by Nazi women for "heroes" hurt in brawls. As the Depression hit Germany's larger towns particularly hard from 1930 onwards, welfare work by women who collected money, cast-off clothing and household utensils, who gave material and moral support to the families of political detainees, and who provided food and warm clothing for destitute Germans, whether they were Party supporters or not, was regarded as vital in both practical and propaganda terms.

As the Party's apparatus and ambitions grew, so it came to create new, permanent institutions to replace the voluntary, *ad hoc* work done by women enthusiasts. The SA in Berlin, for example, developed its own specialist medical corps and increasingly — and ungratefully — rejected the assistance which women's groups continued to provide. The founding of the Nazi welfare organisation (*NS-Volkswohlfahrt* — NSV) in Berlin in winter 1931–2 similarly led to a downgrading of the spontaneous assistance for long provided by women's groups. And in July 1932 the order that the Hitler Youth should have a monopoly of organising Nazi girls threatened to deprive the NSF of its traditional function of bringing the young into the movement, under the guid-

Women for the Fatherland. This Nazi propaganda poster has a beaming young woman, wearing a soldier's helmet, standing bravely at her antiaircraft post. In reality women were relegated to the kitchen, the nursery, or the factory, where they were expected to perform menial tasks in a man's world. (Wide World Photos)

ance of their elders. After tooth-and-nail resistance from the women, this order was enforced in 1933, but only by replacing the existing leadership in the NSF in the first of the series of changes which culminated in the appointment of Gertrud Scholtz-Klink as NSF leader in February 1934. By the time she took office, the women's organisation had been shorn of most of the functions it had exercised in the *Kampfzeit*, and in spite of official propaganda to boost its image it never recovered from these losses. The demarcation disputes in which the NSF became involved, with the NSV and the Hitler Youth especially, during the 1930s and into the war, were a reflection of the extent to which NSF leaders refused to be reconciled to those losses, and to which they recognised the damage they had inflicted on the NSF's authority and prestige. . . .

But if the Party and its women's groups were middle-class in orientation and appeal, this did not mean that all, or even most, middle-class women were attracted to them. There were enthusiasts, and there were also women who joined because they regarded membership as a useful insurance policy, particularly if they had a professional career to conserve. Often enough they merely paid their subscription and were classed, on investigation, as "inactive" members; it was a continuing source of frustration to NSF and Party officials that women from the "educated classes" generally held aloof from the women's organisation. And middle-class women were certainly not in the forefront of those responding to Party and NSF appeals for volunteers to help the German war-effort from 1939. Only a minority of women — in contrast with men — tends to favour single-sex group activity, and a single-sex monopoly organisation with a heavy emphasis on propaganda and indoctrination at once made itself unattractive to large numbers of women, whatever their class. Some women joined no doubt because they wanted to be members of a music group or sports club or sewing circle, and had to choose between the Nazi-sponsored one, under DFW control, or nothing. But, even so, German women were, contrary to the popular view, peculiarly resistant to National Socialism, and probably, because of their relative inaccessibility, much more resistant than men. And there was another reason: German women, like women elsewhere, remained more attached than men to religion. The spiritual authority of the Churches, particularly the Catholic Church in rural areas, retained the allegiance of large numbers of women in the face of competition from the NSF. It was hardly a contest: the Nazis could not hope to win against one of the traditional forces in society which many had believed they were coming to power to safeguard against "atheistic Marxism." Unable to use coercion to win recruits to the DFW, the NSF found, uncomfortably, that it was largely preaching to a converted minority, still cut off from the antagonistic or, more likely, uninterested 90 per cent and more of the female population of Germany.

Annexations before and during the war provided the Party and its affiliates with pastures new, with millions more ethnic Germans to Nazify. If this lifted morale, the effect was only temporary as the same problems emerged in the new territories as had dogged the NSDAP's efforts in the "old Reich." After a wave of initial enthusiasm by a susceptible minority, there remained the mass of the apathetic who, without necessarily being anti-Nazi, wished simply to remain private, unorganised citizens. And attempts to mobilise the organised for extra efforts in wartime revealed a disquieting amount of negativism among even them. It became increasingly clear that many of those who had joined the women's organisation had done so less out of burning enthusiasm for the Nazi cause than because they felt that self-interest would be served by belonging to the official women's organisation; most women of this disposition wanted not so much to be ordinary members as to hold an office of some kind. Favour and status, then, were the preoccupations of many who actually joined the DFW; it may be that the overwhelmingly middle-class character of the organisation determined this, with women who felt they had a position in society to maintain reluctant to be mere ordinary members — working members — of the DFW. The war highlighted the plight of the NSF and DFW by clearly showing up who were activists and who were passengers, and there was no doubt that the former were in the minority. They were left with the unpopular task of trying to maintain morale at home in the face of growing discomfort and the manifest injustice of the way in which the subject of labour conscription was treated by Hitler above all. The NSF's middle-class leaders were highly critical of how the system bore most heavily on working-class women, with large numbers of middle-class women managing to remain immune. The enthusiasts who were left to carry the burden of popular discontent obviously regarded themselves as the representatives of all German women, but government and Party policies had long since worked to deny them the chance to play this role in any way effectively.

It was perhaps fitting that the women's organisation should revert, towards its end, to something akin to what its predecessors had been in the 1920s, small local groups working in difficult circumstances to mitigate distress, this time among fellow citizens who were victims of air raids or the more or less willing subjects of evacuation policies. With shortages and the rupture of the communications' network towards the end of the war, the NSF's activities must have borne an uncanny resemblance to those of the *Kampfzeit*, with little or no central control of individual local policies. And it was clearly in emergency circumstances, in small groups of dedicated activists, that the Nazi women's work flourished. The extent of central authority effectively wielded by Gertrud Scholtz-Klink from her office in Berlin had always depended on the degree to which a Gauleiter had or had not intervened, but the chains of command in the women's organisation had been established at an early stage and had at least nominally held until well into the war. Their purpose had been to try to ensure that the work of the women's organisation throughout the country was conducted in a uniform way, to serve at the local level the demands of the regime as enunciated by the NSDAP and detailed by the staff of bureaucrats gathered in Gertrud Scholtz-Klink's central office. This contrasted sharply with Strasser's creation of the NSF in 1931 as essentially the women's branch of the Party, serving its needs at the local level. Strasser had himself set in motion the centripetal forces, which would ultimately and stultifyingly culminate in a top-heavy administrative centre whose edicts were intended to determine the nature of local women's group activity everywhere. But this conclusion was the logical one only to men, like his successors, with minds less flexible than his own. Unimaginative men with totalitarian aspirations produced a bureaucratic jungle in the women's organisation, as elsewhere; but here they were helped by their choice, as women's leader, of an equally unimaginative woman. No doubt the obsession with order and uniformity — which competing jurisdictions and a barrage of paperwork successfully vitiated — was yet another deterrent to potential recruits to the women's organisation at the local level. Those who joined up and stayed the course had as their reward a brief taste of initiative and freedom from the centrally-imposed straitjacket in the last months of the war, before the total eclipse.

Claudia Koonz

Mothers in the Fatherland

Because Nazi contempt for women was so blatant from the beginning, it would be easy to assume that women ought not share in the question of German guilt. Perhaps women remained pure and powerless, repelled by the racism, violence, and masculine élan of the Nazi Party. But did women really remain immune to what Erich Fromm called "the craving for submission and lust for power" that had engulfed the nation? Voting statistics provide the evidence. Thanks to electoral officials' curiosity about how women would vote in the 1920s, German men were given gray ballots and women, white. We don't have to estimate — we know that women nearly as strongly as men supported the Nazis during the years of their spectacular rise to power between 1930 and 1932.

Women do not appear to have played a role in the Nazi movement before 1933 or the Nazi state thereafter because historians have not defined women's support for Nazi Germany as a historical problem — i.e., a question that needs explaining. After all, the image of politically inert women reinforces cherished myths about motherhood. A fantasy of women untouched by their historical setting feeds our own nostalgia for mothers who remain beyond good and evil — preservers of love, charity, and peace, no matter what the social or moral environment. Against the encroachments of the modern state, we extol women who somehow keep the private beyond the reach of the political. When "feminine" ideals of love and charity flickered and were extinguished in the Third Reich, we assume this occurred because of a masculine assault against women as victims of either force or hypnosis, or of their own masochism. Sylvia Plath's "Daddy" reverberates still.

> *Not God but a swastika*
> *So black no sky could squeak through.*

Every woman adores a fascist.
The boot in the face, the brute
Brute heart of a brute like you.

The Third Reich, which left no serious ideological heritage or political admirers, has bequeathed a powerful reservoir of metaphors to the culture. When Plath hated her father, an image was available. From Riefenstahl to Wertmuller, filmmakers have exploited the erotic tension between the beauty and the brute, creating what some call a fascist aesthetic and others label fascist kitsch. The threat of violence barely contained by fastidious uniforms and martial discipline evokes hatred and love, terror and trust. But we must be wary. The symbolic language of Nazi propaganda, so alive in erotic culture today, misrepresents the real experiences of men and women who lived in Hitler's Germany.

Every woman Nazi in Germany did not "adore" a brute-hearted fascist. The women who followed Hitler, like the men, did so from conviction, opportunism, and active choice. Far from being helpless or even innocent, women made possible a murderous state in the name of concerns they defined as motherly. The fact that women bore no responsibility for issuing orders from Berlin does not obviate their complicity in carrying them out. Electoral statistics charted their enthusiasm, and Party propaganda depicts swooning women as well as marching men. But women did more than faint and vote for the only violently antifeminist party in Weimar politics. And they received more than a "boot in the face."

What did this overtly misogynist movement offer to women? Nazi men inadvertently gave women Nazis a unique opportunity because they cared so little about the women in their ranks. Men allowed women considerable latitude to interpret Hitler's ideas as they wished, recruit followers, write their own rules, and raise funds. In other parties male leaders welcomed women officially, but then curtailed women leaders' independence and chastised them at the slightest sign of separatism. In the service of womanly ideals, Nazi women sometimes behaved in most un-"ladylike" ways: managing the funds they raised, marching, facing down hecklers, making soapbox speeches, and organizing mass meetings, marches, and rallies. While espousing women's special nature and a reactionary view of the family, these women never thought they would retreat to the household. True, they crusaded to take women out of politics, but they did so in order to open up other areas of public life to women. Before 1933 Nazi women viewed the world around them in pessimistic terms, actively working in the public but not the political arena to preserve their nostalgic vision of a world that never was.

What, then, did women do for the men who ignored them? Before 1933, they provided men with an ambience they took for granted, complementing the stridently masculine élan of the Nazi movement and cultivating a homey domestic sphere for Hitler's motley and marginal band. They gave men Nazis the feeling of belonging not just to a party but to a total subculture that prefigured the ideals of the Nazi state for which they fought. Women kept folk traditions alive, gave charity to poor Nazi families, cared for SA men, sewed brown shirts, and prepared food at rallies. While Nazi men preached race hate and virulent nationalism that threatened to destroy the morality upon which civilization rested, women's participation in the movement created an ersatz gloss of idealism. The image did not, of course, deceive the victims, but it helped Nazis to preserve their self-esteem and to continue their work under the illusion that they remained decent.

To a degree unique in Western history, Nazi doctrine created a society structured around "natural" biological poles. In addition to serving specific needs of the state, this radical division vindicated a more general and thoroughgoing biological *Weltanschauung* based on race and sex as the immutable categories of human nature. The habit of taking psychological differences between men and women for granted reinforced assumptions about irrevocable divisions between Jew and "Aryan." In place of class, cultural, religious divisions, race and sex became the predominant social markers. To people disoriented by a stagnant economy, humiliated by military defeat, and confused by new social norms among the urban young, these social categories provided a sense of safety. The Jew and the New Woman, conservatives believed, had become too powerful in progressive Weimar society. The Nazi state drove both groups, as metaphors and as real individuals, out of the "Aryan" man's world.

For women, belonging to the "master race" opened the option of collaboration in the very Nazi state that exploited them, that denied them access to political status, deprived them of birth control, underpaid them as wage workers, indoctrinated their children, and finally took their sons and husbands to the front. The separation between masculine and feminine spheres, which followed logically and psychologically from Nazi leaders' misogyny, relegated women to their own space — both beneath and beyond the dominant world of men. The Nazi system rested on a female hierarchy as well as a male chain of command. Of course, women occupied a less exalted place in Nazi government than the men, and Reichsfrauenführerin Gertrud Scholtz-Klink, who stood at the pinnacle of the women's hierarchy, wielded less real power than, say, a male district chief or deputy minister. Standing at the apex of her own sphere, the woman leader minimized her lack of status vis-à-vis Nazi male leaders above her and instead directed her attention to the battalions of women under her command. As in wartime, women believed their sacrifices played a vital role in a greater cause. Scholtz-Klink saw herself as the chief of a lobby for women's concerns and as the leader of women missionaries who would bring Nazi doctrine "home" to every family in the Reich. Far from remaining untouched by Nazi evil, women operated at its very center. . . .

Where Nazi power reigned, men and women remained separated by function, personality, and responsibilities. Beyond the limits of Hitler's authority, however, in small islands of opposition, women and men formed integrated communities, unified by trust and integrity. After the first wave of isolated and failed protests in 1933, resisters prepared for a long fight. Jews, devastated at their friends' betrayal, created new sources of support that likewise bound together men and women, young and old, rich and poor. To "resist" meant first of all to survive emotionally. It required the inner strength to cut oneself entirely loose from external systems of rewards and punishments and fashion a balance between conformity and opposition. Looking backward, evaluation of very limited information becomes extremely difficult. A wholehearted Nazi might be moved to perform one act of kindness toward a Jewish neighbor, or a diehard opponent would habitually give the "Heil Hitler" (called the "German greeting") salute to avoid suspicion. Next to fear of arrest, apathy was the worst threat. Immobilized rage turned inward produced political depression. Ruth Andreas-Friedrich and her husband, both members of the resistance, wrote: "The time of the lone wolf had passed. . . . Strength no longer depended upon those who appeared powerful. We had to build our own troops . . . what one person needs the other will supply. Everything depends upon our ability to divide up the roles intelligently." We still do not know if hundreds, thousands, or tens of thousands preserved communities of integrity against Nazism, because courage among opponents and victims had to be hidden if it was to exist at all.

Looking back at Nazi Germany, it seems that decency vanished; but when we listen to feminine voices from the period, we realize instead that it was cordoned off. Loyal Nazis fashioned an image for themselves, a fake domestic realm where they felt virtuous. Nazi women facilitated that mirage by doing what women have done in other societies — they made the world a more pleasant place in which to live for the members of their community. And they simultaneously made life first unbearable and later impossible for "racially unworthy" citizens. As fanatical Nazis or lukewarm tag-alongs, they resolutely turned their heads away from assaults against socialists, Jews, religious dissenters, the handicapped, and "degenerates." They gazed instead at their own cradles, children, and "Aryan" families. Mothers and wives directed by Gertrud Scholtz-Klink made a vital contribution to Nazi power by preserving the illusion of love in an environment of hatred, just as men sustained the image of order in the utter disarray of conflicting bureaucratic and military priorities and commands.

Over time, Nazi women, no less than men, destroyed ethical vision, debased humane traditions, and rendered decent peoples helpless. And other women, as victims and resisters, risked their lives to ensure Nazi defeat and preserve their own ideals. . . .

Histories of the Nazi movement generally remained as silent about women in the movement as Hitler himself did. Party officials kept careful membership statistics, aggregated by age, occupation, region, education, and special interests. But they did not bother to separate male from female. For example, we know that 34,000 housewives joined the Party before Hitler took power, and we know that they constituted less than 5 percent of all members, but we have no idea how many women were included as "dependents," "workers," or "white-collar workers." If we had access to the original regional figures, we could recalculate women's participation. It seems clear that after about 1922, women's membership in the Party remained low. Firsthand reports reinforce this conclusion. The initial Nazi meeting in Hanover, for example, attracted a typical mix of people: "two workers, three businessmen, two artisans, two officials, a writer and three housewives." A popular writer described average Nazis as "young out-of-work shopgirls and disillusioned fighters." Alfred Krebs, a district leader, noted, "though our opponents often claimed that Nazis wanted to keep women out of politics, the party never espoused this particular crudeness. In those early days of Nazism, when women were our most zealous agitators, such a position would have been utterly impossible."

Given the paucity of information, a set of records from Hessia takes on added importance. Lists of applications to the Hessian branch of the Party over a three-year period have been preserved in the State Archives in Wiesbaden. Although we cannot know whether this information was typical of the nation, the collection provides a complete sample of data about men and women applicants. Of women who listed their occupations, none defined themselves (or their fathers) as factory workers, and virtually all had worked as sales personnel, office workers, dressmakers, or teachers before becoming housewives. One woman noted that her father had been a foreman in a lace-making factory, but most fathers had been civil servants, office workers, artisans, farmers, or small businessmen — and so were the husbands. It may well be that some of the self-definitions mask working-class origins, but even if that is true, it shows that women applying for membership in the Nazi Party wanted to emphasize their claim to middle-class status.

Membership statistics reveal one contrast between men and women: Women typically were a few years older than men. This might appear odd at first, since Nazi women in the popular image passively followed their men, who, one assumes, were fathers, or husbands, and therefore older. But several factors explain this difference. The Nazi Party was well-known for its youthfulness — over two thirds of all members during the 1920s were under forty when they joined. Women under forty typically found their family responsibilities precluded any political activity. A few young women joined before marriage. Most, however, signed up only after forty, a pattern that, incidentally, holds up for women in all kinds of organizations in any industrialized nation. Young women's low membership rates resulted also from Nazi men's lack of interest in women. The women who did join and paid dues must have defined themselves as especially zealous, probably as leaders within the women's organization. When we compare women Party members' ages with men Party leaders, the age differential disappears. The conclusion seems clear: Women leaders joined the Party. Women rank and file did not.

Once in the Party, women did not integrate themselves within the dominant structure. Instead, they created their own hierarchy. Of course, the women at the very apex of their pyramid exercised far less authority and enjoyed less status than their male counterparts. But since the men ignored them, they could overlook their own relative inferiority and emphasize their status in a separate sphere. What did that sphere look like? Voting behavior and the histories of individual women's organizations provide a rough overview. Throughout the 1920s, women's vote for Nazi candidates lagged behind men's by as much as 50 percent. As long as prosperity prevailed, most women supported moderate and conservative candidates. But with the onset of the Depression, the women's vote caught up rapidly, in some cases growing even more rapidly than men's.

Even the most ambitious women Nazis knew they could never aspire to high positions in a Nazi government after the revolution; nor could they identify with the powerful masculine Nazi élan. But that wasn't all. Some Nazi men routinely insulted women in the crudest terms. The pages of Julius Streicher's magazine for SA Men, *Der Stürmer*, featured illustrated stories of Jewish men raping blond women and derided women as stupid, lustful, and deceitful. Alfred Rosenberg's *Myth of the Twentieth Century* made Nazi misogyny clear to anyone who slogged through its turgid pages. Even in more public forums, Nazi men did not disguise their contempt for women. For example, after a Socialist Reichstag delegate spoke of having lost her son in World War I and of her desire for world peace, a Nazi delegate jeered, "That's all you nanny goats were made for anyway!" Women Nazis managed to overlook the overt misogyny of Party leaders. Jews, after all, and Catholics, to a lesser extent, recognized Hitler's hostility toward them and avoided his movement. Why did women seem not to notice? Several factors played a role. Most Germans, including many of Hitler's supporters, found it hard to take Hitler seriously on the subject of either Jews or women. Because Nazi ideology was a haphazard conglomeration of many shopworn notions, people could (and typically did) agree with Hitler's general views while adding their own vociferous "except." Thus a voter might say, "I, too, believe in authoritarian state, hate Communists, and want to avenge the Versailles Treaty. Of course, the man's racism is crazy. Once he's in power, he will drop such crackpot schemes." Women Nazis told themselves that Hitler would never turn women into brood mares. Power would tame his extremism, they said.

They could also say, with some justice, that Hitler himself did not rage against women, although several of his deputies did. Julius Streicher and Alfred Rosenberg routinely insulted women, but Hitler avoided slurs in public except for diatribes against prostitutes who carried venereal disease. He made it clear that women would confine themselves to reproducing the next "Aryan" generation; but he expected women (unlike Jews) to welcome his program. Women, he insisted, would return to "natural" roles society had for centuries assigned to them. Compared with his rivals' hypocrisy, Hitler spoke forthrightly. Perhaps some women admired the Nazis' frankly conservative position on women. Liberal and Socialist women, by contrast, operated in an ambiguous ambience in which they were simultaneously welcomed and excluded.

Women Nazis operated in a familiar atmosphere, clearly demarcated into male and female domains. Having been raised on the Bible, they had learned to screen out misogyny from a doctrine they respected and still remain faithful to Christ. It was Saint Paul, a mere disciple, after all, not Christ, who made disparaging comments about women; just as Streicher, not Hitler, denigrated women. Although women voted in political elections, they did not enjoy similar rights in their churches, where they accepted their responsibilities within their own bailiwick and obeyed their superiors. Politically, we may find this choice cowardly and wonder why women seemed so happy to settle for second best, but emotionally the prospect of a separate women's world in public life held out the promise of fulfillment. The church, not the state, had for generations been the center of women's public life. And Hitler presented himself as a messiah. Women Nazis found themselves drawn to a vision of the future that was as emotionally appealing as it was practically unfeasible and morally indefensible.

Sarah Gordon

The Ambivalence of Anti-Semitism

Jews represented only a small percentage of the German population in the period 1870–1933, but they were highly visible because of their concentration in large cities, in specific occupations (particularly trade, commerce, free professions, and cultural fields), in higher income brackets, and in political parties of the Middle and later the Left. This exposure made their numbers seem much greater than they were. Both German and immigrating Eastern European Jews attempted to reduce their specific differences from the population by abandoning their customs and even their religion, and through intermarriage. By 1933 Jews in Germany had achieved levels of integration that were indeed impressive, considering that large percentages of them were first-generation immigrants or recent migrants to new cities. Nevertheless, continuing objective differences between Jews and non-Jews made it easy to stereotype Jews as aliens who did not fit into German society. This was standard propaganda for anti-Semites between 1870 and 1945.

Many historians think that intellectual and social anti-Semitism increased during these years in response to the rise of the *"völkisch"* ideology, Social Darwinism, "social conservatism," nationalism, and imperialism. Still, some political parties were at least initially sympathetic to Jews and attempted to insure their fair treatment. Before 1928, parties whose major appeal was anti-Semitism were clearly an electoral failure; no major or minor rights of Jews were rescinded before Hitler came to power, despite the adoption of anti-Semitism around 1930 by some parties that had previously been neutral or sympathetic to Jews. Anti-Semitism does not appear to have been significant as an electoral issue for non-Nazi parties that advocated it sporadically before Hitler's election in 1933. . . .

Since extreme anti-Semitic propaganda often alienated potential voters, Hitler tempered his rhetoric after around 1925 and instead associated Jews with everything that the Nazis themselves disliked or what they assumed the population resented; however, he never outlined his concrete plans for the future treatment of Jews. Since Nazis associated Jews with every conceivable "evil" (internationalism, socialism, communism, parliamentary democracy, Germany's defeat in World War I, the Weimar system, finance capitalism, "interest bondage," reparations, the depression, etc.), the adjective "Jewish" served to focus resentment of these "evils" on a common enemy. This kept the appeal of anti-Semitism at a fairly abstract level of resentment and hostility, which undoubtedly relieved some of the tensions brought on by the depression and attendant political crises and helped to cement the heterogeneous elements within the Nazi party. Nevertheless, Nazi anti-Semitism per se does not appear to have been a major campaign issue except for a minority of voters.

Hitler developed an ethnic theory encompassing all of human history, which he defined as the struggle between nations for living space and world domination. He believed that Jews comprised a nation, albeit one spread out among other nations, and that they participated in the fight for world domination, but not for living space. In his ethnic theory all "subhumans" (including Poles and Russians) must be conquered and their leaders exterminated to prove the historical superiority of "Aryans." All Jews ("nonhuman parasites") must be exterminated because they occupied living space in the East and posed a racial "threat" to other nations, which Hitler thought they were attempting to overthrow from within. He actualized his ethnic theory in World War II when conquered "Aryan" nations were given special privileges, the leadership of "subhuman" nations was murdered, and most European Jews were exterminated.

His attitudes toward Jews also influenced domestic events in Germany before the war. All institutions and political parties that were "tainted" by "Jewish influence" were taken over and those that were suspected of opposing his racial and expansionist goals were purged.

Hitler's psychology was dominated by his misperceptions of the "Jewish threat" and his belief that Jews and all "Jewish inventions" must be "resisted" at all costs. His paranoia was clearly reflected in his ethnic theory, which accounts for his demonic destruction of millions of Jews. His murder of millions of non-Jews, however, did not result so much from paranoia as from his belief that "subhumans" who had been conquered in the past did not deserve anything better than enslavement and selective extermination.

Between 1933 and 1939 Hitler adopted a piecemeal policy to exclude Jews gradually from the political, economic, institutional, educational, social, and religious life of Germany. During the war he exterminated about 130,000 Jews who had remained in Germany and 30,000 who had emigrated to other parts of Europe, along with over five million other European Jews. It is argued here that despite Hitler's consideration of the effects of domestic and foreign opinion, including the attitudes of rabid anti-Semites within the Nazi party, he himself decided upon the timing of persecution and the extermination of Jews and others, because this was a logical consequence of his ethnic theory.

Hitler utilized anti-Semitism for several political purposes: to insure party unity by giving the party a role in racial policies, to dampen party criticism of his failure to implement the socioeconomic aspects of his program, to establish a new racial ideology, to terrorize the population and thus to atomize them socially, to divert Germans from his failure to effect a genuine social revolution, to weaken the power of "reactionaries" in the state bureaucracy, to justify expansion and war against other states that were allegedly dominated by Jews, and, finally, during the war, to include the SS, army, and bureaucracy as complicitors who would have to fight to the bitter end to prevent reprisals.

Anti-Semitic propaganda served many of the same functions, but its most important role was to create a consensus on anti-Semitism by spreading Nazi ideology and blacking out all facts or information about deportation and extermination, as well as other types of persecution, that would have led to questioning of that world view. As it became obvious that this attempt was only partly successful, tighter proscription of news and increased terror became necessary to ferret out real and potential opponents. This was most dramatically demonstrated after *Kristallnacht*, the burning of the synagogues and the general pogrom of November 1938, which was by and large a failure because ordinary Germans now widely questioned the morality and legality of the regime.

There were, of course, shifts in public attitudes toward the Nazi persecution of Jews, and these are reflected in general reports on public opinion. Certain types of measures, particularly legal or pseudo-legal exclusion of Jews from positions of prominence, authority, or economic power, appear to have been fairly well received, although some Germans attempted to aid individual Jews who were friends or neighbors. Before *Kristallnacht* even the Nuremberg Laws were acceptable to many, probably a majority, of Germans. However, the physical violence and brutality of *Kristallnacht* were clearly rejected by the same majority. Apparently anti-Semites and determined opponents of anti-Semitism were polarized around an indifferent or apathetic majority, yet one that was increasingly sympathetic to Jews during and after *Kristallnacht*. Public opinion reports indicate that widespread rumors of shootings in Poland and Russia were badly received by the public, which sometimes even attributed Germany's war losses to Hitler's rumored slaughter of Jews.

There are many possible reasons why so few Germans publicly protested these wholesale murders. Knowledge or even rumors of gassings, which were deliberately kept secret, were extremely rare outside of eastern Germany, so we have little information on German attitudes toward the death camps. Even though shootings of Russians, Poles, and Jews were widely rumored, their extensiveness was not grasped. Moreover, the rumors were apparently discounted as too fantastic to be believed; even if they had been believed, there was little that an individual or small groups of like-minded Germans could have done to halt the destruction. Only the churches and the army might have been able to interfere, and it is very doubtful that their intervention would have resulted in anything more than arrests and executions of protestors and their families. Thus an individual could act on his own, but he could not rely on higher institutions for additional support. . . .

In examining records of Germans who aided Jews it is seldom possible to determine their precise motivations, but a number of values appear to have been at play: patriotism, respect for law, order, and private property, conservatism, religious belief, socialism, and humanitarianism. Although some anti-Semites considered Jews to be totally alien foreigners who had never belonged in Germany in the first place and who had betrayed the country during World War I, some patriots, including Hindenburg, recognized that Jews had contributed to World War I both as leaders of great importance, such as Rathenau, and as front fighters. Moreover, many German Jews were well assimilated into German economic, political, social, and intellectual life; others had even converted and were religiously integrated. Significant numbers of Polish, Russian, and other Eastern European Jews had come to Germany, and they were not as well regarded either by Germans or German Jews. It is conceivable that those Germans who accepted German Jews would nevertheless have favored restrictions on immigration by Eastern European Jews, yet this does not mean that they wanted to expel all Jews from Germany.

Another aspect of patriotism that may have played a role in opposition to Nazi racial policies was the significant contribution of Jews to German intellectual life. Not only had they brought honor to Germany by winning a large number of Nobel prizes, they were also very active in all scientific and cultural fields. Even Goebbels was slow to sever his ties with Jewish artists and performers who were considered first-rate in Germany. Jewish cosmopolitanism (which anti-Semites castigated as internationalism) also extended to their contacts with foreigners, primarily through trade, commerce, and banking. Germans who were not confirmed bigots could easily recognize the importance

The Final Solution. A group of American senators visits the concentration camp at Buchenwald and witnesses the indescribable results of Nazi terror. In this case, surely, one picture is worth a thousand words. (UPI/Corbis-Bettmann)

of Jewish enterpreneurship and international contacts for the German economy. Thus they did not necessarily perceive Jewish contacts abroad as treacherous.

Still another aspect of German patriotic values could also cut two ways. Although it became popular to excoriate "liberal" values after 1890–1900, not everyone believed they were evil. There was considerable diversity on this issue among the middle classes, and the lower classes (which represented almost 50 percent of the population) were in some ways more "liberal" than "socialist." Their complaint was that the "liberal" constitutional monarchy that Bismarck established, and which Jews supported strongly between 1871 and 1918, was not quite "liberal" enough.

In some ways Germany had been a pioneer in granting Jews rights and privileges. German universities had admitted Jews on an equal footing since 1790, and by 1909 and later they had a large percentage of Jewish professors when, for example, American and Canadian universities considered them anathema. Insofar as some Germans still believed the "liberal enlightenment" brought honor to the nation, and insofar as fair treatment of Jews was considered part of that enlightenment, some Germans viewed Hitler's attacks on Jews as a blight on national honor. Many of them equated Nazi violence against Jews with "primitive" countries and Bolshevik Russia. They complained that one might expect pogroms in "backward nations" such as Poland and Russia, but how could they happen in the land of Kant?

Closely related to the question of patriotism is the concept of a nation under law, because there can be no genuine national community without the assurance that laws will provide a stable political and economic order. In most societies law becomes a principle unto itself precisely for this reason. Germans have always had a healthy respect for a nation under law (a *Rechtsstaat*), and this is probably one reason the fall of the monarchy was a traumatic shock. The Weimar government had an entirely new legal foundation, one which challenged and changed past traditions and rights that had become ensconced in the law. The new state was a potential threat simply because it could and did change the law; therefore, it was viewed with fear. Some of this fear was quite rational, and some was hysterical; yet tampering with the monarchy and the old order could only have been expected to produce such fears.

When Hitler came to power, he made certain that his takeover had the appearance of legality; this was his craftiest political maneuver. It prevented the average German from perceiving that he would alter the entire legal system of Germany. Revolutionaries have never been popular in Germany, and Hitler would never have had the full aura of legitimacy he needed had he taken power by force. Accordingly, Nazi violence and illegality after Hitler became chancellor were widely condemned. Likewise, violence against Jews during the boycott of 1933, the summer riots in Berlin in 1935, and the pogrom of 1938 was condemned by many Germans on the traditional grounds that it violated the law. If the state itself authorized wanton illegality in one sphere, such as anti-Jewish measures, how could it maintain its image as defender of the laws in other spheres? Sporadic violent attacks on Jews before 1939 had to be curtailed because the public expected the state to perform its function of maintaining law and order. With the beginning of World War II and the attendant power it gave to Hitler, public indignation at violence against Jews in European lands could no longer have serious consequences. Germans who protested openly about persecution of Jews were treated as criminals because the traditional legal system was destroyed by Hitler, and his war powers could be terminated only with his death.

Omer Bartov

The War, the Final Solution, and the Defeat

The German people did not go to war in 1939 with the same *"Hurra-Patriotismus"* of August 1914. Indicatively, the mood of the nation during the Sudetenland crisis in autumn 1938 was not essentially different from that of Britain and France. Contemporary reports noted that there was "no enthusiasm whatsoever for entanglement in war," that "[m]orale [was] widely depressed," and that there was "overall a 'general war-psychosis.'" As the crisis reached its climax it was reported: "Everywhere there prevailed great tension and anxiety, and everywhere the wish was heard: anything but war . . . expressed with particular vigor by veteran World War front soldiers." Yet once the Munich accords were signed, the public mood rapidly changed into one of admiration for the Führer's "political skill." People had taken Hitler's "peace campaign" of the mid-1930s quite seriously, and had come to believe that he wanted to avoid war just as much as they did. By 1939 the public was so certain of the Führer's ability to extricate

Germany from political crisis without going to war that there was far less "war psychosis" than during the preceding year.

When war did eventually break out, a widespread depression was noted by all observers of the German public. Bernt Engelmann recalls: "No crowds had gathered. We saw no trace of rejoicing, certainly none of the wild enthusiasm that Germans had shown . . . in 1914." An American correspondent found the population apathetic. A Gauleiter who was travelling throughout the country at the time remarked that there was "no happiness, no joy." Instead, he wrote, "everywhere I came an oppressive silence, not to say depression, prevailed. The whole German people seemed to be struck by a paralyzing horror, so that it was capable of neither expressions of approval nor of disgust." Another observer spoke of the "dull obedience of a mass educated to follow [its leaders] blindly and thoughtlessly, but also stupefied and confused by militant propaganda." It has been claimed that the majority of the German population manifested at the beginning of the war a mood of "unwilling loyalty." One might say that the Germans accepted the outbreak of war with the same fatalism that characterized their behavior during the last desperate months leading to the "capitulation."

The great military triumphs in the first two years of the war dispelled much of the gloom. If in 1939 the Germans still believed that Hitler could always avert war at the very last moment, after the victory over France they were sure that he could defeat any enemy. There were other reasons for contentment. During the 1930s the regime had done away with unemployment and was perceived by large sectors of the population as having brought Germany out of what had seemed until the *Machtergreifung* as an insoluble economic crisis. Prosperity and social order under Hitler's rule could be seen as a "return to normality" after the anarchy of the Weimar Republic's last years. Not that the Nazis had created the idyllic *Volksgemeinschaft*; indeed, toward the outbreak of war there were renewed signs of unrest among the workers who wished to make use of the increasing labor shortage to demand higher pay. Yet as long as one did not belong to the political or "racial" categories persecuted by the regime, was not subject to the "euthanasia" campaign, and did not engage in anti-Nazi activities, one was not badly off in Germany of the late 1930s. Furthermore, when within less than a year Germany came to occupy most of Western and Central Europe, the economic prospects of ruling over the entire continent left little room for social unrest. National pride in Germany's military achievements combined with hopes for unprecedented prosperity from which everyone — at least every "Aryan" — would gain. Successful empire-builders have always benefited from this kind of "social-imperialism."

The invasion of the Soviet Union caught not only Stalin, but also many Germans by surprise, and once more unleashed a wave of apprehension and anxiety. On the second day of "Barbarossa" the SD noted that "according to reports . . . from all parts of the Reich the announcement of the outbreak of war with Russia has caused great surprise among the population." By July it was claimed that the "general mood [*Stimmung*] among wide sectors of the population has . . . undergone an increasing deterioration." Of course, stressed the SD, "by and large confidence in victory and trust in the leadership have remained," but "the people are depressed or embittered and incensed by the toughness of the struggle in the East, the criminal conduct of the war by the Red Army, by the noticeable casualties . . . and above all by the consequent difficulties of supply." This was a telling analysis of the public mood, for it encapsulated the most important aspects of the war in the East — which from now on became *the* war — as perceived by the German population. Here was a mixture of irrational, but powerful terror from the Russians, and a very concrete worry about the material consequences of fighting a war on such a scale. Fear of "Asiatic Bolshevism," anchored in long established prejudices and fanned by Nazi propaganda, created the basis for a grotesquely distorted view of reality. Although it was known that Germany had attacked, the Soviet Union was seen as the aggressor; and while the public was promised to gain from the ruthless exploitation and enslavement of the Russians, the Red Army was believed to be the real criminal. Similarly, fears of shortages were accompanied by a widespread zeal for economic expansion which made the idea of a *Raubkrieg* in the East particularly popular among Germany's industrialists and business community. The prospects of power and wealth were greater than ever before, but so were the risks. Hitler's previous triumphs had convinced soldiers and civilians alike that this war too would be won, but the enemy's determined resistance, and the terror from his dehumanized image, filled the Germans with great anxiety. The cause of that fear had to be wiped out by every means available. This was necessary because the enemy was evil; it was bound to succeed, because it was the Führer's wish;

The End of the Thousand-Year Reich. In Hitler's grand plan, Germany's capital city was to have been the center of the world for centuries to come. Instead, after intensive bombing by the Allies, it offered a picture of haunting devastation. (UPI/Corbis-Bettmann)

and it was also to be richly rewarded. In this sense the Germans were indeed fighting Hitler's "war of ideologies."

The war in the Soviet Union demanded increasingly total manpower mobilization. Even the German workers, who throughout the 1930s had resisted the myth of the *Volksgemeinschaft* and had striven to protect their economic, if not their political interests, were now drawn into the war and forced to become part of the no less mythical *Kampfgemeinschaft*. In the Wehrmacht the working class disappeared, only to re-emerge in 1945 after many years at the front as Hitler's soldiers and the representatives of the *Herrenrasse* in the vast territories occupied by Germany. At home some of them might have remained immune to the regime's propaganda, but once in uniform they were sucked into the army's "melting pot" and forged into Hitler's instruments, becoming the executors of his policies, the conquerors of his empire. There were no class-oriented rebellions in the Wehrmacht, indeed, there were no mutinies at all. In the Ruhr industrial region workers might have grumbled against the regime, but in the ranks they numbered among those very same soldiers considered by all observers as Hitler's most loyal supporters. This transformation of Germany's workers into Hitler's soldiers was a measure of the regime's success in mobilizing the whole nation to fight its war of conquest and destruction. Naturally, the soldiers fought for many reasons; they fought for survival, for their comrades, for their families in the rear, and for Germany's victory and prosperity. But workers or not, they also fought against "Plutocracy," "Asiatic barbarism," and "Judeo-Bolshevism," and in defense of "German culture" and "Western civilization." In this sense they fought for Nazism and everything that it stood for.

Perceived as a struggle of all-or-nothing, the war in the East called for complete spiritual commitment, absolute obedience, unremitting destruction of the enemy. As such the war in the East constituted not only the climax of the Nazi regime, but also the most important element of its postwar memory in Germany. Surviving its reality and living with its recollection necessitated a profound process of inversion. When the soldiers returned home, they brought with them the images and horrors of the war, the perverted morality which had formed its basis, and the distorted perception which had made living through it bearable. All of these were combined into Germany's collective memory of the war, for only thus could postwar society "come to terms" with its past. "Auschwitz" could be ascribed to a minority, numerous as well it might have been. Not so the war. Every family had sent at least one soldier to the front. Worse still, the young men who returned from the fighting became Germany's workers and bureaucrats, professors and technocrats, bankers and politicians, and lawyers, writers and poets. It was inconceivable that they had all taken part in a huge criminal undertaking. Thus the same psychological mechanism which had facilitated fighting a barbarous war was employed to facilitate living with its memory. The soldiers' combat experiences were portrayed as unique, the uniquely criminal characteristics of the war were "normalized" as mere by-products of the fighting. Cause and effect were reversed: barbarism was perceived as the outcome of the enemy's bitter resistance to occupation, not as its main trigger. The troops' sufferings were vividly remembered, their victims' were repressed. Nor was this view of the war limited to the soldiers. Civilians too perceived the strategic bombing raids and the occupation of the land by enemy armies as unique manifestations of the destructiveness of war; the industrial murder of millions of human beings was viewed as merely one more aspect of war's evil nature, not something unique to Nazi Germany's very specific war. And, because the bombing and occupation were experienced by many more Germans than the death camps, they remained implanted much more deeply in their memories. Thus the genocide of Jews and Gypsies ceased to be directly related to the Germans, and became something executed not by them, but in their name. The culprits could not have anything to do with the resurrected German people of the postwar era. The war remained a deep, painful memory, but it was a memory of one's own suffering, and it left no room for one's victims. If for Hitler the war had been a vehicle for winning over those Germans who had previously remained aloof from his regime, it served postwar German society to repress the memory of its crimes by lamenting its own fate. The war had made the Wehrmacht into Hitler's army, the Germans into Hitler's people. Defeat converted them all into victims. If Austria was Hitler's first victim, Germany was his last. And victims cannot be called to account. . . .

The German people did not want war. In 1939 most of them preferred things to remain as they had been during the preceding six years of Hitler's rule. Once war broke out, however, they found that much could be gained from it, and the Führer's popularity rose to even greater heights. Germans became anxious when the Wehrmacht invaded the Soviet Union. They did not want that war either. But while at first they expected Hitler to bring them world domination and wealth, later on they came to view him as their only hope for salvation. Instead, he brought them catastrophe. With this, they were released not only from his hold, but also from his crimes. They became his, and his victims' victims. Only now, while these pages are being written, are the Germans liberating themselves from the consequences of the catastrophe they had done so much to bring upon themselves. Ironically, their return to greatness is once more closely tied to Russia's retreat to the East. As the war generation is dying out, a new generation is being born into a reunified Germany. Let us hope that fifty years from now the new superpower emerging in *Mitteleuropa* will have an easier time remembering its past than the two rapidly vanishing German republics have had remembering theirs.

Suggestions for Additional Reading

Every bibliography of the historical literature on Nazi Germany must begin with an obvious disclaimer: This listing can only be selective. The total number of published works runs far into the thousands. Consequently, only a very few can be mentioned here, with apologies to the authors of the many fine books that have been omitted. Although a few classics have been retained, preference has generally been given to more recent studies. Only volumes available in English have been included. Most of them, of course, contain extensive bibliographies of their own, so that the reader can pursue virtually any topic in further detail.

I The Nazi Movement and German History

Berghahn, Volker. *Modern Germany. Society, Economy, and Politics in the Twentieth Century*, 2nd ed. (New York: Cambridge University Press, 1987).

Blackbourn, David, and Geoff Eley. *The Peculiarities of German History* (New York: Oxford University Press, 1984).

Bracher, Karl Dietrich. *The German Dictatorship: The Origins, Structure, and Effects of National Socialism* (New York: Praeger, 1970).

Broszat, Martin. *The Hitler State. The Foundation and Development of the Internal Structure of the Third Reich* (London: Longman, 1981).

Carr, William. *A History of Germany, 1815–1945*, 3rd ed. (London: Edward Arnold, 1987).

Childers, Thomas, and Jane Caplan, eds. *Reevaluating the Third Reich* (New York: Holmes & Meier, 1993).

Craig, Gordon. *Germany 1866–1945* (Oxford: Oxford University Press, 1981).

Herwig, Holger H. *Hammer or Anvil? Modern Germany 1648–Present* (Lexington, Mass.: D. C. Heath, 1994).

Hildebrand, Klaus. *The Third Reich* (London: Allen & Unwin, 1984).

Jäckel, Eberhard. *Hitler in History* (Hanover, N.H.: University Press of New England, 1984).

Kershaw, Ian. *The Nazi Dictatorship. Problems and Perspectives of Interpretation*, 2nd ed. (London: Edward Arnold, 1989).

Kocka, Jürgen, and Allan Mitchell, eds., *Bourgeois Society in Nineteenth-Century Europe* (Oxford: Berg Publishers, 1993).

Kolb, Eberhard. *The Weimar Republic* (London: Unwin Hyman, 1988).

Maier, Charles S. *The Unmasterable Past. History, Holocaust, and German National Identity* (Cambridge, Mass.: Harvard University Press, 1988).

Marrus, Michael R. *The Holocaust in History* (London: Penguin Books, 1987).

Martel, Gordon, ed. *Modern Germany Reconsidered, 1870–1945* (London: Routledge, 1992).

Orlow, Dietrich. *A History of Modern Germany, 1871 to Present*, 2nd ed. (Englewood Cliffs, N.J.: Prentice-Hall, 1991).

Payne, Stanley G. *A History of Fascism, 1914–1945* (Madison: University of Wisconsin Press, 1995).

Peukert, Detlev. *The Weimar Republic: The Crisis of Classical Modernity* (London: Penguin Books, 1991).

Wehler, Hans-Ulrich. *The German Empire, 1871–1918* (Leamington Spa: Berg Publishers, 1985).

Weindling, Paul J. *Health, Race and German Politics between National Unification and Nazism, 1870–1945* (Cambridge: Cambridge University Press, 1989).

II The Seizure of Power

Allen, William Sheridan. *The Nazi Seizure of Power. The Experience of a Single German Town, 1922–1945*, rev. ed. (New York, Franklin Watts, 1984).

Bessel, Richard. *Political Violence and the Rise of Nazism* (New Haven, Conn.: Yale University Press, 1984).

Breitman, Richard. *German Socialism and Weimar Democracy* (Chapel Hill, N.C.: University of North Carolina Press, 1981).

Broszat, Martin. *Hitler and the Collapse of Weimar Germany* (Leamington Spa: Berg Publishers, 1987).

Childers, Thomas. *The Nazi Voter: The Social Foundations of Fascism in Germany, 1919–1933* (Chapel Hill, N.C.: University of North Carolina Press, 1983).

Grill, Johnpeter Horst. *The Nazi Movement in Baden, 1920–1945* (Chapel Hill, N.C.: University of North Carolina Press, 1983).

Gordon, Harold J. *Hitler and the Beer Hall Putsch* (Princeton, N.J.: Princeton University Press, 1972).

Hamilton, Richard F. *Who Voted for Hitler?* (Princeton, N.J.: Princeton University Press, 1982).

Jones, Larry Eugene. *German Liberalism and the Dissolution of the Weimar Party System, 1918–1933* (Chapel Hill, N.C.: University of North Carolina Press, 1988).

Kater, Michael H. *The Nazi Party. A Social Profile of Members and Leaders, 1919–1945* (Cambridge, Mass.: Harvard University Press, 1983).

Kele, Max H. *Nazis and Workers. National Socialist Appeals to German Labor, 1919–1933* (Chapel Hill, N.C.: University of North Carolina Press, 1983).

Koshar, Rudy. *Social Life, Local Politics, and Nazism: Marburg, 1880–1935* (Chapel Hill, N.C.: University of North Carolina Press, 1986).

Merkl, Peter. *The Making of a Stormtrooper* (Princeton, N.J.: Princeton University Press, 1980).

Mitchell, Allan. *Revolution in Bavaria, 1918–1919* (Princeton, N.J.: Princeton University Press, 1964).

Mommsen, Hans. *From Weimar to Auschwitz: Essays in German History* (Cambridge: Cambridge University Press, 1991).

———. *The Rise and Fall of Weimar Democracy* (Chapel Hill, N.C.: University of North Carolina Press, 1995).

Nicholls, A. J. *Weimar and the Rise of Hitler*, 2nd ed. (New York: St. Martin's Press, 1979).

Noakes, Jeremy. *The Nazi Party in Lower Saxony, 1921–1933* (London: Oxford University Press, 1971).

Orlow, Dietrich. *The History of the Nazi Party, 1919–1933*, 2 vols. (Pittsburgh: University of Pittsburgh Press, 1969–73).

Pridham, Geoffrey. *Hitler's Rise to Power: The Nazi Movement in Bavaria, 1923–1933* (New York: Harper & Row, 1973).

Rosenhaft, Eve. *Beating the Fascists? The German Communists and Political Violence, 1923–1933* (Cambridge: Cambridge University Press, 1983).

Waite, Robert G. L. *Vanguard of Nazism. The Freecorps Movement in Postwar Germany, 1918–1933* (Cambridge, Mass.: Harvard University Press, 1952).

III The Personality of the Leader

Binion, Rudolph. *Hitler among the Germans* (New York: Elsevier Press, 1976).

Bullock, Alan. *Hitler: A Study in Tyranny*, rev. ed. (New York: Harper & Row, 1964).

———. *Hitler and Stalin. Parallel Lives* (London: HarperCollins, 1991).

Carr, William. *Hitler: A Study in Personality and Politics* (New York: St. Martin's Press, 1979).

Fest, Joachim C. *Hitler* (New York: Harcourt Brace Jovanovich, 1974).

Fleming, Gerald. *Hitler and the Final Solution* (Berkeley, Calif.: University of California Press, 1984).

Jäckel, Eberhard. *Hitler's Weltanschauung: A Blueprint for Power* Middletown, Conn.: Wesleyan University Press, 1972).

Kershaw, Ian. *Hitler* (London: Longman, 1991).

———. *The "Hitler Myth": Image and Reality in the Third Reich* (Oxford: Oxford University Press, 1987).

Smith, Bradley F. *Adolf Hitler: His Family, Childhood, and Youth* (Stanford, Calif.: Stanford University Press, 1967).

Trevor-Roper, H. R. *The Last Days of Hitler*, 3rd ed. (New York: Berkeley Publishing Co., 1960).

Waite, Robert G. L. *The Psychopathic God: Adolf Hitler* (New York: Basic Books, 1977).

IV The Crucial Role of German Elites

Beyerchen, Alan D. *Scientists under Hitler. Politics and the Physics Community in the Third Reich*, 2nd ed. (New Haven, Conn.: Yale University Press, 1985).

Conway, John S. *The Nazi Persecution of the Churches, 1933–1945* (New York: Basic Books, 1968).

Helmreich, Ernst Christian. *The German Churches under Hitler* (Detroit: Wayne State University Press, 1979).

Hoffmann, Peter. *German Resistance to Hitler* (Cambridge, Mass.: Harvard University Press, 1988).

——. *The History of the German Resistance, 1933–1945* (Cambridge, Mass.: MIT Press, 1977).

Jarausch, Konrad H. *The Unfree Professions: German Lawyers, Teachers, and Engineers, 1900–1950* (New York: Oxford University Press, 1990).

Lewy, Guenter. *The Catholic Church and Nazi Germany* (New York: McGraw-Hill, 1964).

Milward, Alan S. *The German Economy at War* (London: Athlone Press, 1965).

Müller, Klaus-Jürgen. *The Army, Politics, and Society in Germany, 1933–1945* (New York: St. Martin's Press, 1987).

O'Neill, Robert J. *The German Army and the Nazi Party, 1933–1939* (London: Cassell Press, 1966).

Stein, George H. *The Waffen SS: Hitler's Elite Guard at War, 1939–1945* (Ithaca, N.Y.: Cornell University Press, 1966).

Turner, Henry Ashby, Jr. *German Big Business and the Rise of Hitler* (New York: Oxford University Press, 1985).

Ziegler, Herbert G. *Nazi Germany's New Aristocracy. The SS Leadership, 1925–1939* (Princeton, N.J.: Princeton University Press, 1989).

V The Social Impact of Nazism

Angress, Werner T. *Between Fear and Hope: Jewish Youth in the Third Reich* (New York: Columbia University Press, 1988).

Bartov, Omer. *Hitler's Army: Soldiers, Nazis, and War in the Third Reich* (New York: Oxford University Press, 1991).

——. *Murder in Our Midst. The Holocaust, Industrial Killing, and Representation* (New York: Oxford University Press, 1996).

Bessel, Richard, ed. *Life in the Third Reich* (Oxford: Oxford University Press, 1987).

Bridenthal, Renate, et al., eds. *When Biology Became Destiny: Women in Weimar and Nazi Germany* (New York: Monthly Review Press, 1984).

Browning, Christopher. *Ordinary Men: Reserve Police Battalion 101 and the Final Solution in Poland* (New York: HarperCollins, 1992).

Burleigh, Michael. *Death and Deliverance. "Euthanasia" in Germany 1900–1945* (Cambridge: Cambridge University Press, 1994).

Crew, David, ed. *Nazism and German Society, 1933–1945* (London: Routledge, 1994).

Dahrendorf, Ralf. *Society and Democracy in Germany* (New York: Doubleday, 1967).

Friedlander, Henry. *The Origins of Nazi Genocide. From Euthanasia to the Final Solution* (Chapel Hill, N.C.: University of North Carolina Press, 1995).

Gellately, Robert. *The Gestapo and German Society. Enforcing Racial Policy, 1933–1945* (Oxford: Oxford University Press, 1990).

Geyer, Michael, and John W. Boyer, eds. *Resistance against the Third Reich, 1933–1990* (Chicago: University of Chicago Press, 1992).

Gilbert, Martin. *The Holocaust: A History of the Jews of Europe During the Second World War* (New York: Holt, Rinehart and Winston, 1985).

Giles, Geoffrey. *Students and National Socialism in Germany* (Princeton, N.J.: Princeton University Press, 1985).

Gordon, Sarah. *Hitler, Germans, and the "Jewish Question"* (Princeton, N.J.: Princeton University Press, 1984).

Hilberg, Raul. *The Destruction of the European Jews* (Chicago: Quadrangle Books, 1961).

———. *Perpetrators, Victims, Bystanders: The Jewish Catastrophe, 1933–1945* (New York: HarperCollins, 1992).

Kershaw, Ian. *Popular Opinion and Political Dissent in the Third Reich: Bavaria, 1933–1945* (Oxford: Clarendon Press, 1983).

Kitchen, Martin. *Nazi Germany at War* (London: Longman, 1995).

Koonz, Claudia. *Mothers in the Fatherland. Women, the Family, and Nazi Politics* (New York: St. Martin's Press, 1987).

Laqueur, Walter Z. *Young Germany. A History of the German Youth Movement* (New York: Basic Books, 1962).

Large, David Clay, ed. *Contending with Hitler: Varieties of German Resistance in the Third Reich* (Cambridge: Cambridge University Press, 1991).

Mason, Timothy W. *Social Policy in the Third Reich: The Working Class and the National Community* (Providence, R.I.: Berg Publishers, 1993).

Merkl, Peter. *Political Violence under the Swastika* (Princeton, N.Y.: Princeton University Press, 1975).

Owings, Alison. *Frauen: German Women Recall the Third Reich* (New Brunswick, N .J.: Rutgers University Press, 1993).

Peukert, Detlev. *Inside Nazi Germany: Conformity, Opposition, and Racism in Everyday Life* (New Haven, Conn.: Yale University Press, 1987).

Schoenbaum, David. *Hitler's Social Revolution: Class and Status in Nazi Germany, 1933–1939* (New York: Doubleday, 1967).

Stephenson, Jill. *The Nazi Organisation of Women* (London: Croom Helm, 1981).

——. *Women in Nazi Society* (London: Croom Helm, 1975).

Von Klemperer, Klemens. *German Resistance against Hitler* (Oxford: Clarendon Press, 1992).